Advance Praise for *A Paradise to Regain*

"As the title suggests, this volume offers a rich "paradise" from Black women's insights into and from the Black Diaspora. At the same time, there is a nuanced detailing of the loss of paradisal conditions for women leaders and educators historically and in our contemporary post-Obama era. Focusing on teacher education and several sociology fields, these chapters offer a range of storied, artistic, poetic, political, historical, and personal accounts that highlight valuable possibilities to remember, reclaim, and re-imagine legacies and "narratives of hope."

Courtney Lee Weida, Associate Professor,
Ruth S. Ammon School of Education—
Adelphi University, Graduate Program

"In this book, expert and powerful voices deliver impactful and encouraging messages, particularly to those of us who are still trying to figure out our space and place at home, on the streets, in the classroom, on campuses, in politics, and yes, in the world."

Jeanine Ntihirageza, Professor
Northeastern Illinois University

"In *Paradise to Regain*, the paradoxes of the American Dream and the promise of inclusiveness are counterposed against painful exclusion from the full benefits of citizenship, from the mainstream, from leadership, and from equitable access to economic, political and social resources in general. The authors weave a tapestry that tells an intersectional story of the implications of race, class, and gender in the contemporary USA. The book provides an important critique of the status quo and presents some alternative visions of possible futures without sugarcoating. The message that runs through it is that Paradise can be regained, but only through determined, focused, collective struggle. This book is a great contribution to academic and popular analysis and explication of the past and present gendered challenges faced by racial and ethnic minorities in the USA."

Mojúbàolú Olufúnké Okome, Professor of Political Science
African & Women's Studies, Brooklyn College, CUNY

Throughout this volume, the diverse voices of female scholars, educators, mothers, and immigrants from across the Diaspora challenge us to reflect on our cultural heritage – where and how we fit in to this critical time in history. The writings demand that we consider how we can actively create multifaceted opportunities for ourselves and our communities moving forward. Yes We Can!

Adeyinka M. Akinsulure-Smith, Professor
The City College of New York, the City University of New York

A PARADISE TO REGAIN

Post-Obama Insights from Women Educators of the Black Diaspora

Edited By

**IMMACULÉE HARUSHIMANA,
MARY V. ALFRED, AND
R. DEBORAH DAVIS**

Corresponding Author
Immaculée Harushimana
Lehman College, CUNY
250 Bedford Boulevard West
Carmen Hall, Rm-B29
Bronx, NY 10468

Telephone: 718-960-8455
Email: immaculee.harushimana@lehman.cuny.edu

Copyright © 2019 | Myers Education Press, LLC

Published by Myers Education Press, LLC
P.O. Box 424
Gorham, ME 04038

All rights reserved. No part of this book may be reprinted or reproduced in any form or by any electronic, mechanical, or other means, now known or hereafter invented, including photocopying, recording, and information storage and retrieval, without permission in writing from the publisher.

> Myers Education Press is an academic publisher specializing in books, e-books, and digital content in the field of education. All of our books are subjected to a rigorous peer review process and produced in compliance with the standards of the Council on Library and Information Resources.

LIBRARY OF CONGRESS CATALOGING-IN-PUBLICATION DATA AVAILABLE FROM LIBRARY OF CONGRESS
13-digit ISBN 978-1-9755-0111-2 (paperback)
13-digit ISBN 978-1-9755-0110-5 (hard cover)
13-digit ISBN 978-1-9755-0112-9 (library networkable e-edition)
13-digit ISBN 978-1-9755-0113-6 (consumer e-edition)

Printed in the United States of America.

All first editions printed on acid-free paper that meets the American National Standards Institute Z39-48 standard.

Books published by Myers Education Press may be purchased at special quantity discount rates for groups, workshops, training organizations, and classroom usage. Please call our customer service department at 1-800-232-0223 for details.

Cover design by Sophie Appel.

Visit us on the web at **www.myersedpress.com** to browse our complete list of titles.

A PARADISE TO REGAIN

Post-Obama Insights from Women Educators of the Black Diaspora

CONTENTS

Acknowledgments   xi

FOREWORD
Yolanda Sealey-Ruiz   xii

INTRODUCTION
Eight Years of Paradise: An Obama Will Come Again
Immaculée Harushimana   1

SECTION I
THE BURDEN OF LEADING WHILE BLACK

1. "They're Coming for Our Jobs Too!" Double Standards for Black and White Leadership in the Age of Obama and Trump   11
Rosaire Ifedi

2. Does Race Matter in Dissertation Mentoring? A Black Native Caribbean Woman Research Methodologist Genuflects and Reflects   21
Janice B. Fournillier

3. Transformative Leadership–"Botho-Humane": A Wellness Perspective
Meahabo D. Magano   29

4. Mission to Accomplish: A Journey to Math Democracy
Marcia M. Burrell   41

5. Teaching through the Lens of a Mother
Josephine Jarpa Dawuni   49

SECTION II
GENDER EQUALITY AND WOMEN EMPOWERMENT

6. Gender Equality Not of This World: In the Brave New World
Lindamichelle Baron   59

7. Let Hope Ring: Memories of a Black Girl Finding Hope during the 2008 Elections
Ronisha Browdy   67

8. Oppressive Patriarchy: African Women
   Struggle with Gender Inequality
   Gladys Kedibone Mokwena   75

9. Teaching Adult Learners of Color in a Time of Struggle:
   The Impact on Children
   Jaye Jones   85

10. Incivility: Experiences of a Black Widow
    in a Higher Education Working Environment
    Sizakele M. Matlabe   93

SECTION III
HOW BRAVE ART AFRICAN WOMEN IMMIGRANTS?

11. Where Is Justice for Immigrants!?
    "If You Prick Us, Do We Not Bleed?
    If You Tickle Us, Do We Not Laugh?"
    Mary N. Ghongkedze   103

12. "Talking Some and Leaving Some": A Community-Grounded
    Approach to Teaching and Sustaining African Languages in America
    Esther Milu   111

13. When Being Articulate Isn't Enough:
    The Narrative of a French-Speaking African Woman Faculty of English
    Immaculée Harushimana   121

14. Can You Get It If You Really Want? A Jamaican-Born
    Science Educator Reflects on Success Attainability
    Ellie Williamson   131

15. Beware of False Consciousness: A Letter to My Son
    Shirley Mthethwa-Sommers   139

SECTION IV
BLACK SELF-AFFIRMATION

16. Standing with Barack Obama:
    The Need for Black Scientists in STEM Education
    Diane Price Banks — 149

17. "Yes, I Can; Yes, We Can!" Reflections of a Caribbean Immigrant Sistah in the Struggle with a Legacy of Determination, Strength, and Empowerment
    Mary V. Alfred — 157

18. Writing Ourselves into History:
    Examining a World of Black Imaginings and Possibility
    Tracy Cook-Person, with Djenaba Dekkatu and Quincy Merrill — 167

19. On Being a Biracial Woman of Black and Puerto Rican Descent:
    A Mother Reflects on a Mother-Daughter Conversation
    Patricia Isaac — 177

20. To Dream the Impossible Dream
    Lindamichelle Baron — 187

SECTION V
CAN A BLACK MALE CHILD DREAM BIG IN A MELANIN-PHOBIC WORLD?

21. Hope: President Barack Obama's Legacy to Black Children
    Eleanor T. Campbell — 199

22. Dreams for My Son: Dreaming Big in America
    Faith Muturia — 207

23. Dreams Shattered and Restored: President Barack Obama Confronting the Shadow of Absent Fatherhood and the Pursuit of a Healthy Relationship
    Faith N. Maina — 217

24. The Black Male as World Citizen and Cultural Ambassador:
    Embracing Multiple Identities
    Rasheeda Ahmad   223

SECTION VI
PARADISE TO REGAIN: CHANGE MUST COME AGAIN

25. "Oh, Mercy, Mercy Me"—"A Change is Gonna Come"... Again
    Gillian U. Bayne   235

26. Yes, She Did: Following Queen Mother Sanford Wherever She May Go
    Lindamichelle Baron   247

27. As Long as There Is Life: Elections That Shaped My Transnationality
    Immaculée Harushimana   255

28. From Barack Obama to Donald Trump:
    Two Extremes at Making History
    Aminata Diop   263

29. Supporting the Village That Raises the Children:
    From the Perspective of a Community Advocate
    Patricia Mason   273

30. "We Danced in the Streets:"
    Obama Era, Civil Rights Generation, and Voting Rights
    Mary E. Dillard   281

CONCLUSION

Looking Back to Move Forward: A Black Women's Collective
(Re-)Imagining and (Re-)Membering Hope and Change
Sherry L. Deckman   289

Contributors   297
Index   309

Acknowledgments

WHENEVER A PROJECT of great magnitude, such as a book production, is brought to fruition, it is customary to look back and think about all the people who have made ultimate sacrifices while the project was being built from inception to completion. As lead editor, I wish to thank the contributors, starting with the initiators of the project, Drs. Gillian Bayne and Sherry Deckman, and the co-editors, Professor Emeritus R. Deborah Davis and Professor Mary Alfred, for your unconditional acceptance of my invitation to join me on such an uncertain journey. Without that first step that you supported me to make, nothing guarantees that this book would have seen the day.

I ALSO WISH to thank each of and all the contributors to this book for the enthusiasm you expressed about the project and the messages of encouragement and endearment that kept coming from many of you. Without your occasional sisterly messages, this project would have been a lonely endeavor. Allow me also to make special mention of a particular contributor, *lmb*, for your willingness to contribute as many chapters as needed to ensure that this book happened.

AND, TO MY sisters from the African continent, for your bold decision to share your personal stories despite your awareness of the likelihood that your message might be subject to intense scrutiny, I say thank you.

FINALLY, TO THE great leader who inspired this book project, President Barack Obama, son of an African father and American mother, thank you for being the force behind the unity and univocality that characterize this collaborative endeavor.

Foreword

Yolanda Sealey-Ruiz

> "Well, son, I'll tell you: Life for me ain't been no crystal stair.
> It's had tacks in it, And splinters, And boards torn up,
> And places with no carpet on the floor—Bare."
>
> (LANGSTON HUGHES, "MOTHER TO SON")

The protagonist in Langston Hughes' "Mother to Son" poem explains to her child how life has been for her as a black woman. She encourages her son to keep pressing on, particularly when life becomes most challenging. She uses her story as an example of how black people persist and make it through the most difficult moments in their lives.

To be sure, life has been "no crystal stair" for black women in particular and black people in general. Despite this reality, they continue to rise. An example of this is seen in the election of President Barack Hussein Obama. In 2008, Obama became the first African American to be elected president of the United States—a country built on the backs of black slaves who were involuntarily brought to America in bondage, and forced to remain in bondage for centuries until their emancipation in 1863. Obama's presidency created a major shift in the mindset of the black community. Although it has been proven that racism increased against blacks as a result of his eight years in office—a 2011 American Press survey showed that 51% of Americans now express explicit anti-blackness—black people across the world, and certainly in the United States, had a new image for what was possible.

A new generation of young people now could look to a tangible example of a black person who had reached the highest political office in the country. So, when asked by adults to answer the obligatory question: "What would you like to be when you grow up?" a generation of black children can now say "president of the United States" and follow an actual precedent. With Obama's election, access to formerly white-dominated, severely restricted places like the White House suddenly opened. While black folks did not suffer amnesia about the racism they had historically experienced and endured daily, Obama's election shifted how they saw themselves as a collective, and what they thought possible to achieve despite opposing systemic forces.

Obama's presidency and his marriage to Michelle LaVaughn Robinson were significant to black folks. Together, with his wife, Michelle, and their daughters, Sasha and Malia, the image of the First Family of the United States was recast. Black girls and women in America were suddenly centered, in part because when the nation looked at its first black president, it also had to see his family. With the Obama girls and Michelle in the media spotlight, the beauty and grace of black girls and women were a constant for all to witness and appreciate.

This volume honors the significance of Obama's elections by reflecting on lessons learned during and in the shadow of his presidency. The book's chapters elevate the voices of black women educators who bring an important and particular lens to his presidency. The volume's editors have assembled a cadre of authors who powerfully use the tool of storytelling to present provocative and thoughtful essays on issues that are important to black women, but should matter to everyone. These chapters provide insight into various important fields and areas of study that are vital to examine for their impact on black women over time and through the present day. The voices in this volume offer varied perspectives that provide robust research and gut-wrenching commentary on black people's reality before, during, and after Obama's presidency. Although multiple and inherently different, what is consistent across all of the writing is how black women have carried movements on their backs and been the motivator and interpreter of change throughout history. Black women, like the black women scholars who share their stories in this book, have experienced struggle and met it with resistance and resilience; they continue to rise in spite of all that is against them. As I read through this volume, I was inspired and felt invigorated by the particular themes of struggle, resistance, resilience, and rising up, which so elegantly and eloquently show up in the following ways:

In her **Introduction**, Immaculée Harushimana takes us through a metaphorical retrospective of what we learned while in "Paradise" during Obama's eight years in office. The introduction lays the foundation for the book, which is an odyssey of facing reality and finding hope—what black people have always had to do since they were brought to this country.

In **Section One: The Burden of Leading While Black**, Rosaire Ifedi, Janice Fournillier, Maheabo D. Magano, Marcia Burrell, and Josephine Jarpa Dawuni address some of the challenges black women face in leadership positions. They tell stories of navigating systems that have placed obstacles before them based on their gender and race. These stories offer sharp reflection and also a way forward as they reveal the resilience and brilliance of black women leaders.

In **Section Two: Gender Equality and Women Empowerment**, Lindamichelle Baron, Ronisha Browdy, Kedibone Gladys Mokwena, Jaye Jones, and Sizakele M. Matlabe delve into an examination of intersectional racism. Each author offers a compelling essay on how gender inequality manifests in various ways for black women. They share stories about how they have individually and collectively persisted, achieved success, and helped others gain personal success in the face of sexism and racism.

In **Section Three: How Brave Art African Women Immigrants**, Mary Ghongkedze, Esther Milu, Immaculée Harushimana, Ellie Williamson, and Shirley Mthethwa Sommers deftly add to the relevance of this book by focusing on the anti-immigrant environment that has intensified in this country during the post-Obama years. Through their own stories, black immigrant women reveal how they were never fully accepted in this country in ways other immigrants have been over time.

In **Section Four: Black Self-Affirmation**, Diane Price Banks, Mary Alfred, Tracy Cook-Person, Patricia Isaac, and Lindamichelle Baron stand firm on the necessity for black women to stake their claim in the field of education as well as in society, despite fierce objection. They evoke lessons taught to them from history and from their own lives about how a black woman's assertion and determination to succeed have allowed her to overcome obstacles with precision, grace, and persistence with dreams for herself and others in her community.

In **Section Five: Can a Black Male Child Dream Big in a Melanin-Phobic World?** Eleanor T. Campbell, Faith Muturia, Faith Maina, and Rasheeda Ahmad discuss how black people should prepare their children to navigate an anti-black world. They examine the realities that racism has created within black families and suggest how we hold on to the hope that Obama infused in society and in black lives.

And finally, in **Section Six: Paradise to Regain: Change Must Come Again**, Gillian U. Bayne, Lindamichelle Baron, Immaculée Harushimana, Aminata Diop, Patricia Mason, and Mary E. Dillard remind black women of their strength. They assert that black women will be the ones to lead their communities through the current political storms and reintroduce the hope and promise that Obama's presidency brought forward. The stories in this section close out this volume by prompting black women to remember their power and reimagine a world worthy of them.

Taken together, these women tell a collective story that inspires their contemporaries and the black women who will follow in their footsteps. In her **Conclusion**, Sherry L. Deckman brings forward the theme of looking backward to go forward in full view. She draws on the black feminist principle of collective memory, and invites the reader to consider what it means for black people to reimagine the world they live in, restore hope in our communities, and bring about the continual change needed for themselves and those who share their world. In all, the women educators who have contributed to this book successfully fulfill the role of "interrupters"—interrupters of the oppressive status quo, interrupters of the oppressive patriarchy, interrupters of black male vilification, interrupters of the oppressive white supremacy, interrupters of immigraphobia.

INTRODUCTION

Eight Years of Paradise
An Obama Will Come Again

Immaculée Harushimana

As women of African descent who also happen to be academic scholars and teacher educators, we are constantly haunted by the scantiness of the African and African American story in the U.S. educational curriculum. It is a well-known fact that the majority of school textbooks around the world are authored by Westerners and promote one tale—the tale of Western civilization and Western history. This approach to teaching and learning has produced generations of black intellectuals who believe that to be successful means to adopt the Western way of thinking, lifestyle, and language. Yet, once upon a time, before the Western invasion, Africa was a fertile land ruled by powerful kings. The feats and deeds of these great kings were recorded and well preserved in the Timbuktu library until they disappeared without a trace, leaving generations and generations of children in the dark concerning their roots and history. There is no doubt that the Eurocentric perspective that permeates the curriculum and academic textbooks bars black and brown children from uncovering the greatness of their ancestors, their self-worth, and their inventiveness. We are saddened to watch young generations of black and brown children, our children's generations, denied the right to hear and read tales of the greatness of their ancestors before they were robbed of their humanity through slavery and colonization. Above all, we have the greatest fear that, by virtue of being black, Barack Obama's story as the first African American president of the United States of America and one of the most inspirational world leaders will not receive the attention it deserves in the United States history. The history of Obama's presidency needs to be presented in its unabridged and unobliterated form—and allocated as much space in history textbooks—so that black and brown children can realize that political power is within their reach.

The victory of Barack Obama sent shock waves around the world, from his father's native country of Kenya, which declared that day a national holiday (Berger, 2008), to the small Obama Island, in Japan, whose "girls" performed a special dance to celebrate his victory (Alabaster, 2008). President Barack Hussein Obama's history-making election as the first black president of the so-called first world in 2008 was a surprise to many black people, especially those with an understanding of how deep rooted white racism is. Reverend Martin Luther King may have dreamt of equality of the races, but he did not predict the black man's ascent to the presidency of a Western nation. The Western narrative had been successful in painting the image of the black man as a descendant of apes, incapable of syllogistic thought, incapable of being "articulate," and, therefore, destined to serve.

Establishing a strong connection between President Obama and the African continent, many African leaders welcomed his victory with a strong sense of hope and optimism. For former interim South African president, Kgalema Motlanthe, Obama's election "carrie[d] with it hope for millions of [American] countrymen and women as much as it is for millions of people, particularly of African descent, both on the continent of Africa as well as those in the Diaspora" ("Motlanthe Joins Leaders", 2008, n. pag.). For Bishop Desmond Tutu, speaking on his behalf as well as that of other people of color, Obama's victory gave assurance and confidence to people of color. Because of his election, black people in South Africa "have a new spring in our walk. [...] Obama stood so that our children can fly" ("Conversations with Archbishop," 2009, pp. 46-47). In a world where the black race is associated with failure, whenever a person of color stands out through success, s/he communicates a message of hope to millions of young brothers and sisters who are plagued with self-doubt that they can achieve the same or more. The same message was conveyed by Nelson Mandela in his congratulatory letter to Obama. Feeling proud that Obama followed in his footsteps in fulfilling a dream previously thought impossible, Mandela seized the opportunity to rule out any excuse that any "person anywhere in the world should not dare to dream of wanting to change the world for a better place" (Kannings, 2008, n. pag.). Another trailblazer from Africa, the Liberian president Ellen Sirleaf, perceived the milestone as "a realization of the dream of Dr. Martin Luther King, not only for the African-American citizens of the United States, but also for those all over the world who hold dear the values of liberty, dignity and equal opportunity" ("Liberian Leader Congratulates U.S. President," 2008, n. pag.).

That Obama's victory carried a special meaning for African Americans was echoed by Condoleezza Rice, former secretary of state under the George W. Bush administration. On the one hand, she acknowledged the milestone, saying, "As an African-American, I'm especially proud, because this is a country that's been through a long journey, in terms of overcoming wounds and making race less of a factor in life" ("Remarks on the Outcomes," 2008, n. pag.). At the same time, she cautioned those who might use the victory to claim that race is no longer a factor: "That work is not done, but yesterday was obviously an extraordinary step forward." Both Rice and Sirleaf alluded to the painful memories of Jim Crow and slavery, and the ultimate sacrifice paid by the leaders of the Civil Rights Movement. The question now becomes, how does this narrative of "more work remains to be done" get transmitted to and cemented in the minds of the young generations of black and brown youth through education?

Whereas Obama's back-to-back victories, 2008 and 2012, were historical in the minds of people all over the world, it is not evident that they will be so in textbooks so that younger generations of black and brown children in the world will get a chance to learn about that pivotal moment in their history. It is only fitting that the electoral victory of the first black president should be recorded in history books as a significant chapter in the U.S. history, one that all the children, regardless of race or country of origin, should learn about. It is a tale that is worth telling all over the world to capture and immortalize the feelings that it generated worldwide. It is a tale that should inspire a wonderful bedtime story that all black and brown children should grow up hearing and seeking to emulate—instead of telling them about fictional kings of Zimunda or Wakanda.

As all good things come to an end, Obama's presidency expired after two terms set by the Constitution. He and his First Lady campaigned hard for the Democratic candidate who, if she had won, would have marked another historic milestone, as the first woman president of the United States of America. The irony of fate was that Obama was to pass the rein of his presidency to the very man who led the movement which undermined the legitimacy of his candidacy during the two consecutive election terms. The presidential campaigns for presidents 44 and 45 will go down in history as the most memorable in U.S. political history and, perhaps, in the world. On the one hand, there is Barack Hussein Obama, an African American presidential candidate who, after defeating his Democratic challenger, a white female senator (and former wife of a president), defeated his Republican opponent, despite his popularity as a war hero. On the other hand, there is Mrs. Hillary Rodham Clinton, a white woman, former wife of a president, who was hoped to be the first woman president of the United States and, at the last minute, lost to her populist opponent, Donald Trump, whose campaign slogan "Make America Great Again" earned him massive support by white nationalists and led him to unanticipated victory.

Mrs. Clinton's loss was hard to accept by women voters, especially white liberals, who took to the streets to express their discontentment by organizing anti-Trump demonstrations throughout the country, which were also echoed by feminist movements all over the world. Less heard and less visible at the pro-Hillary rallies and anti-Trump demonstrations were the voices and faces of black women in the demonstrations. What message does such a silence send to African American children and children born to African-descent immigrant parents? How are the children who, for eight years, had come to believe in the "yes we can" slogan going to adjust to policies of a government which seems determined to sink their hopes by taking away all the funding for programs that made possible the dream that led to the first black president of the United States of America? Who can convince them that it will not take another two hundred years for their descendants to witness another change in the racial identity of the president of the United States? Narratives of hope, comfort, and empowerment from educators and parents of color are direly needed, and this book fulfills that goal.

This volume is edited by three black women educators—an African-born and naturalized U.S. citizen, a naturalized American citizen of West Indian descent, and an African American woman and U.S.-born citizen of the U.S. As women educators of color, we have all agreed that the socio-political climate prevailing in the United States of America since the aftermath of the 2016 election requires unprecedented agency. We acknowledge that we might actually be holding onto experiences that could educate and inspire our children and those like them. We also believe that there are other sisters and colleagues out there who have stories like ours that need to be told. We, therefore, are determined to collect those stories and publish them in the form of an edited volume that educators at all levels—K-12 and beyond—will find worth reading and interpreting for their students.

This volume comprises 32 chapters, which include the introduction and the conclusion. The chapters have been organized into six sections, each of which centers on a theme of pertinence to the experience of being black and/or a woman either in a white-male-dominant or a once-white-suppressed patriarchal society elsewhere.

The first section, **The Burden of Leading While Black**, tells of the feeling of frustration and powerlessness felt by black Americans and black immigrants in the position of power. In the same way that President Obama was not allowed to govern by those who did not want to face the truth that the black race may be intellectually as capable (or even more) than the white race, blacks in leadership positions have to work under hostile work environments deliberately created by white saboteurs to make them either resign (see Rosaire Ifedi), look for employment at other institutions (see Maheabo Magano), or simply feel uneasy (see Janice Fournillier; Josephine J. Dawuni), unless someone develops a tough skin like Queen Sanford (see Lindamichelle Baron in section six) to fight all the way or self-affirm (see Marcia Burrell; Mary Alfred in section four). The burden of leading while black becomes even heavier when it involves intersectionalities of gender (woman), race (black), place of birth (Africa), parental status status (mother) and professional status (academic), as in Dawuni's case. She found it rather difficult to reconcile the authority figure and the humanity of motherhood, but why?

The second section, **Gender Equality and Women's Empowerment**, denounces the repressive patriarchy, which considers itself entitled to ruling over the world while women are relegated to subservient roles and positions. Two chapters in particular (see Sizakele Matlabe; Kedibone Mokwena) denounce the incivility of male-dominated institutions and norms toward widows. Lindamichelle Baron makes sure that the world does not lose sight of the cruelty of the patriarchal system toward strong women, like Hillary Clinton or herself, who vie for male-coveted positions. Josephine Dawuni in section one also alludes to the issue of gender imbalance when she evokes the dilemma of reconciling mother-nurture female nature with the dry academician persona. In the same vein, Jaye Jones highlights the critical responsibility of women who were fortunate enough to achieve an education and have a voice in society to help those not so fortunate to improve their condition.

Section three, **How Brave Are African Women Immigrants?**, projects the feelings of hurt, scarred immigrant women, who are frustrated by the unanticipated racism and discrimination they incur upon arrival in the United States.

Both Mary Ghongkedze and Immaculée Harushimana are widowed women who, while trying to transcend the tragedies of losing a loved one and being left alone to raise male children, were disappointed by the insensitivity of the world around them, which, instead of showing them appreciation for their strength, sought to break them further. Esther Milu brings hope to the situation through her narrative of determination to safeguard her linguistic and cultural identity and imparting it in her children, an attribute she tends to share with Immaculée Harushimana in her determination to tap into her cultural knowledge during her teaching. Ellie Williamson's story epitomizes the resilient mind of the black immigrant woman by never giving up on her dream to become an educator despite the many obstacles she met on the way.

Chapters in section four, **Black Self-Affirmation**, raise the importance of self-affirmation of people of the black race. Diane Price Banks exposes whites' malicious intentions in stealing credit from black scientists to propagate their false theories of black inferior intelligence; she rallies behind Obama's call for the strengthening of STEM education in all schools, including those serving underprivileged children. She, along with other strongly grounded women (see Mary Alfred, Tracy Cook-Person, and Patricia Isaac's Melissa), relate their narratives of strength and unwavering determination which led them to success in domains that are usually closed to blacks, especially women. Tracy Cook-Person has a clear message for minorities of color who wish to be acknowledged for their capacities: "we must write ourselves into history." Lindamichelle Baron brings the conversation together by reminding us that no dream is impossible, as Barack Obama and Martin Luther King have demonstrated.

Section five, **Can a Black Male Child Dream Big in a Melanin-Phobic World**, takes the conversation of hope and possibility to young ones (see Eleanor Campbell; Ronisha Browdy in section two), both males and females. Through her memories of a black girl finding hope during the 2008 elections, Ronisha Browdy in section two gives black girls in the United States and beyond the message that their vote and voice matter. The importance of voting is cemented by Historian Mary Dillard in section six, who uses the voice of her parents— forebearers of today's generation—whose nostalgic narratives evoke the price paid by civil rights leaders and activists for black people to have the right to vote. Mothers of black male children (Faith Muturia and Shirley Mthethwa-Sommers in section three) seize the opportunity to write powerful letters to their black sons urging them to remain vigilant and vision-oriented so as not fall into the trap of the white distorted narrative of black ignorance. They exhort them to follow in Obama's footsteps as well as in the footsteps of other strong black men who came before him (as discussed in Rasheeda Ahmad's piece). Faith Maina follows and detangles Obama's trajectory from an uncertain childhood to a glorious adulthood to remind young boys who grow up in fatherless households like Obama that they can still achieve great things if they put their minds to it. Rasheeda Ahmad completes the conversation by reminding black males that they are destined to be world citizens and cultural ambassadors.

The sixth and last section, **Paradise to Regain: Change Must Come Again**, contains chapters that convey a message of hope that, despite the disappointment that followed Obama's exit from the leadership of America and the entrance of his stark nemesis to the White House (see Aminata Diop), hope for the regaining of the paradise should never be lost. Despite palpable pain behind their words due to the negative encounters they have witnessed, Gillian Bayne and Immaculée Harushimana believe in possible dreams and the possibility of recapturing the Obama era paradise. Patricia Mason reminds communities, educators, and advocates for young people of color that they have a big responsibility to support the village that raises the next future generation. In conclusion, Sherry L. Deckman highlights the importance of reconciling past memories and present occurrences as catalysts for the remembering of where one has been and (re)imagining the future that lies ahead.

The messages contained in this book, while primarily targeting educators, will be of interest to faculty outside of schools and colleges of education, especially in the social sciences domain (Immigration Studies, Black/Ethnic Studies, Humanities, Anthropology, Sociology, Political Sciences, Philosophy, etc.). The volume will also appeal to the general audience, particularly any person who believes in a fair and just world for all.

References

Alabaster, J. (2008). Japan's Obama Town Celebrates Namesake's Victory. Available: https://www.telegraph.co.uk/news/politics/local-elections/3384122/Barack-Obama-victory-sends-Japanese-town-of-Obama-wild.html

Berger, S. (2008). Kenya Declares National Holiday in Celebration of Barack Obama's Presidential Victory. Available: http://www.telegraph.co.uk/news/worldnews/barackobama/3385610/Kenya-declares-national-holiday-in-celebration-of-Barack-Obamas-presidential-victory.html

Conversations with Archbishop. (2009). Conversation with Archbishop Emeritus Desmond Tutu. The Rotarian, 42-48.

Kannings, A. (2014). Nelson Mandela in His Own Words. New York: Little, Brown and Company.

"Liberian Leader Congratulates U.S. President." (2008). Liberian Leader Congratulates U.S. President-Elect Barack Obama. Retrieved 09/18/2017, from http://emansion.gov.lr/2press.php?news_id=938&related=7&pg=sp

Motlanthe Joins Leaders. (2008). Motlanthe Joins Leaders in Congratulating Obama. Available: https://mg.co.za/article/2008-11-05-motlanthe-joins-leaders-in-congratulating-obama

Remarks on the Outcomes. (2008). Remarks on the Outcome of U.S. Presidential Elections. Retrieved 09/10/2017. From: https://2001-2009.state.gov/secretary/rm/2008/11/111569.htm

SECTION I
THE BURDEN OF LEADING WHILE BLACK

Chapter 1

"They're Coming for Our Jobs Too!"
Double Standards for Black and White Leadership in the Age of Obama and Trump

Rosaire Ifedi

WHO SAID POST-RACIAL AMERICA?

> *Storytellers are a threat. They threaten all champions of control; they frighten usurpers of the right-to-freedom of the human spirit—in state, in church or mosque, in party congress, in the university or wherever.*
>
> —CHINUA ACHEBE (1987)

THE LAYERS OF discrimination that African-born females have encountered in society and the workplace are well documented. As black women in academia, our sheer presence challenges accepted norms in leadership. The contradictory and jarring ascendancy of Obama and then Trump to the highest office has served to highlight the discomfort toward black leadership. In the U.S. and globally, Obama was celebrated and his blackness and identity were touted as proof of acceptance of black leadership. On many fronts, it appeared to be the end of an era of racism, leading to many a talk about post-racial America. Careful observers of history knew otherwise, and yet couldn't have predicted what was to come after a second Obama term. It was a backlash. The resulting response to Obama's successful presidency—not to talk about his personal integrity, charm, and character—was that the U.S. did an about-face to elect someone completely different in personality, character, and skills. A big chasm suddenly emerged, or maybe it had always been there—underneath it all. Minorities, immigrants, their supporters, and the political Left tried to find solace together.

As we mourned the turn of events in November 2016, we were confronted with the resurgence of latent racism that seemed to have gone underground and been fairly silenced during Obama's leadership. The fact is Obama had shouldered much of the weight of the racism in the eight years in office; and now, it was going to be unleashed on all non-whites. This is the account of my own personal experiences that reflected the hidden yet resurfaced racism as President Obama began to step away and President Trump emerged as the voice of anti-immigrant America.

THE CONTEXT: SOMETHING IN THE AIR

Rendered Invisible

Black leaders' experiences of being undermined and denied credit for their successes was on full display after 2008. The unsung and hidden heroines of NASA, finally brought to the screen in *Hidden Figures,* are but an old metaphor for everyday occurrences of the same phenomenon. The syndrome of black people working triply hard to get the same accolades easily given to their white counterparts is not new. For President Obama, the visibility of the office granted him no protection or immunity from this disease. While Obama was in charge, he hardly received the credit due to him—not for economic stabilization, not for healthcare, and not immigration for the Deferred Action for Childhood Arrivals act (DACA) children. His actions to fix immigration, which were similar to actions taken by previous presidents like Reagan, became a constitutional offense. The noise from the political hard right was shrill and unbearable. Every step Obama took was questioned. Loudly. As Africans, we all recognized not only the tinge of racism in the birtherism but also the reality of a double standard: a standard that rewarded anything white with praise (no matter how mediocre, as in the response to Trump) while undermining and disdaining black excellence. We just didn't think the opposition would be so personal and blatantly bigoted. Bill Maher, a comedian whose political truths resonated with me, would tell it like it is: As *R* (Republican), one could get away with anything—practically, anything. The unfolding events of 2017/18 in this Trump era continue to prove Maher right.

Leading with the Heart

> *The forces that unite us are intrinsic and greater than the superimposed influences that keep us apart.*
>
> —KWAME NKRUMAH

In spite of the toxic environment created by the opposition, Obama was not to be swayed from his humane style of leadership. The significance of his presidency to young people, black males, Africans, all of the U.S. and the world, was not to be lost. He was the embodiment of the legacies of proud and thoughtful leaders from the past, such as Dr. Martin Luther King Jr. He was the continuation of legacies that predated him. He lived out and modeled his truths and convictions with a distinctly Afrocentric-influenced personality—with resilience and calm—what would come to be called "No-drama Obama." The impact of his ethos on young people was and still is far-reaching.

Then came November 8, 2016; it seemed like everything came crashing down. It has remained one of those days in history that, if you were old enough, you remembered precisely where you were. Dreams were deferred; expectations shattered. I remember waking up and unburdening myself, my frustration, angst, and fears into a blog, surmising that:

> *The cover had been blown. This is the America we always knew existed, but silently wished had been mitigated by modernity, exchange with other cultures, and even the Obamas' legacy. The truth for me is that while economy, gender, race, terrorism, the Supreme Court, white working middle class disenfranchisement, and immigration were all on the ballot, the overwhelming sense of America's rejection of immigrants like me cuts across all the others.* (Ifedi, 2016)

As I reflected on the turn of events, there was no singular factor that could explain the stunning victory of Trump. Regardless of the fact that it was an Electoral College win rather than a popular vote one, our feelings of estrangement were not assuaged. Should we attribute his election solely to the equally surprising rise of the rust belt, the economically left-behind, the disenfranchised Americans? That alone couldn't explain it all. There was the gender vote and then the white

Christian vote. I opined in another blog post that the Evangelicals and, indeed, the American Church was in dire need to exorcise, discern, and soul search (Ifedi, 2017). What do I have to do with all this?

MY STORY: WHAT HAPPENED

Not long after Trump's victory, I was asked to give the invocation at a faculty meeting. My faith was surely being tried. I didn't know how else to be but to be true to myself. I voiced my thoughts from the blog as an opening to prayer, highlighting the new feelings of being unwelcomed, the fears, and the estrangement I and the rest of the immigrant community were experiencing. Yet, it's also in times like these that we experience clarifying moments. When we talk about racism, there is never an intention to castigate all members of any one race or the other. Racism can be either individualistic or systemic. A pattern of unjustified discriminatory utterances and actions can qualify persons or systems as racist. After the invocation, a dear colleague of mine was so moved he wouldn't let me leave the hall till he gave me the biggest bear hug of my life. My friend passed away barely two weeks after that encounter, suddenly. I would forever be thankful for the love and peace we shared in that moment of understanding and solidarity. There truly is more that binds us than separates us.

Leading with Truth

The way we have to measure progress is not, "Is there ever going to be an incident of racism in the country?" It's, "How does the majority of our country respond?"

—BARACK OBAMA

"I am the least racist person there is."

—DONALD TRUMP (JAN. 15, 2018)

We are necessarily telling these stories to elucidate, educate, encourage, and empower. Positioning ourselves in these challenging times is speaking our truths to power. During a very constraining experience of undermining, I had to fight to maintain self, sanity, and strength. In my work educating teachers, I always present themes of affirmation, efficacy, and self and group identity and their impact on black students. Facilitating discussions on self-identity meant that if teachers recognized and owned their own identity (with all of its hidden advantages and disadvantages), they would be better prepared to recognize and affirm the identities of their students: black, white, immigrant, indigenous, minority, majority, and all. Immigrant and transnational students deal with much more in terms of academics, language learning, and cultural adjustments. The current climate makes this even more burdensome. How do we, as blacks, self-affirm that indeed we are? How do our neighbors react to implicit or blatant racism expressed toward our blackness? Unfortunately, extreme polarizations have offered no answers.

In an interview with Oprah Winfrey, Nelson Mandela cautioned us that "sometimes a leader has to criticize those with whom he works—it cannot be avoided. I like a leader who can, while pointing out a mistake, bring up the good things the other person has done" (2016, n. pag.). What Mandela said next could very well have been said by President Obama, a mentee of his: "If you do that, then the person sees that you have a complete picture of him. There is nobody more dangerous than one who has been humiliated, even when you humiliate him rightly" (2016, n. pag.). Obama himself was appreciated for his ability to listen, accommodate others, and be patiently thoughtful, acknowledging:

> *One of my strengths is I have a pretty even temperament. I don't get too high when it's high and I don't get too low when it's low. And what I found during the course of the presidency, and I suppose this is true in life, is that investments and work that you make back here sometimes take a little longer than the 24-hour news cycle to bear fruit. (Obama, 2015, n. pag.)*

Mandela and Obama were role models for leading with truth and humility. I had always prized myself as someone who could handle tough verbal attacks. Admittedly, it wasn't the narrative most people would expect, but that had been my experience. I typically responded to racist attitudes and behaviors directed at me with a shrug and a prayer.

Set in context within these presidential leaderships, something in the air was changing, however. The U.S., as I stated before, had gone from the shock of a two-term President Obama to questioning what that meant and trying but failing to come to terms with it. The hornet's nest of resentment had been stirred.

As black people, we work to counter the myth that black is inferior while white is right and beautiful. America subconsciously began to respond as such to Obama's leadership. When presented with policies that they themselves had previously championed, the opposition balked. The hostile and irrational sentiments accompanying the infamous "You lie" from Congressman Wilson and "We'll make him a one-term president" by Senator McConnell persisted. Looking back, it still baffles me. These incidents were not imagined but real. The "offense of black leadership" would ripple out to all areas of American life. The police relations with black communities deteriorated, and the unwarranted slaying of innocent black men escalated.

Leading While Black and Immigrant

In academia, black faculty would not be exempt from the assault of being black. At some point after I made tenure, I was approached to lead my college's re-accreditation process. Five years into the process, things seemed in disarray. Faculty were worried. The new process of accreditation was a change in paradigms from a checklist process to a performance-based, mixed-methods process. The old way would not work anymore. As God would have it, I attended one of the conferences offered to all faculty who had an interest. Even before going, I sensed in the spirit that I was going to experience a shift in my career. At breakfast on the last day, some of my colleagues confided in me that I had to somehow take the leadership because I truly understood the process and had the personality to create much needed collaboration. I politely said "No" to them. Four weeks or so later, I was invited to lunch. My suspicions were right. Before we were done eating at this fine Ohio Amish restaurant, I had said "Yes" to the request to lead.

With a two-course release, I jumped into the work with all I had. I reorganized the entire process, created sub-committees, coached faculty and staff, and put together new teams and leaders. It was, even to me, amazing how everyone cooperated. Indeed, maybe I had underestimated my people skills. Yet, I always knew that empowering others and pulling on their strengths was an asset. Everybody was on board, and hard work was getting done.

Did I say "contradictory experiences" before? I had almost everybody on board but of course had to deal with teaming issues and personalities. I had enough thick skin and felt strengthened to persist. Like I said, inspiration came from Obama's "No drama" personality in the face of stifling opposition from congressional Republicans. The college underwent several leadership changes, one of which was to create a new position to oversee accreditation and quality assurance. I mean that's what I was already doing, right? Wouldn't it naturally be something I would switch over to, after having done all this work? That's when matters took a different turn.

While I was still at a conference, my colleagues voted for someone else to take the position. Granted I didn't want a fully administrative position like that and certainly loved my teaching and researching, but I did feel the underlying message of rejection of my leadership. I began to receive reassuring texts from a number of my colleagues who called out the wrongheadedness of the vote. But not so fast. The reorganization required that I continue the accreditation preparation while someone else not previously engaged with the process would take the position. Wait—take the title! It was unbelievable. Seriously, I would be doing the work and someone would get the leadership title/position. I had heard and read of similar stories: the black person doing the job while a less qualified white person had the title! I was bemused. Somewhere they forgot they were dealing with an African woman.

At first, I spoke up and proposed other options: either separate the two positions and I finish up with the assignment, or I totally step down and the new person takes over—all of it. I look back and thank God for the courage as I prayerfully communicated my decision. I received an affirmative answer but after a few more weeks in the readjusted leadership structure, the undermining got worse. It was tangible and visible. Another colleague even called it out at one of our meetings. I checked myself to see if I was an illegal immigrant trying to take a job that belonged to someone else. Was I stealing a white woman's position? The demonization of immigrants who come to steal jobs from black, and now white Americans, was alive and well! Laugh if you will, but that's exactly what it felt like.

Leading with Persistence and Love

"No one can make you feel inferior without your consent."
—ELEANOR ROOSEVELT

"No matter what anybody says, we can't have it all. Not if you are a woman. Not yet."

—AMA ATA AIDOO

For the good of the unit, I made my decision to step away. It was important for me to share the evolving story with family and church members (without names or titles, of course) to show them how to endure under pressure, how to affirm who you are and what skills you bring to the table—any table—and how to never allow yourself to be judged by bigoted, double, or different standards. It's literally funny as I look back that I made this statement in my resignation email, "It's just tiring. I am no Obama. :)"

Did I give up? Am I contradicting my message about endurance? Of course not. Many wonderful outcomes came out of this experience. For one, if you don't live it, you can't tell the story. If we pay careful attention, we can see that effective black leadership should not threaten white people. The sense of superiority may be challenged, even dethroned, but the outcomes for all outweigh these sensibilities. Similarly, immigrants should not pose a threat to the native-born—black or white—people. In stark contradiction to the Western idea of competition that creates winners and losers, there's room enough for excellence from any and all peoples. Denying goodness when it comes from a source other than white can leave persons, communities, or nations worse off. Conversely, mediocrity from any leader should not be rewarded, period. The dominant society needs to do away with the tendency to ignore or reward white mediocrity and *always* denigrate it when black. Likewise, excellence and competence should always be acknowledged, regardless of skin color.

AND THE MORAL OF THE STORY IS...

It remains important that we encourage ourselves and our children about what they are likely to face in the workforce, in the marketplace, or in society in general. I articulate these enduring lessons with students, teachers, and mentees of color, particularly. Do your work with excellence, and even when it's not acknowledged or when it's judged with double standards, do not give up. Follow the right channels to make your case without becoming obnoxious. Whether the playing field is leveled or not, and while we strive to erase different standards for black leadership, I call on young emerging leaders to be the best they are created to be. Obama did; so can you. My encounter with the implicit biases and overt double standards at work did not stop me from being me. I rejected retaliatory bitterness and, when necessary or called upon, continued to be a voice of reason and peace. We refuse to live under man-made weights; rather, we rise above them to build community with all who are willing to be part of a loving, interconnected humanity.

References

Achebe, C. (1987). *Anthills of the savannah*. London, U.K.: Heinemann.

Ifedi, R.I. (2016). "Welcome no more." Accessible at www.drrosaire.wordpress.com

Ifedi, R.I. (2017). *Christianity and the American Presidents.* Accessible at https://drrosaire.wordpress.com/2017/07/08/christianity-and-the-american-presidents-taking-our-faith-through-a-much-needed-soul-searching/

Mandela, N. (2016). *Transcript of Interview with Oprah*. Accessible at http://www.oprah.com/world/oprah-interviews-nelson-mandela/all#ixzz5GusvUJpG

Obama, B. (2015). *Transcript of Interview with Jon Sopel*. Accessible at http://www.bbc.com/news/world-us-canada-33646542

CHAPTER 2

Does Race Matter in Dissertation Mentoring?
A Black Native Caribbean Woman Research Methodologist Genuflects and Reflects

Janice B. Fournillier

> *Started the day with an early morning inspirational phone call with my major professor, Dr. Janice Fournillier. She said, "No one can stop what you're called to do." I needed it more than I realized, embraced it, and had a fun, amazing day. Choose your mentors wisely!* (Elston, D., February 26, 2018).

> *Through it all was a dissertation chair committed to the process of honest, objective research singularly focused on a policy discourse and produced new knowledge celebrating the subaltern voices adversely affected by that discourse. "Think small, dig deep." I was never more proud than what resulted. Thank you.* (R. Maltese, personal communication, 2018)

I INTENTIONALLY BEGIN this narrative with two remarks from former graduate mentees whose work propelled me during the Obama and post-Obama era, as I worked at coming to know what it means to be a mentor in a foreign space at a higher education institution. I do so because what they wrote resonates with the kind of legacy that is and will always be important to me, as a self-identified black Afro-Caribbean woman in the academy.

In the Caribbean, being black meant very little to me other than it was the color of my skin. My parents, friends, and family looked like me and no one challenged my identity. Yes, we had different shades of black, but I learned that my grandmother's father was from China, and her mother was born in

Venezuela. My great-grandmother Mena worked on the cocoa plantations in Gran Couva, and so did my great-aunts and -uncles. A calypsonian/historian/teacher made me aware that the government owed my grandparents back pay for all the free labor they provided for the white plantation owners. I attended a Catholic secondary school where I had my first contact with students who did not look like me and seemed to be affluent. But my mother taught me to hold my head up high and be proud of who I was, so they did not bother me.

In 2000 I migrated to the USA and moved between various identities: an alien immigrant, an international student with legal status, a permanent resident, and a naturalized citizen. One black male student put me in my place when he told me that even if I had citizenship I would never be American. Anyone who knows me would know what my quip response was. Looking back on my five years in graduate school, I realize how fortunate and/or privileged I was to have had such a "smooth ride." This would be made even clearer as I mentored a graduate student who made issues related to immigrants the focus of his dissertation.

I also came to understand that I was not just a woman with African roots; but that I was also supposed to accept a minority status. However, there was no turning back when a supposedly black man decided to put his hat in the U.S. election ring during my tenure at a higher education institution. I was forced to recognize what it means to be black in the United States of America, where I was now a researcher/methodologist/evaluator at a predominantly white institution (PWI) in an urban region. I struggled to accept that I had to be and become somebody else to be accepted by the institution's faculty and students. I insisted that I was black and a woman from the diaspora and had nothing against African Americans, but that it was not how I self-identified. I also resisted being identified by faculty as a "Brit" because of how I taught and my high academic expectations of all the students I taught. I responded to faculty stating that although I was from an English education system, I was also filled with French, Spanish, and Chinese heritage and so refused to be characterized as British because I expected assignments to be creative, thoughtful, clearly expressed, and reflective of author individuality. I did not just give grades; those grades had to be earned.

The election of the first black president put a lot of things in perspective and became even clearer when the next president, a white man, came into power. Having been granted citizenship in 2006, I could now vote. So, I paid close attention to the discourse, listened to the conversation about the first black family who was moving into the White House, and felt a sense of pride and boldness. The discussions circled around whether or not the president was claiming his identity as a black president, what was the role of this black wife/mother figure, and whether she helped to make more of this mixed-race man. Was he to, or could he, do enough for the black community?

In the meantime, President Obama was trying to be the president of the United States and not white or black America. The First Lady had to also fight against how she was being identified and had to constantly defend her positioning of herself as first and foremost the mother of two girls and the wife of the president. The tensions of being a black leader were very evident. The black community and, indeed, many of the members of the Democratic Party felt that the president was more committed to big businesses and the white community and not enough was being done for them. The following hypothetical questions plagued me as I thought of my role as mentor/advisor at an urban institution in the South:

> "Were whites therefore going to (dis)engage because they were not in power?"
>
> "What would be done for the millions of immigrants who were looking up to the president to ease their pain and anguish? "
>
> "How would I now be able to advise and mentor students at my university given the changing pre- and post-Obama environment?"

There were lots of changes taking place within and outside of the higher education institutions where supposedly there was academic freedom. I too began to reflect on what seemed to be the place I occupied in the institution. Of course, there were more questions than answers. I wondered whether I was being viewed as a black professor who could take care of the black students. I questioned whether my presence on their committees identified me as a black mother to others. I pondered about the many students who looked like me and came knocking on the door of the office I occupied for advice on their research methodology. I often deliberated on the issue that only the dissertation chair was recognized when evaluations were being done. During those initial years, I dared not ask to be the chair since I thought you needed to want me rather than I wanting to be it. In hindsight I speculated about what might be considered "a Caribbean mentality." Eventually I came to the realization that I should have known that "you can't play mas' and fraid [dialect spelling of the word afraid] powder." If you throw your hat in the ring, be prepared for the consequences.

Finally, one young man was bold enough to ask me to be his dissertation chair. I guess he did not regret it given his Facebook comment many years later, and which I used to open this narrative. The student was dealing with a touchy issue that might implicate the university that housed large numbers of black and white students who now felt minoritized. It, according to the graduate student, was a "tipping point." When asked during my process of writing this narrative to reflect on his process, Dhanfu stated:

> Upon entering the doctoral program, I had already thought extensively about a topic of race and equity that I knew would require guidance and mentorship from someone that could assist me in navigating the sociopolitical structures of the institution being studied. I needed more than a committee member. I needed an advocate. (personal communication, 2018)

I believe my role is not only to provide academic advice, but to also protect the students from harm and ensure that their career and post-graduation goals and dreams would not be adversely affected. The institution's Institutional Review Board (IRB) took care of the participants who were being studied, and as the advisor, I took on the role of the graduate student protector from harm. This experience would be repeated years later during the post-Obama/Trump era, as another self-identified male, black student came to realize during one of my writing retreats that his passion was for issues related to immigrant students who were being impacted by the American immigration policy, Deferred Action for Childhood Arrivals (DACA). According to Ryan,

> In the summer of 2015, as the presidential election process was only just beginning to unfold and candidates were still caricatures, I came to you with a proposal for a research article that was the result of an earlier paper I'd written on the lack of access to post-secondary education for undocumented students. When the consolidation of GSU & GPC was announced a couple months before, I wanted to interrogate the issue further, perhaps from multiple viewpoints at

> state and local levels. I had only a cursory awareness of the plight of undocumented students, the DREAM Act, and had only JUST begun to look at either the existence or importance of DACA, all of which were mentioned in my 8-page outline. It took you about 5 min to look at me and say, "This is not an article. THIS is your dissertation." (personal communication, 2018)

As I reflect back, as a trained methodologist, it was easy for me to spot errors in terms of how the dissertations were being framed and the types of data were being collected and analyzed. In contrast, I did not have much convincing to do, and the students accepted the advice. As the dissertation chair, I felt called on to stand in the gap when this second dissertation proposal was sent to the University Legal Counsel for review without my knowledge. I wondered about how I was to interpret this in an institution that supposedly valued academic freedom. I felt challenged about the kind of advisor I was being called to be in situations like these. My goal was still the same: Ensure that the students achieved their goals of becoming the kind of scholar who did not just reify the institutions but did rigorous, credible, authentic scholarship that spoke to issues for which they had a passion and which would make a difference to the worlds in which they reside and would continue to work as scholars. The mentee further reflected,

> Over the course of the next 18 months, I went through a variety of research questions, interrogation topics, and entry points for the research. At the same time, there were cases working their way through the courts demanding interpretation of USG policies as they related to in-state tuition for DACA students. What seemed at first to be a rather benign overview of the plight of undocumented students instead became a direct interrogation of a university system policy and its adverse impact on social justice, access, and equity. (Ryan, personal communication 2018)

Similarly, my mentoring approach was appreciated by Dhanfu, my other mentee. I needed that advocate on my doctoral journey in the late 2000s, and Dr. Fournillier became that person for me. For one of the first times, she taught me that I could be free in what I had to say and write. It was more than a teacher-student relationship; we learned how to academically dance with one another. I would discuss the political land mines of writing about race and injustice at the institution where I worked and she emboldened me to use a voice that was personally comfortable from my own cultural lens and relevant for the individuals that I wanted to share my research, whether it be readers, fellow scholars, or university administrators. (Dhanfu, personal communication, 2018)

Being unfamiliar with the immigration and higher education policies, I looked to the graduate students to "teach" me, like I taught my dissertation committee members during my process. I wanted to ensure that they were becoming the "experts" in the area that they were researching.

Having adopted the *Ubuntu* mantra that *I am because you are*, I was committed to ensuring that justice and beneficence were not only for the participants who volunteered to be in the study but those who were bold and brave enough to make those controversial topics the focus of their dissertation studies. I thought I knew what I was doing, but their words say it much better than mine and I humbly accept them. And in so doing, I am proud to make them integral to this story.

According to Dhanfu's observation below, my role as dissertation mentor goes beyond methodological guidance, something I had not anticipated. I could not help being part of the deep conversation on race, power, and injustice. Thus, Dhanfu commented,

> Dr. Fournillier helped to realize that voices of people of color sometimes become inconsequential and it is critical that our stories and voices be heard. We frequently discussed how historical context always influences the future; thus, requires a holistic approach to race and equity, otherwise institutions fall into a cyclically regressive pattern of racial identity relationships. People of color are now faced with challenges of maintaining the gains that former members of their communities fought so hard to achieve. I learned then and watch now, in my professional career, how historical foundations and resulting demographic changes have resulted in White

> colleagues' perceptions of the increasingly racially diverse space. As experienced during that earlier period, individuals are talking equity without actually doing equitable work. Equally as complex. Watching the language but policies that disenfranchise. They want [to] make changes, but on their own terms and without inclusion from those most affected. (Dhanfu, personal communication, 2018)

The first line of Dhanfu's dissertation reads, "As the United States of America becomes progressively more diverse, at what point do previously underrepresented groups become the new racial majorities?" (Elston, 2011, n. pag.). According to Dhanfu, "The dream has not shifted, as much as we realize that it will continue to be difficult to attain in the current political environment" (personal communication, 2018). Still seven years later, there continues to be a need for the amplification of alternate voices of people of color, as presented in Ryan's work (Maltese, 2017), and other disenfranchised populations for those in power to truly hear the impact of their policies, actions, and thoughts.

These are some of the important lessons I learned as a dissertation advisor from my graduate mentees who were teaching me as much as I was teaching them. Little did I know that as a dissertation advisor/mentor I would silently become embroiled in controversy related to what should have been a scholarly developmental process. But I guess it was related to the political time in which I was operating as a mentor to upcoming scholars who dared to challenge the status quo and to *"think small and dig deep"* (my advising mantra for which I have become known). But I know that I was, am, and continue to be the kind of advisor who has an interest in social justice issues and not in research just for the sake of obtaining academic qualifications. And, indeed, if I am to be the kind of advisor who sees the events and activities involved in the process as what I am called to do, it will continue to be because of who these graduate students are and continue to be. Yes, dreams really matter and it is okay to be dreamers; however, it is also okay to be doers of good to self and the communities in which we have been privileged to be members. I learned that I am more than the black lady in the academy, and it is okay to be a mother in the white academy house. But we have a responsibility to be true to self and community and do what intuitively we know to be the honest, good, and right thing, even if it does not get recognized by the institutions, the people themselves for whom it is done, and in spite of the IRB's rules and regulations.

And so, I end with the belief that governments and administrations come and go. This process has helped me achieve a better understanding of Obama's bravery in tackling the conversation on race relations and crisis in America, especially given the climate that has prevailed since his successor took office. The work never ends, and as Christ Tambu Herbert, the Trinidadian calypsonian, reminds me, "The journey now start!" And so, I continue to take into consideration the present discourse as I do my mentoring work and accompany students on their journey within and outside the hallowed walls. As Dhanfu noted,

> Many of our mentoring conversations related to the tribalism that exists when policies and practices are questioned. That recognition continues to guide my personal life and professional trajectory. Change requires a strength and emboldened behavior that few are willing to sacrifice. The students taught and advised by Dr. Fournillier are challenged to determine where they will stand—not only now, but in the future. (personal communication, 2018)

The narratives of these mentees now scholars and those with whom I work continue to provide the impetus and motivation for me to do the work I feel called to as the light from within guides me throughout the process. Indeed, I dare say, I can do no less as an authentic scholar/mentor/advisor that I aspire to be and become....

References

Elston, D. E. (2011). *Tipping point: The diversity threshold for white student (dis)engagement in traditional student organizations.* Unpublished dissertation. Georgia State University, Atlanta. https://scholarworks.gsu.edu/eps_diss/75

Elston, D. (February 26, 2018). Posted to Facebook.

Maltese, R. Z. (2017). *They, too, sing America: A critical analysis of USG policy 4.1.6 and its perceived impacts on DACA students in the state of Georgia.* Unpublished doctoral dissertation. Georgia State University, Atlanta. https://scholarworks.gsu.edu/eps/diss/159

CHAPTER 3

Transformative Leadership—"Botho-Humane": A Wellness Perspective

Meahabo D. Magano

Introduction

THROUGH THE WORDS of former president of the United States of America (USA) Barack Obama who said, "Yes we can," young academics regardless of their skin color are also wishing to make a mark. The post-apartheid era (post-1994) necessitated a transformed educational landscape in South Africa. Prior to 1994, white males predominantly led South African universities while blacks who were employed by universities occupied lower ranks. It was rare to find black professors in the corridors of universities; instead, black people were serving as lecturers, administrative staff, cleaners, or messengers. I joined academia in 2007 as a senior lecturer because I had already obtained a doctoral degree. What appalled me was that there was minimal transformation and blacks did not have a voice in faculty meetings; their ideas were ignored. It was heart wrenching for me to see some young black women who were mentored by white female professors being turned into administrative staff, or instructed to pack assignments, rather than being supported in the writing of articles or book chapters. There was white hegemony and prevailing myths that blacks were not good enough in leading or coordinating programs. That is when I decided to act in a way of transforming the lives of black academics in higher education.

In an attempt to transform the situation, I took a standpoint theory and humanness as a transformative lens. Indeed, the journey was marked by antagonism just like most black leaders, such as former presidents, Nelson Mandela and Barack Obama, and their First Ladies, Winnie Mandela and Michelle Obama, experienced. However, I took a stance of resisting oppression through hard work, developing others while I was also developing myself and showing kindness (*botho* in Sepedi). Servant leadership is what I cherish, with—an element of "botho"—humane, as the South African saying suggests, "Motho ke motho ka batho", meaning, *I am because you are*—if you want to go fast, go alone; if you want to go far, go together with others. As a black woman leader in academia, I have embraced going with other young academics and being a change agent.

Background

John Maxwell (2005) underscores that one secret of leadership is the principle of leading oneself well and learning self-management. The principle is seen in people who left a legacy like Nelson Mandela, who said: "What counts in life is not the mere fact that we have lived. It is what difference we have made to the lives of others that will determine the significance of the life we lead" (Forde, 22 July 2014). Furthermore, Maxwell (2005) states, "championing the vision is more difficult when you did not create it" (p. 64). This chapter is written in an attempt to reflect on my journey as a black South African woman to becoming a leader in an academic world that was predominantly dominated by whites.

Leaders in academia are rated differently from other sectors. In academia, publishing is seen as an important thing since it distinguishes one either as a scholar or not. I am proud to say that in South Africa, there are black women leaders in academia, like Professor Mamokgethi Phakeng, who is a B2-rated Scientist by the National Research Foundation (Ancer, 2018). Having such women in academia inspires other black women that it is possible to work hard and be recognized nationally and internationally. Besides being a renowned scholar, Professor Phakeng was a vice principal of research and innovation at the University of South Africa and, currently, she is vice chancellor of the University of Cape Town. Other South African women who have inspired me, with their resilience and assertiveness, are Dr. Mmaphele Ramphele, who was an academic and a political leader; and the political icon Winnie Nomzamo Madikizela Mandela, who faced all sorts of oppression and alienation but fought for the nation's liberation to the end of her journey. Outside South Africa, in particular in the U.S., I see Michelle Obama who became the first black First Lady in the history of her country and inspired many people inside and outside of America.

Michelle Obama, as the first black First Lady, had numerous transformative initiatives, such as "Let's Move" in challenging childhood obesity, "Joining Forces" in supporting military families, "Reach Higher" in career emancipation, and "Let Girls Learn." Other inspirational American women are Maya Angelou through her shared wisdom, and Rosa Parks, who refused to be undermined as a black woman. I take lessons from such women that it is possible to transform society. They were transformative leaders in their own right. It is also upon this background that I am embarking on an autoethnographic chapter looking at how I played a role in academia and my community to transform the lives of women, in particular young black academics.

Theoretical Framework

My story was informed by three theories brought together through an integrative lens. These are a feminist theory, standpoint theory by Dorothy Smith (2005) and Patricia Hill Collins (2000), the wellness theory by Hettler (1980), and the *Ubuntu* (humane) principle.

Standpoint theory. Smith (2005) argues that when one uses a standpoint, it simply means that the researcher is located within existing social relations and may have subjective experiences. Whereas Collins (1997) sees standpoint theory as a historically shared group-based experience, she also acknowledges that groups may be historically subject to discrimination or prejudice. Collins (1997) looks at the construction of self and negotiation of multiple identities within one's self in a standpoint theory. The standpoint theory resonates so well with my experiences in that having a voice matters in a group where black woman power is erased. I found that in certain situations in academia, I had to make my voice heard in a white-dominated environment. As a black woman, I also consider what Collins (1990) calls alternative epistemology—that is, an epistemology centered not just on the woman but also on the black woman. This epistemology challenges the Eurocentric masculinity knowledge. Other forms of knowledge, in particular those of the oppressed, need to be recognized.

Collins' notion (1990) of epistemologies of the oppressed resonates so well with me. As I ascended the ladder in the faculty as manager of teaching and learning, I experienced some opposition as the university was transforming the curriculum and we embarked on Africanizing the curriculum by bringing in indigenous knowledge. There were some white academics who openly said that there was no written literature on African psychology; for them African knowledge was not viewed as scientific. Now that advocacy initiatives on Africanizing the curriculum are ongoing, I trust that the oppressed epistemologies will finally be recognized. Another point that is suitable for this chapter within the standpoint theory is the ethic of caring, which is vital for the transformative leadership. As a black scholar emerging in academia, I realized that without the ethic of caring, other young scholars will not be able to grow in academia as people may be self-centered and ignore young emerging academics.

Central to transformative leadership is the ethic of caring, which makes a leader care about others. Lastly, what I noticed in the standpoint theory is the personal accountability and the assessment of an individual's integrity. As a transformative leader, it is important to assess how I am accountable in my duties and mentoring of other young black women as they grow academically.

Wellness theory. In my story, I also draw from Hettler's (1980) wellness theory. Through this theory, Bill Hettler asserts that wellness is a state of being in which one's potential to live, work, and contribute to society is expanded through positive personal choice for optimum and integrated levels of the intellectual, social, emotional, spiritual, occupational, and physical dimensions of wellbeing (Hettler, 2002). As a leader believing in transforming mentees' lives, I found the wellness theory relevant to this ethnographic study. I pondered on how the protégés, especially black women who are new in academia, should develop optimally as leaders.

Ubuntu. The third theory that served as a lens was the Ubuntu principle derived from an African ethic philosophy. According to Letseka (2013), botho or humaneness comes from the saying "Motho ke motho ka batho," meaning a human being is human because of other people. Ubuntu shows an interdependent relationship that each of us needs as human beings. It ties well with the standpoint theory, which has an element of an ethic of caring. The ubuntu/botho (humane) philosophy helps me not to ignore the needs of young academics that I see developing. I always ask myself, how am I accountable to these young academics? How can I make a difference in their development? How can I play a transformative role in their lives?

Methodology

I am locating my ethnographic account in a transformative paradigm. Chilisa and Kawulich (2012) define *transformative paradigm* as an emancipatory paradigm which rests on the premise that myths need to be destroyed and one needs to empower people to change society radically. My account is located in the transformative paradigm as a black woman in academia who witnessed many cases of discrimination and injustice and took a stance to change the situation, though on a small scale. I draw from my promotion to associate professorship in my sixth year in academia to dispel the myth that undermined blacks, in particular women, claiming that one cannot publish if new in academia.

Qualitative methodology, especially institutional ethnography, was deemed suitable for this study since the occurrences are in a naturalistic environment, and my account is based on experiences of a number of years. Creswell (2009) describes *ethnography* as a strategy of inquiry of an intact cultural group in a natural setting studied over a prolonged period of time. The cultural group in this study is the academic world in which I have lived over years. To be more accurate, the design is *institutional ethnography*, which Smith (2005) defines as an alternative to the objectified subject of knowledge from the mainstream academic discourse. Institutional ethnography seeks to discover the actualities of people's everyday lives and experiences. The study is more flexible and also evolves contextually owing to the realities encountered (Le Compte & Schensul, 1999). In this chapter, I allude to everyday lives and experiences of black women academics, the challenges they go through, their tenacity and the way they aspire to win battles. Participant observation was used throughout this study as Wagner, Kawulich and Garner (2012) point out that in ethnography, one is participating in the cultural activities and simultaneously observing others as they live their lives.

Research Setting

The study took place in two universities where I was employed over a period of 10 years. Both universities were undergoing transformation since it was a prerogative from the post-apartheid government that all institutions were compelled to transform. Indeed, there was transformation regarding student numbers; more black students who could not access higher education were now allowed to study at universities owing to funding that was availed to children from disadvantaged communities (Council on Higher Education, 2016). Regarding staffing in higher education, the numbers were still skewed, especially on the side of professors. There were still few black professors; white professors were in the majority. It is against this background that the ethnographic study evolves, with a particular focus on the transformative leadership role that one can play in higher education.

From Theory to Story: My Institutional Standpoint Ethnography

The naturalistic inquiry carried out in my academic environment, supported by the three theories discussed above—standpoint, wellness, and ubuntu—revealed three key leadership traits that I associated with transformative leadership. The traits include the mentoring stance, leading by example, and servant leadership.

Mentoring. Upon leaving my one institution and joining another university as an associate professor, my goal was to grow and mentor other women in academia who were young scholars. I did not want to see them suffering and swimming upstream without any guidance. Stepping into action, I invited black women and men to the community engagement projects that I was leading, which had a research component. I also initiated book authoring projects and invited young academics who had never written an article or a book chapter in their careers to join as contributors. With encouragement, they contributed chapters in three books that I edited. Currently, I am supporting nine mentees, and they are proud to have single-authored chapters and articles.

Leading by example. I realized that as black women in academia, we work twice as hard as black males and white females to make a statement, and that it is through research outputs, book or chapter writing, and academic presentations that we can make a mark. I continue to mentor and show "botho" by taking students to conferences where they present, and encouraging young academics to present and publish papers so that we could proactively transform the landscape of higher education and ensure that black females' voices are heard.

Inclusive approach. I use an inclusive approach in my leadership and mentoring so that lives of my fellow academics can be transformed. Using the standpoint theory I ensure that both women and men are assisted in their academic development. When colleagues in need of mentoring approach me, I provide guidance irrespective of their gender.

Selfless leadership. At times when I assist young scholars, I take a stance that other people need development, and they need somebody to show them direction, especially when they are new in academia. This is in line with the African saying that "when your neighbor's house is on fire, you need to put out the fire"— "*Matlhaku go tsha mabapi*" in Setswana. By assisting and supporting young academics, I am also helping myself. It does not matter how long it takes to keep on assisting; what matters is making a difference in gender and race representation in South Africa's academia.

Servant leadership. As a black full professor, it is difficult at times when I lead some of the projects in the faculty.[1] I have experienced antagonisms from some white males who undermined my leadership in some portfolios, but I made it a point to raise the matter with the relevant authorities to transform the situation. I am happy that the outcome was positive. I took a standpoint of being a servant leader by serving others with humility and in an excellent way so that others could become better people. It is always humbling when you see that the service that you render in a faculty is actually bearing fruit. My office has become a consulting room for those who need help academically and others who just need someone to guide them in understanding the institution. I believe, like Maya Angelou (1994), that people may forget what you said, but they will never forget how you made them feel.

Assertiveness and power relations. A level of assertiveness is necessary for a black Pedi woman in academia. When I was new in academia, I observed some anomalies that I endured for some months until I gathered courage to be assertive and tackle the matters. Once, a white female lecturer who undermined blacks coordinated the course that I was teaching with two other black lecturers. Even though the three of us were allowed to teach the course content, the white female coordinator neither allowed us to set the question paper nor choose tutors. She would call us to a room and type the question paper as she was dictating the questions while we were seated there as if we knew nothing. Through her domineering approach, we were reduced to ordinary workers with little to no knowledge, who observed a white woman who knew everything.

---

[1] Faculty is the equivalent of "school" or "division" in the United States higher education structure.

After she did that twice, I decided to change the situation in my second year of being a course lecturer by acting proactively. I decided to set the question paper and sent it to her and other two colleagues to critique it. Comments were given and from there onward, I took the leadership of transforming the situation. She was not pleased at all about the stance that I took, so she tried to find fault in what I had done and influence the students. Fortunately, I related well with the students.

Level of independence and invading publishing space. The main initiative that I took was to lead a research and community engagement project in the early stages of my development in academia. This giant leap actually contributed to me not being dependent on senior academics, as most senior scholars were whites and they supported other white young academics. Black academics were undermined owing to lack of scholarship, especially publications. I therefore decided to initiate a research project and a community engagement project on my own without any mentorship. I applied for ethical clearance, and permission was granted. I also started to write articles from my doctoral thesis so that my voice could be heard.

The exercise of publishing in accredited journals changed the perception of some, though others were not impressed, particularly seeing a black woman claiming her space in academia. When my publications and supervision of my master and doctoral students increased, I was promoted to associate professorship. That angered some white females whose applications had been declined. Consequently, I joined another university as an associate professor, with my set goal to grow and mentor other women in academia who were young scholars. As indicated earlier, I did not want to see young black women academics suffering and swimming upstream without any guidance. Therefore, I invited black women and men to the community engagement projects that I was leading. Through encouragement, they contributed book chapters in the three volumes that I edited.

Promotions and myths dispelled. Regarding promotions, it was a struggle to be promoted as a black woman. The institution that I joined as a young academic had only one female black associate professor and few black male associate professors in the faculty of education. The challenge was to meet criteria in teaching and learning, research, and community engagement. Student evaluation was also critical in this case, since it was a requirement stipulated by the university's center for continuous professional development to approach your students during your lecture period and have them complete a questionnaire assessing your teaching, the course materials, and your preparedness for all the lessons. The outcome of the student evaluation depended on the relationship that one had with the students. I was advantaged because I taught a mixed class of black and white students. I related well with all races and I spoke both English and Afrikaans so well that even white students did not have anything against me. Hence, I was rated high as an excellent teacher, which added value to my portfolio for promotion. I also had a good supervision record for master and doctoral candidates. I met and satisfied all the criteria for promotion toward an associate professor in a university that was previously a unilingual (Afrikaans-speaking) institution. My promotion angered some white colleagues, so that one even resigned as a result. Still, the myth that a black woman will not be promoted in a university that was previously dominated by white Afrikaners had been dispelled. I was the second black woman to be an associate professor in the faculty.

Self-develop as you develop others—show botho. Michelle Obama and Winnie Mandela are women whose footsteps I try to follow as they both led by example, showing botho to all people while driving the transformation agenda of women. Immediately after my promotion in that university, I resigned and joined another university that was driving the transformation agenda and looking for blacks who were hard working to be promoted. In my current research and community engagement project, I am mentoring colleagues who are young in academia and, bi-annually, we must co-author a book. With them, I co-supervise master and doctoral students and guide them on marking processes and on how comments are given. Recently, I was promoted to lead teaching, learning, and student support portfolio in the faculty. There are a number of initiatives in place, and I encourage everyone to participate and transform the space of higher education, which was dominated by one race in the past. Currently, there are nine mentees whom I am supporting, and they are proud that I have led them to producing publications. I am also on the executive committee of the Women's Forum in the university, where we drive the agenda of transformation and give every woman a voice. Apart from academic work, I initiated a project of knitting blankets with women janitors, i.e., who clean the offices in the university, and we donate them to orphanages in showing kindness. These women who knit blankets were so happy to be approached by a black professor and to work together in that project; their self-esteem was positively reinforced.

Conclusion

Many black women are still marginalized, especially in their homes, communities, and workplace. This ethnographic chapter was just an attempt to highlight some of the evidence of transformation that one can cause in the workplace environment. I still believe that women can make a difference if we empower one another and show kindness to others instead of pulling other women in leadership positions down. Leadership starts with oneself and occurs at all levels. From being a follower, one can ascend to leadership and succeed at it. Confucius says, "If you wish to move the mountain tomorrow, you must start by lifting stones today." My mountain is seeing transformation in academia and black academics, women in particular, having a voice in a positive way. I have started lifting stones by empowering a few black women and men, and by resisting failure and any form of hegemony. As teacher educators, we should cultivate in our mentees the spirit of leadership and self-reliance and encourage them to do the same in their classrooms.

References

Ancer, J. (2018). Mamokgethi Phakeng: The professor who pushed. *Sunday Times*, 27 May, P12.
Angelou, M. (1994). *Wouldn't take nothing from my journey now*. Bantam Books.
Collins, P. H. (1990). *Black feminist thought: Knowledge, consciousness, and the politics of empowerment*. Boston: Unwin Hyman.
Collins, P.H. (1997). Comment on Hekman's "Truth and Method: Feminist Standpoint Theory revisited": Where's the power? signs: *Journal of Women in Culture and Society*, 22(2), 375-381.
Collins, P.H. (2000). *Black feminist thought: Knowledge, consciousness, and the politics of empowerment*. Rev. 10th anniversary ed. New York: Routledge.
Council on Higher Education. (2016). *South African higher education reviewed. Two decades of democracy*. Pretoria: Council on Higher Education.
Creswell, J.W. (2009). *Research design: Qualitative, quantitative, and mixed methods approaches*. Los Angeles: Sage Publishers.
Forde, D. (22 July 2014). Mandela's life inspires service community. Retrieved from http://www.nelsonmandela.orgnews/entry/mandelas inspires-service-community
Hettler, B. (1980). Wellness promotion on a university campus. *The Journal of Health Promotion and Maintenance*, 3, 77-95.

Hettler, B. (2002). *Bill Hettler home page*. Retrieved from http://www.hettler.com

Le Compte, M.D., & Schensul, J.J. (1999). *Designing and conducting ethnographic research*. Walnut Creek, CA: AltaMira Press.

Letseka, M. (2013). Educating for Ubuntu/Botho: Lessons from Basotho indigenous education. *Open Journal of Philosophy*, 3(2), 337-344.

Maxwell, J.C. (2005). *The 360° leader: Developing your influence from anywhere in the organisation*. Nashville: Thomas Nelson Inc.

Smith, D. E. (2005). *Institutional ethnography: A sociology for people*. Lanham, MD: Alta Mira Press.

Wagner, C., Kawulich, B., & Garner, M. (2012). *Doing social research*. London: McGraw Hill Higher Education.

Chapter 4

Mission to Accomplish
A Journey to Math Democracy

Marcia M. Burrell

THE NARRATIVE OF Obama's historic ascent to power can be interpreted as a narrative of opportunity and access to success. The narrative of my journey to success in mathematics is about my reclamation of deep interest in doing mathematics and of feeling confident in my inborn ability to do math. Also, it is about the use of my privilege and influence to ensure that the next generation has every opportunity in our democracy to learn through problem-solving in general and more specifically in mathematics. The struggle through any math problem appears to parallel the processes in building any democracy. Democracy and mathematics learning are constructed by building confidence in the learners (citizens), hard work (campaigning and passing laws), and building teacher trust (re-election) in a guided collaborative process, where all are included, as in President Barack Obama's words (2008),

> This is our time—to put our people back to work and open doors of opportunity for our kids; to restore prosperity and promote the cause of peace; to reclaim the American Dream and re-affirm that fundamental truth that out of many, we are one; that while we breathe, we hope, and where we are met with cynicism, and doubt, and those who tell us that we can't, we will respond with that timeless creed that sums up the spirit of a people: Yes, we can. (Obama, 2008 Victory Speech)

If one believes that "everyone can rise above their circumstances and achieve success if they are dedicated to and passionate about what they do" (Nelson Mandela Foundation, n.d., n. pag.), then what about those of us socialized differently? I was socialized to be humble in a society that is different than the dominant culture; I believe that I missed out on some of the opportunities offered to me. I never thought that I belonged on a college campus until I graduated from one. My lack of confidence and my socialization about who I was may have affected my learning to my full capacity. Inhibitions and self-doubts affect one's education. Sometimes students of color, those from lower socioeconomic populations, girls, and young women cannot meet their full capacity because of emotional issues around self-efficacy and self-worth. Math learning requires trust in oneself and others around us, including peers and, of course, the teacher. Learning around higher-order thinking and problem-solving is stifled if one is not aware of the emotional and dispositional factors that are involved in learning.

My learning experiences were not unlike those of other black girls, immigrants, and English language learners. Do we, as teachers, trust these audiences to make decisions with the information we give them? Do we believe in allowing these populations to try and fail? Do we have the same patience and trust for those who are not considered talented to learn as well as some elite groups in the dominant culture?

The tendency to give only our most talented students the opportunities for success in math or other content areas stifles our democracy. Our democracy depends on full participation—participation from the elite and those labeled as not as talented—with equity. Problem-solving approaches provide all students with opportunities to build mathematical knowledge and strengthen their ability to contribute to their learning process. In a democracy, where equal treatment and inclusion are priorities, and the responsibility of the educators is to teach all students, how can we make sure that every student can make evidence-based decisions as they learn? We have to teach and reinforce those democratizing behaviors where all students have permission to learn as much as they can and to make decisions about the learning process through their errors. These democratizing behaviors map mathematical ways of knowing (Cuoco, et al. 1996).

Building mathematical ways of knowing, where students are builders, describers, tinkerers, and visualizers (Cuoco, et al. 1996), requires creativity in our approaches to teaching. Some members of the dominant culture are encouraged to participate more than other populations. But those considered to be "talented" may have been purposefully taught to exercise their habits of mind

(Cuoco, et al. 1996), but our democracy requires that all members of the society deserve to have access to the hidden curriculum too. Unveiling the hidden curriculum is the paradise regained. Everyone has a right to instruction often relegated to only a small portion of the population—the talented.

I remember in grade 6, our physical education was a class in square dancing. It felt like the same students were selected to demonstrate the square-dancing moves. Those students were allowed to make mistakes as part of the demonstration. They had a lot of time with the square-dancing music on the floor of our classroom. I wanted to be on the floor too, but each time I was finally allowed an opportunity to try what I had only observed, I was not successful. The short time on the dance floor always ended in disappointment because as soon as I made a mistake, I was removed and replaced with the demonstrator groups. I observed intently, but it was never right. I had little time to make mistakes and to recover from only watching. The demonstrators had a chance to try and fail and to try and to succeed. The rest of us just watched. Learning mathematics successfully is like square dancing. You cannot only watch. You have to participate, and the participation has to be a part of the process at all times. The teaching of math has to involve all the students. Using a problem-solving approach in teaching and learning mathematics has to be done via interactions. Students have to be socialized to accept the mistakes as part of the process. As Thomas Edison said about inventing the light bulb, "I have not failed; I have just found 10,000 ways that won't work." You learn far more from your failures than from your successes, as long as you remain patient, persistent and thoughtful.

Educational inequities are not only found in the United States. In fall 2017, while on sabbatical in Budapest, Hungary, I witnessed the Lajos Pósa problem-solving methods being implemented in math classrooms. The methods were meant to encourage gifted students to engage in mathematics. As soon as I learned about the Pósa methods, I wondered why Pósa was only encouraged for talented students but not all students. After meeting a Hungarian teacher working on her Ph.D. in math education, I learned that her research project was investigating the Pósa method for all students, not just talented ones. It encouraged me in that someone else was thinking about the general population, not just about a chosen few.

Back in the U.S., my context as a teacher educator follows a social justice conceptual framework. While this social justice framework is not new to our institution, my time away helped me to understand it better, as well as to better understand my responsibility to future math candidates and fellow citizens. While the Pósa method began as a method for engaging talented students, I wondered, why in the U.S. we had created an education system just for the most talented. Aren't we part of a democracy? Don't we care about all citizens and the entire voting population, who make decisions about our communities?

As a human being, I wondered: Why can't all students have access to the best learning typically only reserved for the elite and talented in our population? How is it that we choose a problem-solving approach to teach our students perceived as "gifted" but we often use rote learning and more content coverage for everyone else? As a human being, I pondered: Could I have been a more successful math student if my teachers trusted me to use the problem-solving approach to learning? Would my trajectory toward math have been different if I had had more opportunities to try and fail?

My observations of the Pósa method reminded me of my math journey that began with my 7th-grade teacher, Ms. Madura. Ms. Madura challenged us 7th graders and taught us how to study math. I loved her because this was the beginning of my math understanding and enjoyment. On the other hand, I did not like Mrs. Weissbrod, my geometry teacher, because she stood for memorizing theorems and I could not understand everything she was asking us to do until the end of the course. In the end, I learned geometry well, but I wonder what if the teacher could have trusted me enough to explain what was happening at each stage of the learning. Also, I wish I had believed in Mrs. Weissbrod more. My freshman year at college, I was placed into a college algebra course based only on a low placement test score. I was angry because I believed that I did not belong in a college algebra course. I ignored the placement test and registered for a pre-calculus course. I ended up earning an A in the pre-calculus course. I remember needing to prove to everyone that the placement tests did not represent my capacity for doing mathematics. That experience did not make me want to do more math. To the contrary, that experience made me less confident about my math abilities. I think I was afraid to fail; I wanted to succeed but was often afraid. I recognize the fear now because I have observed it in my daughter. I take full responsibility for not being more successful in knowing what I needed to do to be successful. I did not know how to study, and I was afraid to fail. Being afraid to fail is not the way to study mathematics or any subject successfully. I was scared to give everything of myself, because I felt invisible, and did not do everything I should have done to succeed. I needed more help with how to be successful in mathematics, and many other students needed the same encouragement. I had experienced some difficulty with the placement test, and so the course was not recommended. I needed someone to take me seriously and help build on my small successes.

I did not study math seriously again until I was a senior, when I met a professor, Dr. Howard Johnson, who encouraged me to explore even more mathematics. He took a chance on me and helped me gain confidence in the benefits of hard work and questioning. However, it was not until I took graduate math courses almost five years later that I finally figured out mathematical thinking through my work with symmetries and abstract algebra. By then, I had had some teaching experience, but I wanted to do a better job of teaching, so I was taking more math classes. I already had a master's degree, but I wanted to explore more content. I began to trust myself and trust the university teachers who accepted my work. What changed?

I have learned that math is a content area that requires participation in learning. You have to know something to participate. Learning math is an interactive process of struggle and success and not knowing. Teaching in a way that encourages these characteristics requires trust from all sides: teachers, students, and parents. In most of the classes in college, I always felt like I was on the sidelines looking in, not knowing the answers and not knowing how to find the answers. I was the only black woman in my university classes; I never saw anyone else who looked like me in my classes. It was when I was teaching adult students in their first college-level math course that I realized that my perceptions were common. While teaching, I helped them learn how to overcome their socialized approaches to thinking they could not do math; I provided them with the emotional and technical support they needed to succeed, to be a member of the college community. I trusted these students to learn, and I gave them every indication that I expected them to learn.

Many colleges require that students take and pass a basic algebra course, and without that compulsory course students are not allowed into the "club." Without passing through this arbitrary gate, many students have no access to certain privileges in our democracy. Sometimes students lose their confidence in their ability to do mathematics, and that lack of confidence sometimes spreads across to how they cautiously move through the next phases of their education. I believe all of us can do mathematics, and we should not use math as a barrier to building problem-solving. The entire process of creating a space for all students to do mathematics makes for a citizenry prepared for solving math and other problems.

I realize that my role in this process is to introduce others to the ways they can participate in our democracy. It requires a belief in the process and trust in one another to engage in the process. Everything about preparing students in math involves faith, trust, confidence, and diligence. The following list of 10 principles represents what I did and suggest that students do to take responsibility for becoming successful at mathematical learning:

Principle One:	Believe in yourself
Principle Two:	Take risks
Principle Three:	Work in 20- to 30- minute intervals
Principle Four:	Make sense of the theory and read the text
Principle Five:	Work on math a little bit every day
Principle Six:	Investigate your creativity
Principle Seven:	Know your study downfalls
Principle Eight:	Expect to succeed
Principle Nine:	Trust your teacher
Principle Ten:	Have patience

These principles are essential, simple, and frightening at the same time. Can math learning be as straightforward as just knowing and understanding one's responsibilities in the learning process? No. Successful math learning also requires high teacher expectations and a problem-based curriculum, as documented well in *Adding It Up* (National Research Council, & Mathematics Learning Study Committee, 2001). *Adding It Up* discusses a curriculum that reinforces conceptual understanding, procedural fluency, strategic competence, adaptive reasoning, and productive reasoning. These abilities can be learned and built into the teaching process.

"Paradise regained" to me is about assisting all learners in the pursuit of their innate mathematical abilities. The steps to success, the how to study math, and the reminders about one's capacity all connect to a way of approaching learning and thinking. When placing students in tracked groups, however, based on standardized tests, we deny them the inherent nature of what it means to be mathematical. Learning mathematics is a collaborative problem-solving way, where peers rely on one another while the teacher, working as a facilitator of learning, strives to empower the students' increasing abilities in mathematics. We have to think about how learning math involves cooperative processes, which engage students' emotions, pre-conceptions, and strengths. We can teach students how to push through the struggle of not knowing all the steps to the answer, and show them how the creative process of engaging the unknown with their innate abilities to do mathematics is essential. My journey to math is my paradise regained. The entire process of solving a math problem is "the journey" to math.

The discoveries I found helped me grow into my belief that I am a math person, a mathematician. I have a larger capacity for math than I believed I had. I have math capacity, and the discovery process for learning math is at the heart of how one comes to understand problem-solving. Roger Bacon, English philosopher and naturalist, claimed, "Mathematics is the gate and key of sciences [...]; neglect of mathematics works injury to all knowledge since one who is ignorant of it cannot know the other sciences or the things of this world" (MacTutor History of Mathematics, 2013, n. pag.).

In an environment where everyone is involved in ensuring that the full community has every opportunity and support to succeed, using a problem-solving approach to learning mathematics is ideal. As math educators, we have to think about how learning math involves cooperative processes as a means to engaging students' emotions, pre-conceptions, and strengths as learners. We can teach students how to push through their reluctance toward the challenge found in math. This approach takes encouragement.

There is a respected knowledge base about how to learn mathematics. Creating lessons for students to learn mathematics is not easy. Learning math well requires conceptual understanding, procedural fluency, strategic competence, adaptive reasoning, and productive reasoning (National Research Council & Mathematics Learning Study Committee, 2001). I had a chance to engage in these processes via my mathematics educator blog, and I can say that these skills take practice.

I see myself as a mathematician now, and a capable member of the academic community. I am confident about the errors I make to learn more mathematics as well as to address complex problems of day-to-day working and living. I believe that teaching with a problem-solving approach in mathematics is an avenue to building a democracy. To build a democracy, we must grow citizens who can problem solve, not just in math, but also in other parts of their lives. Using a problem-solving approach can be taught through theoretical math problems, puzzles, and brainteasers. Through applied problems students will find opportunities to extend themselves beyond the memorization and rote learning as they build their capacity. Paradise regained calls upon us all to rethink our potential in the work we do, but also to rethink our interactions with one another as we learn together. We are all born with an ability to do mathematics, but we must reclaim it.

References

Cuoco, A., Goldenberg, E. P., & Mark, J. (1996). Habits of mind: An organizing principle for mathematics curricula. *The Journal of Mathematical Behavior*, 15(4), 375-402.

MacTutor History of Mathematics. (2013, December). Quotations by Roger Bacon. http://www-history.mcs.st-andrews.ac.uk/Quotations/Bacon.html

Matsuura, R. (2014). Budapest Semesters in Mathematics Education: Study Abroad Program. http://www.ams.org/about-us/governance/committees/Matsuura.COE2014.pdf

National Research Council & Mathematics Learning Study Committee. (2001). *Adding it up: Helping children learn mathematics*. Washington, DC: National Academies Press.

Nelson Mandela Foundation. (2009, December 17). Selected Quotes. https://www.nelsonmandela.org/content/page/selected-quotes

Barack Obama. (2008, November 4). *Barack Obama Victory Speech*. Available: https://www.c-span.org/video/transcript/?id=909

CHAPTER 5

Teaching through the Lens of a Mother

Josephine Jarpa Dawuni

> *Any classroom that employs a holistic model of learning will also be a place where teachers grow and are empowered by the process.*
> —BELL HOOKS (1994, P. 21)

Introduction

THIS CHAPTER EXAMINES the nexus between education and mothering by exploring the challenges and opportunities arising from the multiple roles women academics occupy in classrooms. Women educators, more so than men, must constantly juggle their roles as mothers, educators, and other intersecting identities. Therefore, I discuss the ways in which women educators have a role of educating not only their students, but also their children on what it means to be a woman of multiple identities in a new America. Drawing on my personal experiences, I discuss what it means to be a woman educator occupying multiple identities in a post-Obama America. I situate this study within bell hooks' (1994) work on emancipatory classroom environments, as spaces that provide learning opportunities for all parties involved. I also draw on the experiences and legacy of President Barack Obama and Michelle Obama in situating the black family within the broader discussion of what it means to be a successful black parent. The value of education, which informed the parenting of the Obamas, is captured in this statement:

> Michelle and I know that our first job, our first responsibility, is instilling a sense of learning, a sense of a love of learning in our kids. And so, there are no shortcuts there; we have to do that job. And

we can't just blame teachers and schools if we're not instilling that commitment, that dedication to learning, in our kids. (Obama, 2011)

Teaching and Learning beyond the Classroom

The Obama presidency ushered in a pivotal shift in race and gender consciousness in the United States and the world, providing many teachable moments. The presidency signaled different things to different people. For those interested in race issues, it was the affirmation that being black did not erase one from achieving the highest goals they set for themselves. For political scientists and presidential historians, it was in some ways a prediction that many did not see happening anytime soon. Thus, with the domestic and global euphoria came many challenges the new president of the United States had to deal with. To say that President Barack Obama had extra layers of challenges he had to deal with is an understatement. To a faculty at a historically black college and university (HBCU), the Obama presidency provided a whole set of topical issues to discuss, and these issues found their way to the classroom, irrespective of what subject matter one was teaching.

As a woman scholar who finds myself embodying and simultaneously mirroring different identities, what the Obama presidency meant to me was multifaceted—at some points liberating and other times challenging. I found myself at the center of two classroom environments during the eight years of the presidency. The first half of the eight years, I was teaching at a predominantly white institution (PWI), a small liberal arts college in Georgia where I found myself having to constantly navigate multiple boundaries in and out of the classroom. I was at once and the same a black woman, an immigrant (African) woman, a mother, a doctorate holder, a young scholar, a lawyer, a feminist, and this list goes on. The intersecting and overlapping identities I found myself navigating personally were also apparent in the classroom, in the way I taught and engaged with my students. In my attempts to provide a liberating and emancipatory learning experience, I had a classroom policy in my syllabus on intra-peer respect for all political and personal opinions.

Here I was, teaching an undergraduate course on American government that provided room for practical application of the concepts we learned in the class to the real-life situations that were happening around us daily. To make the learning experience emancipatory, students were required to link the concepts learned in class to the different news items in their favorite media. It soon became evident how students' ideological leanings filtered into their processing of the concepts discussed in class. For most of my students, the political happenings in the country were nothing but "politics as usual." On occasion, some of these political leanings reared up in class, leading to some unpleasant debates among my students—often bothering on race relations.

As I moved to an HBCU in 2015 during the last stages of the Obama presidency, I carried with me the same teaching methods and policy on political and personal opinions. However, I noticed a shift in the ways in which my students viewed the political climate. For most of my students, the daily political happenings were much closer to home for them for two reasons. First, the location in Washington, DC, was in the heart of all the political institutions and events happening in the country. Second, the politics of self—most of my students experienced the American presidency under the first black president as a life-changing development.

As a scholar, I had to position myself in different contexts in teaching my students—considering the different locations I embodied at different times. How were my intersecting identities of being a woman, a mother, a black person, an African, a lawyer, a Ph.D. holder informing my teaching? I also identified as a feminist/womanist scholar who was a self-trained critical thinker within the framework of critical studies—postcolonial, critical race, and critical legal studies.

Did the Obama presidency provide avenues for employing critical thinking and consciousness raising in our classrooms? How was a feminist/womanist critical thinker like myself to engage with the Obama presidency both in and out of my classroom? In my quest to be critical of what was happening in politics, I endeavored to provide a space in my classrooms for students to become conscious of their perceived weaknesses, as well as owning the transformational power in them. I had to adopt an inclusive teaching strategy that was simultaneously critical, yet emancipatory. This teaching strategy safeguarded my students from focusing on their multiple injuries, but also to be conscious of their multiple capabilities. It was a teaching strategy grounded in the fact that education should be seen both as a human right, and the key to freedom and liberation of the human mind and being.

To achieve the goals implicit in my strategies, I had to give my students voice. The voice of the student was not only limited to the oral but also the written and, sometimes, the non-verbal modes of communicating. I encouraged my students to find their voice and their place in history—to question the known and unknown. What did the Obama presidency mean to you? Was it the beginning of endless possibilities or an end to past historical marginalization? The Obama-era slogan of "yes we can" resonated with many of my students, who saw the presidency as the beginning of many possibilities and the endless opportunities for them to achieve their dreams. For others, however, it meant little to them as they had to grapple with their personal daily challenges, thereby creating a chasm between what is and what ought to be.

In an earlier publication (Dawuni, 2017), I noted that the teacher plays multiple roles in and out of the classroom—some consciously and others unconsciously. In *Teacher Man*, McCourt (2005) enumerates different hats worn by a teacher:

> In the [. . .] classroom you are a drill sergeant, a rabbi, a shoulder to cry on, a disciplinarian, a singer, a low-level scholar, a clerk, a referee, a clown, a counselor, a dress-code enforcer, a conductor, an apologist, a philosopher, a collaborator, a tap dancer, a politician, a therapist, a fool, a traffic cop, a priest, a mother-father-brother-sister-uncle-aunt, a bookkeeper, a critic, a psychologist, the last straw. (p. 19)

I, too, felt like I played multiple roles as a mentor, therapist, and sometimes the unwitting mother to students, in addition to being a mother to my own daughter.

To her, I was a teacher mom, who also had human emotions. In reviewing videos for my classes, I invite my children to watch with me and together we discuss the content. On one occasion as we were reviewing the documentary *Pray the Devil Back to Hell*,[1] I could not hold back my emotions and wept through the movie. This reaction prompted my daughter to ask me why I was so sad and crying. As an educator and a mother of a child born in the United States, I had to take time to educate her on the challenges women face in some communities in Africa, but more so their resilience and creativity in resolving matters.

---

[1] *Pray the Devil Back to Hell* is a movie about the mobilization of women in Liberia across ethnic, religious and social class, led by Leymah Gbowee, to end the civil conflict in the country.

How was I to reconcile my multiple identities while maintaining my role as *the* instructor? Playing multiple roles required tact, as well as a great deal of reflexivity on the part of the instructor. These roles require striking a delicate balance between being the authority figure, on one hand, and the emancipatory teacher, on the other hand, with many other roles in between. While I could be vulnerable to my daughter by crying while watching a documentary, the same cannot be the case with my students in the classroom. The questioning gaze of my gender identity as a woman professor will no doubt be in question, were I to express such emotions in the classroom. After all, even President Obama teared up in public on a few occasions.

The Obama Legacy and Black Motherhood

Barack and Michelle Obama have left an indelible legacy in the minds and hearts of people—not only in the United States, but around the world. Despite the efforts by political opponents to erase the Obama White House legacy, (her) history has been made, and what is written and engraved on the heart cannot easily be blown away, even with the best of military bombers. In this section I focus on three main legacies left by the Obama presidency—motherhood, family and education.

Motherhood. Sociologist and feminist scholar Oyeronke Oyewumi in her new book *What Gender Is Motherhood?* asks a provocative question on the shared responsibility of parenting. Oyewumi (2016) challenges the Western conceptualization of motherhood, often understood to be a category where "motherhood is perceived to be embodied by women who are subordinated wives, weak, powerless, and relatively socially marginalized" (p. 58). While Oyewumi's premise is based on critiquing imported Western notions of motherhood, the underlying ethos of her argument broach a larger debate on the definitional quandaries that loom large in the African American family. In *Rise Up Singing* (Berry, 2005), the authors remind readers of the role of women and motherhood in the African American family experience—singing praises to matriarchs of the black family, while also acknowledging and paying homage to the many challenges and triumphs of black motherhood and mothering. Situating motherhood in the works of black feminist scholars such as Patricia Collins (1987), we see the relevance of motherhood as a central defining force of what it means to be part of a larger community beyond one's immediate family.

Barack and Michelle epitomize the multifaceted ways in which motherhood and mothering transcends biology. Barack, who was largely raised by his maternal grandparents after his mother died, had to grapple sometimes with his identity as a "black" child in a white family. Do these experiences help explain his positionality and his drive for not only diversity but inclusiveness? Michelle, on the other hand, was born to two African American parents and was raised by her mother after her father died. Though she did not have to struggle with questions of her racial identity within the family, her social class of being raised by a "single" black mother must have also had some effects on how she identified herself as a woman and later as a mother of two young black girls.

The contrasting identity formations of Barack and Michelle provide us with glimpses not only into their upbringing, but help to frame through a broader lens what family means to them. The fact that Barack had a half-sister, whose father was from Indonesia, and his own father from Kenya, no doubt impacted his worldview on multiculturalism and inclusivity. As academics, not many of us will have such multicultural experiences; yet, in our classrooms, we may be confronted with dealing with, and/or addressing, issues of multiculturalism and inclusiveness. How do we deal with our own inefficiencies in handling these issues? Does one's exclusion from such multicultural family experiences prevent one from attempting to listen, understand, and learn from other people's experiences? The art of teaching involves using the skills of motherhood to listen, to learn, and to direct.

Family. The Obama family showed unequivocally the value and essence of family. The universal appeal of the first black family in the White House sent powerful signals around the world, challenging the gendered received knowledge of what it means to be a man in a black family. The close-knit ties between Barack Obama and his half-sisters (Auma Obama and Maya Soetoro) and the special bond he had with his maternal grandparents and his paternal grandmother were powerful portrayals of what family meant to him. Although Barack Obama did not live with his father, we get glimpses of his family life in his book *Dreams from My Father* (Obama, 2004). On Michelle Obama's side, the strong bonds between her mother and brother were moving depictions of the grounded black family, even in the absence of a father who was deceased.

The most extraordinary part of the Obama family legacy is in the show of love and affection for their two young daughters—Malia and Sasha, who the world literally watched as they matured into beautiful young black women. Above all, Barack and Michelle Obama did not shy away from their love for one another, showing affection in public for the whole world to see and experience the value of family to them.

Education. The Obamas have no doubt left a strong legacy for the education of our youth, both through various philanthropic and grassroots organizations they worked with before the presidency and after the presidency, such as the My Brother's Keeper Initiative, and their personal achievements—both trained as lawyers in some of the top law schools in the country—despite their relatively modest backgrounds. Their educational accomplishments are yet another indication of endless possibilities for all who aspire to attain educational heights. In a final speech as First Lady, Michelle Obama reiterated her belief in the power of education as a step to freedom and liberation. She noted,

> My final message to young people as first lady is simple. I want our young people to know that they matter, that they belong [. . .]. Don't be afraid, be focused. Be determined. Be hopeful. Be empowered. Empower yourself with a good education [. . .] then build a country worthy of your boundless promise. (Taylor, 2017, n. pag.)

The transformative power of education and the opportunities presented by having an education are depicted in the numerous achievements of Barack and Michelle Obama. To the Obamas, education is power, and at no time in history is such power needed more than in this age of global competitiveness.

Concluding Thoughts

I love to teach. I see teaching as my calling. Teaching is like parenting, in that you make a choice to enter the vocation, and you have to resist the temptation to ask yourself if you made the right decision. As academics, we must grapple with being objective, putting our subjectivities in check and providing an environment conducive for teaching and learning. As I teach my students about transnational feminism, I strive to highlight not only the negativity and oppression women face, but more so their resilience, creativity, and triumph in the face of challenges. As I explain to my students the tenets and foundations of transnational feminism, I hope to instill in them a strong sense of self, choice, voice, and liberation. The Obama family has provided a living classroom experience and a legacy of hope, resilience, and triumph. Through their legacy of strong family ties, motherhood, and the emphasis on education, we are constantly reminded to make good choices, choices that empower us and our communities. Will the Obama legacy signal the beginning or end of a paradigm of what it means to learn, to love, and to succeed? I can't say; you make the decision.

References

bell, hooks. (1994). *Teaching to transgress: Education as the practice of freedom*. New York: Routledge.

Berry, C (ed.). (2005). *Rise up singing: Black women writers on motherhood*. Harlem Moon.

Collins, P. H. (1987). The meaning of motherhood in Black culture and Black mother/daughter relationships. *SAGE: A Scholarly Journal on Black Women*, 4(2), 3–10.

Dawuni, J. (2017). Beyond the accent: navigating the multiple intersections in a foreign trained instructor classroom. In Budryte, D. and Boykin, S., (eds.), *Toward a transformative classroom: Creating reflective identities in multicultural settings*. Rowman and Littlefield.

McCourt, F. (2005). *Teacher man: A memoir*. Simon and Schuster.

Obama, B. (2004). *Dreams from my father: A story of race and inheritance*. New York: Three Rivers Press.

Obama, B. (2011). Remarks by the President on No Child Left Behind Flexibility. The White House, Office of the Press Secretary. Retrieved from https://obamawhitehouse.archives.gov/the-press-office/2011/09/23/remarks-president-no-child-left-behind-flexibility

Oyewumi, O. (2016). *What gender is motherhood? Changing Yoruba ideals of power, procreation, and identity in the age of modernity*. New York: Palgrave McMillan.

Taylor, D. (2017). More than "mom-in-chief": Michelle Obama bows out as dynamic first lady. Available at: https://www.theguardian.com/us-news/2017/jan/06/michelle-obama-legacy-first-lady

SECTION II
GENDER EQUALITY AND WOMEN EMPOWERMENT

CHAPTER 6

Gender Equality Not of This World:
In the Brave New World

Lindamichelle Baron

I FOUND MYSELF in a room of attractive young women of color. We were various shades of black, from deep, dark brown to darn near white. One of us, however, looked more like a Miss America contestant than an applicant for a position as a textbook salesperson. She was the "darn near white" one, with long straight hair swooped into a loose bun. I, on the other hand, was less than gorgeous, browner, with a short "natural." While I sat, waiting to be called, I considered what would be the determining factor for a job as an educational textbook salesperson, in an industry that had traditionally hired white men.

What I didn't know while I sat was what precipitated the publishing industry's transformation, in the mid 1970s, to include women of color. It seemed the 15 members of a newly founded National Alliance of Black School Superintendents (NABSS) enlightened the industry. Collectively, they made the purchasing decisions for millions of dollars spent for textbooks and ancillary materials in their school districts. They used that backdrop as an economic incentive to encourage the textbook publishing industry to hire minority sales representatives. Based on the representation in the waiting room in which I found myself, and what I encountered later in the world of publishing, some companies intentionally hired black women, who could be counted as two "minorities," both black and a woman. On this day, there was only one job opening. Obviously, according to the gender and race of those in the waiting room, this job would go to a black woman. It was my intention to be *that* black woman.

I was fairly confident that each of us in the room had some years as a teacher. That was a basic qualification. I was uncertain of the academic background of my competitors. I had a master's degree, which was necessary had I been applying for a position as educational consultant. A consultant was required to have in-depth knowledge of the academic discipline, usually reading or math, and of the textbooks that were sold by the sales representatives. At the time of my interview, there were a handful of consultants who were of African descent in the industry nationally, but only one who was a saleswoman.

While I waited to be interviewed, I had time to think about the reality of leaving my life's purpose as a teacher in order to make a living. I had planned to be a public school teacher forever. Had there not been a financial crisis in New York City, and the politicians' answer was to "lay off" teachers and other city workers, I would probably still be a teacher. My husband and I had recently purchased a house in Long Island. Our capacity to get a mortgage had been calculated based on both of our salaries. At that time, I made a bit more than my husband, which created a dilemma for our real estate agent, who suggested I lower my salary on the application so that it would not make my husband's slightly lower salary look bad. Interesting suggestion in that we needed to show the highest possible salary in order to get a mortgage! Male chauvinism? Even as our salaries grew, my husband's growing significantly faster than mine (although I had a master's degree, and he had not completed college), neither salary was enough to pay the mortgage. I needed a job for us to keep our life intact.

Thanks to a colleague's husband, I considered an occupation in the world of educational publishing. He was a textbook salesperson and helped me to prepare by arranging for me to spend a day with one of his coworkers. Actually, I was not initially interested in sales; I thought it beneath me. My concept of a salesperson was based on my experiences with car salesmen and door-to-door vacuum and encyclopedia salespeople. I didn't realize that a sales position is actually one of the best jobs to have as a woman in the world of business. Your success is quantifiable. The numbers speak for themselves.

Paradoxically, 40 years later, I would learn that getting the job of president of the United States of America, even when the outcome is quantifiable, could still be a losing proposition. Hillary Rodham Clinton, although the first female presidential nominee in the United States, was highly qualified—in fact, the only qualified candidate in a two-person race against a man who celebrated his lack of knowledge and experience as an advantage. She did not get the job. Millions of the electorate's votes did not actually count. An Electoral College was the arbiter, rather than the popular vote. Actually, there were those who questioned the extent to which gender did count in the election.

In sales, success is unquestionably quantifiable, although getting a job, particularly your first job as a salesperson, can be much more subjective. Whatever the job requirements, and whatever "Miss America's" qualifications were, based on my experience in other circumstances, I believed she would be my primary competition if men were doing the hiring. And men were doing the hiring. I'd have to dig deep and bring my very best self to the interview. All things being equal, all things are not equal. Outward attractiveness could trump the most qualified person for the job.

I brought my confidence, my personality, my experience, my knowledge, my smile (yes, one of my best characteristics), and the capacity to look a person in the eye and give a firm handshake. The benefit of what I perceived as my competition made me up the ante. I used my persona along with my teaching pedagogy to "sell" a textbook during my five- to- 10- minute mock presentation to a fictional administrator. It worked. I was invited back a few days later and told I had the job. At some point during the conversation my intuition was confirmed by my soon-to-be-manager. "Miss America" had been my competitor. But I had won!

I also went above and beyond the call of duty after I was hired. My success in the field was recognized by managers at a competing company who invited me to join them by offering me a significantly higher salary. I accepted. This time neither my ethnicity nor my gender seemed to be the consideration. My ability as a salesperson is what mattered. What was interesting and perhaps disturbing was when I was informally introduced, with accolades, to some of the salesmen at my new company. One of my colleagues then took the opportunity to "put me in my place." "Enough of all that," he said. "When do we go to bed?" I almost gave an answer rooted in my cultural background, "Why don't you ask your mother?" But I didn't. I just turned my back to him, ignoring his ignorance, and began speaking to one of my other male colleagues. I did wonder if any of the other men heard. Certainly, none came to my rescue. Which was fine. I felt I had handled it. Done. Had it been today, though, I would have perhaps added his name to the #MeToo list.

Thankfully, I experienced few additional inappropriate remarks or actions over time. I don't know that I can take credit for that. The word spread about my six-feet-two, muscular husband, who rarely, if ever, smiled at others. The "black man fear factor" probably protected me. He accompanied me to many of the national venues. We would link our vacation to the location, often arriving a few days earlier. During the inevitable welcoming social event, he would stand silently, away from others, surveying the room, just long enough to make an indelible impression into any potential ignorance, by word or deed, that might have been considered. I was thankful for that protection. But later, as I matured, I took responsibility for my well-being. I "manned up" and became a strong woman, who would do as William Ernest Henley (1919) wrote: become the master of my fate and the captain of my soul. The poem below is a representation of my evolving self-efficacy.

I'm the Man

I don't have to live large to know I'm in charge.
I know where I stand.
I have a purpose and a plan.
So I say, "Hey, I'm the man."

I have not gone insane.
Woman is my true name.
But, I won't give up my self-control,
Or place my dignity on hold.
I will take a stand and get what I demand.
There is no "I can't," just "I can."
So I say, "Hey, I'm the man."

I'm definitely a she,
But I see beyond the gender of me.
I'm not on your case.
I don't want to take your place.
But I've made a decision to elevate my position.
I have the power...
This is my hour.
I've taken control...
So, don't assign me to a role.

I'm not playing a game,
So don't call me out of my name.
It's about me and the Higher Authority.
We walk hand in hand.
So I say, "Hey, I'm the man."

—Lindamichellebaron (Baron, 2007, 22-23)

We entered a field in which men ruled; however, as new entrants into the profession, we believed that the women hired, whether white or black, were better dressed, better looking, and better prepared than most of the men who had been in sales for years. We had to be better to get the job in the first place, or attractive enough for it not to matter to the men who hired us even if women's dress code and look mattered to them. We were superior regarding our knowledge of content and educational methods. We realized that we stood on the shoulders of those who had taken a stand for us. We honored the trust placed in us.

Being your best and excelling did not mean there were not gender differences in how textbook sales were consummated. Although many of the men, at that time, were retired principals or other administrators, few of them were expected to know the product. Consultants, specialists in the areas, could be called in when necessary. Most of the women made sales based on proficiency in product knowledge. A man's sales pitch could be over a game of golf, or over drinks. Woman, for the most part, did not have that luxury. And in many situations product knowledge was a "nice to," not necessarily a "have to." What was universal, if you were to be successful, was the capacity to withstand being turned down, ignored, and told "no" multiple times every day. You had to develop the capability to listen to your customer and direct your product's benefits to the needs they expressed, even when the needs were not clearly articulated, and do so within minutes. Tenacity, drive, independence, resilience, and work ethic were premium for both men and women in the field.

My experience of being hired and working in a "man's position" informs some of my reflections on the 2016 race for president. I've come to agree with the saying that sometimes "the best man for the job is a woman." We have to bring our best self to the job, even when the competition has unearned advantages. Secretary of State Clinton was in the position to win the presidency because she earned it. She had impressive experience beyond having been the First Lady. She had been, among many things, a lawyer, a senator, and, of course, *secretary of state*. She was not only prepared, but she over-prepared for every encounter. Nevertheless, she was expected to adhere to nuances of gender-related requirements.

For instance, attractiveness matters, particularly if you are a female. Hillary was not considered beautiful in the eyes of many, but she had to make certain she looked good enough; make certain her hair was coiffed enough; her style fashionable enough; her voice moderated enough—powerful but not shrill. She had to be strong but not too strong. In order to be seriously considered, she had to be overqualified for the job. Clinton lost the race for president to a man who seemed to be freed from the constraints of those who actually cared about winning. She lost to a man who coalesced a constituency who, as he said, to paraphrase, "could shoot somebody in the middle of Fifth Avenue and not lose any voters." There is an adage that says, "He who cares least wins." He represented that maxim. He was a consummate salesman who sold his product, himself, to his constituency. He brought to his constituents features and benefits that directly correlated to their perceived needs and wants. He won the election because he also received large numbers of votes from those who didn't necessarily buy his product, but who weren't buying the idea of a woman as president.

I have felt as if most of the country and much of the world have been shot in broad daylight as we enter the second year of this 45th administration. We, as women; we, as immigrants; we, as citizens with Muslim and Latin American heritage; we, as Indigenous Americans; we, as African Americans; and we, as a country have been assaulted and maligned by hate-filled, oft times misogynistic rhetoric, wide-ranging lies, half-truths, misappropriations of truth, alternative facts, hyperbole, and exaggeration that is anything but literary.

I am a product of the Civil Rights Movement. I was in Washington with my parents during the March on Washington. I went to college on a Martin Luther King Jr. Scholarship. I am love filled. I love life and all people. So, I applaud our First Lady, Michelle Obama's entreaty that "When they go low," we display more integrity, more veracity, more uprightness and "go high." I will admit that I also come from a deeply ingrained oral tradition I referenced earlier in this chapter. The African American tradition fights back verbally when attacked, using harsh witticisms we call "playin' the dozens." That convention would dictate that, instead of going high, you look the abuser in the eye and say,

"Mr. President, yo' mama!'" But I won't. Instead I will defer to Maya Angelou, my shero, through the excerpts below.

> You may write me down in history
> With your bitter, twisted lies,
> You may trod me in the very dirt
> But still, like dust, I'll rise.

I'll continue to quote her, my shero…

> You may shoot me with your words,
> You may cut me with your eyes,
> You may kill me with your hatefulness,
> But still, like air, I'll rise.

And then continue with her reference to our honored and honorable past,

> Out of the huts of history's shame
> I rise
> Up from a past that's rooted in pain
> I rise
> I'm a black ocean, leaping and wide,
> Welling and swelling I bear in the tide.
>
> Leaving behind nights of terror and fear
> I rise
> Into a daybreak that's wondrously clear
> I rise
> Bringing the gifts that my ancestors gave,
> I am the dream and the hope of the slave.

I would then add, yes, as you go low, I will go high…

> I rise
> I rise
> I rise.   (1978)

As we witness the increasing involvement of young people and women and so many others in response to this current incursion, it is clear that still we rise!

Now, since I am an educator and a black female educator on top of that, I have the following message for my fellow female educators.

But, it's not just about me.

It's about we.
We have the power.
This is our hour
To take control
Of our mind, body, and soul.
Together we stand
With a purpose and a plan.
And we be the man.
Yeah!
We be the man,
Yeah!
We be the man,
Yeah!!!

—Baron, 2007, pp. 36-37

This is the type of self-affirmation message we need to communicate to the girls in our classrooms— that "they be the man. They be the wo-MAN!"

References

Angelou, M. (1978). And still I rise. In *And still I rise*. New York: Random House.
Baron, L. (2007). Poem about a teacher, *I'm the man*. In *For the love of life: Life lyrics from an oral tradition*. New York: Harlin Jacque Publications.
Henley, W. E. (1920). Invictus. *The Musical Herald*, (873), 3-3.

CHAPTER 7

Let Hope Ring
Memories of a Black Girl Finding Hope During the 2008 Elections

Ronisha Browdy

IN 2008, I was 18-years old and had just graduated from high school. Like the character Zoey Johnson from the television sitcom *Grown-ish* (Barris & Wilmore, 2018), I was a girlish black woman ready to escape the overprotection of my parents and the monotony of my hometown to taste the freedom of adulthood and take on the challenge of college life. By August I was unpacking boxes and preparing for my first semester as a freshman at the University of Florida. The campus was alive. A sea of orange and blue covered the college town; students flooded onto busses and into buildings on every corner, and promoters for clubs, student organizations, and campus events could be heard from the Hub to Turlington Plaza and all the way down to Library West. It was an exciting and overwhelming time in my life—a time where I could barely manage the basic tasks of grocery shopping and remembering to get a roll of quarters for laundry, let alone contemplate the major—adult—responsibility of voting for the first time.

The presidential election created a unique buzz on campus. I had anticipated chants of "Go Gators," but that year the school spirit seemed to be accompanied by messages of "Hope," "Change," and "Yes We Can." My deep interest in the power of words made those slogans difficult to ignore, especially during those very lonely first few months in college. In many ways, those words along with the political messages coming out of the Obama administration reminded me of home, of my parents, and of my community. For example, when I was a little girl my parents would take me to church. As I sat there in my ruffled socks and shiny black shoes, I would spend a majority of praise and worship looking for candies and peppermints in my daddy's pockets, while anticipating the sermon portion of the service. I enjoyed listening to the Word. I liked how a good Word could move a congregation to reflection, to singing, to clapping, to shouting, to praying, to crying, to change.

Within African traditions throughout the diaspora, there are rhetorical discourses and literacy practices that are unique to our cultural communities. One particular practice referred to as "call and response" is commonly noticed within black churches. It is an exchange and creation of knowledge (truth) between speakers and audiences through communal participation (Alkebulan, 2003; Smitherman, 1977). In the church, a good Word requires both the powerful message of the pastor that moves the audience to mental/physical/emotional action—the call—and the participation of the congregation who confirms (or denies) the preacher's Word through their own verbal and nonverbal languages (e.g., shouting "Amen") and willingness to make changes in their daily actions—responses.

When I first heard Barack Obama speak, it reminded me of the black churches I had attended in my youth. His message of "Hope" and "Change" related to me spiritually. It seemed like, along with a governmental and social change, Obama was also calling for an internal shift in how we understood ourselves as individual citizens, how we defined our relationships with one another, and the ways we took responsibility for ourselves and each other. In his announcement of his candidacy for the presidency in 2007, Obama talked about the importance of unity and collaborative efforts to inspire change and hope. He said:

> *That is why this campaign can't only be about me. It must be about us—it must be about what we can do together. This campaign must be the occasion, the vehicle, of your hopes, and your dreams. It will take your time, your energy, and your advice—to push us forward when we're doing right, and to let us know when we're not. This campaign has to be about reclaiming the meaning of citizenship, restoring our sense of common purpose, and realizing that few obstacles can withstand the power of millions of voices calling for change. By ourselves, this change will not happen. Divided, we are bound to fail. But the life of a tall, gangly, self-made Springfield lawyer tells us that a different future is possible. He tells us that there is power in words. He tells us that there is power in conviction. That beneath all the differences of race and region, faith and station, we are one people. He tells us that there is power in hope.*[1]

(Associated Press, 2007, paras. 32-38)

---

[1] The use of Italics throughout the essay is intentional.

As I passed by campaign signs on my walks home from campus, a tension filled my chest. I was nervous about voting. I felt unworthy. This message of solidarity and citizenship was appealing to me, but it was difficult for me to feel a sense of unity with anyone or any cause while navigating the everyday loneliness of being on my own for the first time. Attending another predominantly white school did not exactly help ease these feelings. My parents always instilled in me a sense of pride about my identity as a black person, but they never shielded me from the realities of systemic and everyday oppression. My mother, born and raised in Florida, recalled the normalcy of segregation, and how remnants of Jim Crow laws were a part of her everyday life as a kid. For example, she would tell me about going to movie theaters as a child and having to sit in the balcony sections above the white customers, or the racial distinctions between water fountains and bathrooms in town. Her experience contrasted with my father's, who grew up in upstate New York. He shared stories about his youth where he seemed to be surrounded by family members who owned their own businesses and homes. They were proud people but seemed to prioritize upholding images of black respectability. On the weekends, my parents and I would watch movies about black history, typically biographical drama series and films like the 1977 miniseries *Roots* (Chomsky, Erman, Greene, and Moses, 1977), Spike Lee's *Malcolm X* starring Denzel Washington (1992), *Ghost of Mississippi* (Reiner, 1996), and *Rosewood* (Singleton, 1997) which was historically based on the 1923 Rosewood Massacre in Florida.

Reflecting on how these stories impacted my life as a youth, I believe they served as oral and visual teaching materials used by my parents to talk to me about what it means to be black in America. Given that a large majority of my education has taken place within predominantly white spaces where I was (and continue to be) "the only black person," my parents (like most parents of children of color) did not have the luxury of shielding me from racism and discrimination. These stories allowed them to teach me how to value our history and engage in the practices of looking back, remembering, and honoring those who came before me. By looking back, I could think about how my foremothers' and forefathers' lives could inform my own experiences and actions in contemporary society—in my world. Although I felt pride in the strength of my community, and was thankful that through their sacrifices I could obtain so many opportunities that they could not—like going to college and voting—up until 2008. I had primarily relied on my parents to draw the connections between our past as a black community and my/our present circumstances. What was sparking this nervousness inside of me was the realization that I would now have to envision and interpret those connections for myself. Instead of being a passive bystander, casually observing history and the contributors within it, as a young black adult and American citizen, I was now responsible for being an active participant in our society—a voter. I was now a participant in a moment that would impact my future. This was terrifying. *What if I made the wrong choice?*

**

My uncertainties and insecurities about my realities of adulthood clearly were not just about the election, but the anxiety of possibly electing the first African American president in U.S. history was real. A prominent image that was displayed everywhere in 2008 was the Obama Hope campaign poster. Created by LA street artist Shepard Fairy in late 2007, *Obama Hope* is a portrait of Obama looking upward and outward, as if he is staring off into the future. Fairy shaded the entire portrait in the patriotic colors of red, white, and blue. The Obama campaign logo was shown on Obama's lapel, and the bolded and capped words "HOPE" were printed just below his image like an exaggerated caption. When I first saw this poster, it captured my attention. When I observed *Obama Hope*, I saw a black man. I saw the United States of America. I saw a story that I was familiar with—a black man *in* America. I also saw a story that was less circulated and under-represented especially within the dominant and popular culture—a black man *as* America(n). For me, this image that is now iconic and has been replicated, repurposed, satirized, and memorialized all over the world provided an image to Obama's message of hope that spoke directly to who I was in that moment. It made visible the reality that I, as a black girl, not only *live here* in the United States of America, but I *belong here*.

Since starting school, every February in observance of Black History Month, or during the one to two weeks of history classes set aside to talk about black folks, I would hear audio-clips of Dr. Martin Luther King Jr.'s "I Have a Dream" speech. I loved this speech. For fun, I would print out the transcript and read it aloud, mimicking Dr. King's cadence and trying to make my voice boom when he said:

> *I have a dream that one day this nation will rise up and live out the true meaning of its creed: "We hold these truths to be self-evident, that all men are created equal" [...] I have a dream that my four little children will one day live in a nation where they will not be judged by the color of their skin but by the content of their character. I have a dream today [...] This is our hope. This is the faith that I go back to the South with. With this faith we will be able to hew out of the mountain of despair a stone of hope. With this faith we will be able to transform the jangling discords of our nation into a beautiful symphony of brotherhood. With this faith we will be able to work together, to pray together, to struggle together, to go to jail together, to stand up for freedom together, knowing that we will be free one day [...]* (King, 1963, paras. 12-18)

In 2008, I did not believe, and I still do not believe, that we had reached a moment in American history where Dr. King's dream had (has) finally come true. But, the *Obama Hope* image and campaign message reminded me of Dr. King's dream and gave me hope that we, as a people, were a little bit closer to that dream than we were in August 1963. *A part of that hope was seeing my likeness presented not as lazy, not as a criminal, not as uneducated, not as a slave, not as a problem, not as the help, not as an animal, but as a human, a leader, a citizen, as qualified, as whole, as complex and proud, as equal, as what people should see and think about when they envision America and what it means to be American.* Instead of erasing the intricacies of Obama's identities—black, Hawaiian, Chicagoan, bi-racial, African (Kenyan), American, male, Ivy-leaguer, husband, father, lawyer, senator, young, Christian, etc.—all of these stories and experiences could exist together. This wholeness is humanness. What I saw at the core of the Obama campaign and into his administration was this emphasis on accepting our differences as a necessary component of our humanity and citizenry. The hope was that we could reimagine ourselves collectively—under the banner of American—in a way where, instead of seeing our differences as barriers, they could be resources for change—for freedom for us all.

**

I do not remember hearing about the election much in class, but the conversation was ongoing around campus. In October 2008, Michelle Obama visited University of Florida. The Hippodrome Theater and the neighboring blocks were flooded with spectators. Local coverage of the event emphasized her call for early voting. Her message reminded me of the regular phone calls I received from my mother that year. Besides being reminded to eat and pay my rent, I got constant reminders to register to vote and then actually, "Go vote, Ronisha." I, of course, procrastinated and avoided the actual act of voting for as long as possible. One afternoon as I was exiting campus, I was approached by a volunteer, from the Obama campaign, who was helping students on campus register to vote and providing a shuttle to a location downtown for early voting. The nerves raced in my stomach as I talked to that volunteer: *Am I ready for this?*

After making some poor excuses, I was filling out registration paperwork and then being shuttled five minutes away from campus to go vote. The whole experience was a blur. I made sure to fill out each bubble precisely and to complete the entire voting sheet. Like a good student, I double-checked my responses. I took a moment to savor the moment—my vote. I looked at the printed names and my marks. It seemed like such a small and simple task. I thought about all the people who had boycotted, who were beaten, who were arrested and died for me to feel the mundaneness of this moment. I turned in my ballot, received a smile and an "I Voted" sticker from the woman supervising the voting location, and returned to the shuttle. My nerves had settled. I felt proud. I felt hope. I felt whole.

The challenge since this moment, and long after Barack Obama was elected the 44th president of the United States, is to hold on to these feelings of pride, hope, and wholeness. One of the immediate concerns following President Obama's election was his safety and the safety of his supporters, especially people of color. In the midst of our celebration, there were also attempts at intimidation and inciting fear. By the time Obama's first term drew to an end and the country started gearing up for the 2012 election, I had completed my undergraduate degree and was starting graduate school and a teaching position at a university closer to my home. I wanted to go home. I wanted to be closer to the nest, to feel the warmth and security of family, although I was too bold to admit this to my parents.

On February 26, 2012, just two hours away from my hometown, a 17-year-old black boy named Trayvon Martin was murdered (Blow, 2012). I was stunned by the reports of what happened—the blatant attack and disregard for a black life. I found solace with two other black women students and teachers in my graduate program. Following Martin's murder, they invited me to attend a rally and march in Sanford. People in the streets wore black hoodies and raised their fists chanting

Let Hope Ring 73

"No Justice—No Peace." I remember being handed two fun-size packs of Skittles and seeing people holding cans of Arizona Iced Tea in the air. I watched the rows of signs that read "I am Trayvon Martin." There was sadness, anger, and frustration—a desire for change. A desire for justice. A desire to not be racially profiled. To have our lives valued. To be young black people who were "not judged by the color of our skin, but by the content of our character" (King, 1963, para. 15). I watched the George Zimmerman trial with my mother on television. I watched Rachel Jeantel, Martin's friend, get criticized and belittled by prosecutors, and then attacked again by commentators on television and online for her physical appearance and language. I saw the bloody sweatshirts that Martin fought for his life in, and ultimately died in. I saw the images of Martin's parents who sat in the courtroom helpless as a verdict of *not guilty* was read in favor of the man who had murdered their son. *How does one have pride, hope, and wholeness in these moments?*

Reflecting back on these earlier times in my life, and even looking at the current political climate that has replaced messages of "Hope," "Change," and "Yes We Can" with the mantra "Make America Great Again," I understand that these attacks against women and men of color in our society—via police brutality, terrorism, sexual assault, mass incarceration, poverty, gentrification, immigration policies, travel bans, failures to provide relief to our communities during times of crisis and natural disaster, insistence of building pipelines through our communities, and the everyday acts of racism that we prepare ourselves for every morning—are attacks on our humanity. It is an attempt to disrupt our feelings of wholeness, to make us feel less than human. It is also an attempt to divide us as individuals from each other, so that we cannot see, empathize with, and assist each other. When Dr. King talked about the potential greatness of America, he talked about us—all of us—coming together. Similarly, Obama's campaign and administration tried to reiterate this message of unity and communal efforts to make positive changes for us all.

As an educator, and a black woman with occasional girlish tendencies, I encourage my generation and the generation after me (including my students) to practice holding on to themselves and each other. This means critically engaging and acknowledging our stories and experiences in the bodies that we occupy. This means seeing our voices and our words as legitimate and powerful weapons, especially when accompanied with our collective physical action (whether that is voting, rallying, writing, volunteering, etc.). This means finding ways to unite with others with similar experiences and concerns, as well as those whose identities and stories may be different because we all have partial lenses for understanding the world and acting in it. It is through combining these viewpoints and abilities that we all can truly see, make a difference, and be free.

References

Alkebulan, A. (2003). The spiritual essence of African American rhetoric. In E. Richardson & R. Jackson II (Eds.), *Understanding African American rhetoric: Classical origins to contemporary innovations* (23-39). New York: Routledge.

Associated Press. (2007, February 10). Illinois Sen. Barack Obama's announcement speech. *The Washington Post*. Retrieved from http://www.washingtonpost.com/wp-dyn/content/article/2007/02/10/AR2007021000879.html

Barris, K. (Creator/Producer), and Wilmore, L. (Creator/Producer). (2018). *Grown-ish* [Television Series]. Burbank, CA: Walt Disney Company.

Blow, C. (2012, March 16). The Curious Case of Trayvon Martin. Retrieved from https://www.nytimes.com/2012/03/17/opinion/blow-the-curious-case-of-trayvon-martin.html

Chomsky, M.J. (Director), Erman, E. (Director), Greene, D. (Director), & Moses, G. (1977). *Roots* [Television series]. Hollywood, CA: American Broadcasting Company.

King, M.L. (1963). *I have a dream, address delivered at the March on Washington for Jobs and Freedom* [Transcript]. Retrieved from https://kinginstitute.stanford.edu/king-papers/documents/i-have-dream-address-delivered-march-washington-jobs-and-freedom

Lee, S. (Director). (1992). *Malcolm X* [Motion picture]. United States: Warner Bros.

Reiner, R. (Director). (1996). *Ghost of Mississippi* [Motion picture]. United States: Castle Rock Entertainment.

Singleton, J. (Director). (1997). *Rosewood* [Motion picture]. United States: Warner Bros.

Smitherman, G. (1977). *Talkin and testifyin: The language of black America*. Detroit: Wayne State University Press.

CHAPTER 8

Oppressive Patriarchy
African Women's Struggle with Gender Inequality

Gladys Kedibone Mokwena

Introduction

"FAT. PIG. DOG. Slob. Disgusting. Animal." These epithets have become synonymous with Donald Trump, the current president of the United States, who habitually uses derogatory words to characterize women. It is Trump's tendency to criticize women for their looks, and he has been widely repudiated for his objectification of women. Leaders like Trump and the endless list of men who have been exposed in the #MeToo movement prove that gender equality is perceived as a pipedream. In an ever-dominant patriarchal society, women's oppression is an indisputable fact. Currently, women continue to face oppression of various kinds at home, work, schools, and in society (King Jr., 1993).

This excerpt from Martin Luther King's famous speech at the mountaintop, "I have a dream that my four little children will one day live in a nation where they will not be judged by the color of their skin but by their content of their character..." (King Jr., 1993), provokes me to pose the following questions:

- What is the plight of women and girls?
- Does gender equality also apply to an African girl?
- Will women ever realize the dream of equality in this world dominated by patriarchy?

To address these questions, I have identified eight women (W-8) who experienced oppression in the U.S. and South Africa and highlighted their struggle to illustrate how the changing role of women has contributed to disturbing patriarchy's established tradition. These women are Coretta Scott King, Maya Angelou, Hillary Clinton, Michelle Obama, Winnie Mandela, Albertina Sisulu, Graca Machel, and Nkosazana Dlamini Zuma. All the women highlighted in this chapter have played a very important role in fighting oppressive practices either in South Africa or in other parts of the world.

The late *Coretta Scott King*, the widow of the late Martin Luther King Jr., experienced oppression while her husband was alive (Tutu, 2007). She continuously picked up the telephone, receiving call after call threatening her life, the life of her husband, and the lives of her children. After the assassination of her husband, she managed to raise four children single-handedly and remained an activist. Like Coretta Scott King, my husband was killed, and I experienced widowhood at a very young age of 26. As young widows, we both stayed the course despite the hardships of raising our children single-handedly.

Another woman figure, *Maya Angelou*, the civil rights activist and world-renowned poet, survived rape and racism but remained joyful. In her book entitled *Wouldn't Take Nothing for My Journey Now*, Maya Angelou (1993) makes the following assertion:

> The woman who survives intact and happy must be at once tender and tough. She must have convinced herself, that she, her values, and her choices are important. In a time and world where males hold sway and control, the pressure upon women to yield their rights-of-way is tremendous. And it is under those very circumstances that women's toughness must be evidenced. (p. 7)

Maya Angelou's experiences of racism and oppression enabled her as a working-class single mother to challenge traditional and Western viewpoints on women and family life "and rise" to become one of the most influential women in the world. Her strategies of economic survival and experiences of family structure present a model for black families to survive economically. A recurrent theme in Angelou's autobiographies mirrors the independence I dream of for womenfolk. Consequently, I have taken many of her life lessons to reflect on mine to have a purpose-driven life.

Hillary Clinton became the first woman to become a U.S. senator of New York. She was the first-ever First Lady to win an elected seat in public office. She served as the secretary of state from 2009 until 2013 and then became the first woman in U.S. history to become the presidential nominee for a major political party. During the presidential campaign, she received an onslaught of sexist remarks by Trump, was demonized by society as emotional, and blamed for her husband's actions *because she is a woman*. However, in her book *It Takes a Village*, Hillary (1996) pointed out that our existence depends on relations that influence all aspects of socialization and these relations are responsible for what our children ultimately become in life. As the presidential nominee, she shattered the stereotype that women cannot lead; rather she demonstrated that women, like their male counterparts, can have a political agenda and perform any task, despite the unfair and oppressive treatment by men.

In the same breath, *Michelle Obama,* married to the 44th president of the U.S., Barack H. Obama, blended purpose and policy with fun and was able to reach beyond Capitol Hill as the First Lady of the U.S. from 2009 to 2017. Her emphasis is for women to stand up for ourselves, for each other, and for justice for all (Obama, M., 2009). In one of her landmark speeches, Michelle said this of oppressive men like Trump, "When they go low, we go high." She continues to be *the feminist* idol, who is brave enough to take on Trump's utter disrespect toward women. In addition, yes, Michelle Obama seems to be the only woman able to shut Trump down.

In South Africa, one of the W-8 figures whose role in the struggle is recognized worldwide is *Winnie Madikizela Mandela*, the anti-apartheid fighter and international symbol of resistance. When President Mandela divorced her in a brutal letter, critics accused her of attempting to use Mandela's surname for political mileage. Her reputation as Mother of the Nation was marred after she was accused of the kidnap and murder of a suspected 14-year-old spy in 1991. However, throughout her life, she remained resolute and steadfast in the face of adversity.

The other South African female politician, *Albertina Sisulu*, spent most of her adult life under house arrest and was psychologically tortured in solitary confinement. She symbolizes the Rock in South Africa for her famous quote, *"You tamper with women, you tamper with the rock."* It is in the context of W-8 women that Chilisa (2012) explains the importance of motherhood within African feminism and identifies several proverbs to illustrate the changing role of women in society.

A Historical Perspective

My reflection on the era in which I was born draws from some significant historical events with regard to human rights in South Africa. One such right is the Freedom Charter of 1955, which is unique in that people were involved in creating their own vision during the oppressive times of apartheid[1] in South Africa. The Freedom Charter pledged that, "All shall be equal before the law" (South Africa, 1996). A year later, on 9 August 1956, 20,000 women in all their diversity organized their first ever and biggest march to that time in South Africa to the Union Buildings of Pretoria, without seeking permission from the authorities. Women protested against the apartheid government led by Afrikaaner and male leaders who epitomized patriarchy. Chakkalakal (2004) asserts that patriarchy gives more value to men than women. She explains: "Patriarchy has turned woman against herself, her daughter, her daughters-in-law, her sisters, her mother and her mother-in-law" (p. 19). I agree with Chakkalakal's statement as it carries multiple truths and calls for the deconstruction of patriarchy.

Deconstructing Patriarchy: Theoretical Framework

Drawing from this history, this chapter takes the deconstruction theory as a lens to draw upon proverbs that establish the place of African women in broader society. The deconstruction theory propounded by Foucault and Derrida (Culler, 2014) may be defined as a theory of literary criticism that questions traditional assumptions about certainty, identity, and truth. It asserts that words can only refer to other words and attempts to demonstrate how statements about any text subvert their own meaning. Most importantly, deconstruction theory opposes the status quo in the sense that an individual or persons take it upon themselves to free themselves.

An individual or group seeking to emancipate themselves can relate deconstruction with Paulo Freire's (1996) notion of pedagogy of the oppressed, as both theories underpin the urge for individuals to liberate themselves. Through deconstruction theory and critical feminism, women who have been denigrated by a patriarchal and misogynist society are encouraged to free themselves (hooks, 2003).

[1] Apartheid / ə`paːtheit/ (in South Africa) refers to a policy or system of segregation or discrimination on grounds of race.

It is in the spirit of deconstruction that this chapter focuses on how (South) African society has been socially engineered to view women as sexual objects rather than human beings with the same worth as their male counterparts.

Oppressive Patriarchy: African Women Struggle with Gender Inequality

Women in Africa, and South Africa in particular, have had their space and identity trampled upon, not only by apartheid, but also in the name of tradition. The death of Winnie Mandela in early 2018, and all that has been revealed posthumously about her, has opened the debate in which women sat down and asked themselves, "How could we not have seen?" a rhetorical question asked by Winnie's daughter to which she responds, "Because we never did." The daughter further asked mourners at the funeral: "Why did you people wait until my mother is gone to vindicate her?" Evidently, silence is one kind of oppression women go through and nobody seems to care. In the modern time, social media do not seem to dig more into this misogyny and abuse of women leaders. Therefore, we have to speak out for ourselves.

Disrupting Patriarchy: A Critical Feminist Deconstruction of Gender-Biased Proverbs

The first place to start is through challenging the institutionalization of female objectification through African proverbs. Mieder (1993) as cited in Sebate (2001) points out that proverbs are important and provide basic and universal experiences. Furthermore, Sebate (2001) supports this view and postulates that proverbs are relevant to humanity today in the same manner they were during the early years. African women must unite and disrupt the patriarchal mindset that perpetuates the image of the woman as an inherently disposable object.

A newly wedded bride is taught from the onset that *Monna selepe o a adimanwa* (a man is like an axe so he can be shared) (Chilisa, 2012). Through cultural transmission, a girl grows up knowing that men have the right to engage in infidelity and live promiscuous lives whereas the wife/wives must forever be grateful to men and stop whining and ranting. Imagining an axe, I see a heavy bladed head attached to a handle. Its uses vary, and include shaping, splitting, and cutting wood. An axe causes pain, paralysis, and even death. However, the value of an axe in the African tradition outweighs the negatives attached to it. During Lobola[2] (dowry) negotiations, an axe is used for the two families to share tasks and strengthen the bond between them. Well, the same way the axe can cut a powerful tree down is the same way it can destroy the livelihoods of women.

Another patriarchy-loaded proverb that South Africans swear by is *Lebitla la mosadi ke bogadi* (a married woman dies and is buried at her in-laws' homestead). Divorce is not an option for a married woman in (South) Africa. One woman who stood up to the tradition is *Graça Machel*, second wife of Nelson Mandela and former wife of Samora Machel, former president of Mozambique. Even though she was the president's wife, she was not persuaded to adopt Mandela's surname; she stuck to her original in-laws' name. She is a perfect example of patriarchy deconstructed to benefit posterity. By refusing to take Mandela's last name, she refused to be her new in-laws' property. Why should she even have to go through the agony of fighting with two in-laws? Widowhood is harder on women than it is for men (Mokwena, 2016). Chilisa (2012) is right when she points out that gender-biased proverbs do not allow women to question possible abuse by the husband or his family.

Nkosazana Dlamini Zuma, the eighth chosen woman among the W-8 figures, was in a polygamous marriage with the former president of South Africa, Jacob Zuma, until they divorced in the late 1990s. As the former African Union Chairperson, and a medical doctor by profession, Nkosazana brought victory for Africa's women; yet society continues to perceive her as the former president's ex-wife. With her political accomplishments, her name as a presidential nominee, she presented a dilemma for many South Africans for another Zuma to take the presidency. She lost the bid. The pit of patriarchy (Chakkalakal, 2004) continues to haunt women.

---

[2] Lobola—a African custom in Southern Africa by which a bridegroom's family makes a payment in cattle or cash to the bride's family shortly before the marriage.

Reconceptualizing My Identity as a Widow

On the eve of my husband's burial, Fr. Michael D'Annucci (God bless his soul) of the religious Congregation of the Sacred Stigmata (CSS) gave me an opportunity to say my marriage vows to his stone-cold corpse. Placing his wedding ring on his chest in a coffin, I made a commitment that when I should die, I would surely be buried with him in the same grave, not "in my in-laws' homestead." I summoned my courage to have a voice and to stand up for myself. True to my statement, I deconstructed the proverb *Lebitla la mosadi ke bogadi* (a married woman dies and is buried at her in-laws' homestead) by getting a homestead for my children and grandchildren. When my late husband paid Lobola, the elders in his family conveyed the strong message that I would be married to the family and live with my children at my in-laws' homestead. My in-laws, however, respected my wish to raise my children in my own homestead, and I am forever indebted to them. Hopefully my children will grow up in an era where they do not have to seek anybody's permission to be themselves.

Overlooking the fact that he could have been an *axe*, I have dedicated special moments to Molefi, my late husband, such as visiting his grave, particularly twice a year—on his day of birth and his day of passing. On these occasions, I courageously write down my pain; I allow myself to be mournful and emotional, as I read from my grieving diary,

> It is 36 years since his passing,
> He would be turning 65 years of age,
> I visited his grave; I lit a candle in his memory
> I was a bit perturbed by the state of vandalism occurring in our gravesite;
> As I cleaned the tombstone, I found myself singing his favorite Dobbie Gray song.
>
> I cried a soulful cry; it felt so good; it felt so very bad.
> In the midst of my crying, I felt my freedom coming. (Vanzant, 1998)
> *Molefi, the love of my life, Love never dies!* (13 February 2018)

As a widow, I am proud of the changes that I was able to effect in my widowed life, and I am determined to leave it as a legacy to my children.

Learning Conversations with Our Sons and Daughters

The life of the W-8 figures, and my own life, in small ways highlighted in this chapter depicts strong women—*"lions in dresses"* (Attwood, Castle, & Smythe, 2004)—who are committed to female empowerment. Women globally, and in Africa, are part of a culture, tradition, and history, that can never be eradicated from us even though we are not happy with some of the practices (Chilisa, 2012). This said, women are primarily educators. We play an important role for initiating interactive learning through learning conversations.

Magano, Mostert, and van der Westhuizen (2010) view learning conversations as people learning about themselves, from the other person and about the other person. Methodologically, *learning conversation* has been defined as "a process where practitioners can speak to each other to gain a greater understanding of the theory and practice of their work in a collaborative partnership that supports mutual learning about improvement" (Saunders & Gowing, 1999). This process can be applied to family conversation, as well.

Ubuntu, a South African word that means humanity, is essential in learning conversations. With Ubuntu, "I am because we are"; I am apt to believe that conversations will occur in a humane manner, where the self cannot be self without the selves (Tutu, 2007). We can therefore draw from the past to help us understand the present and move to the future.

Conclusion

As an African female, I am committed to the development of self, other women, and vulnerable children. Service in humanity is essential for me. Women worldwide are primary nurturers in the family and broader society. We not only keep fires burning but also collect the wood and light the fires. It is therefore important that we women hold hands to appreciate the initiatives of our predecessors in the political sphere as well as in broader social circles.

The National Research Foundation of South Africa supported this work fully (GN: 110927).

References

Angelou, M. (1993). *Wouldn't take nothing for my journey now.* New York: Random House.

Attwood, G., Castle, P.J., and Smythe, S. (2004). 'Women are lions in dresses': Negotiating gender relations in REFLECT learning circles in Lesotho. In A. Robinson-Pant (Ed.), Business in Society Conference, May 15, 2017.

Chakkalakal, P. (2004). *Discipleship a space for women's leadership? A feminist theological critique.* Mumbai: Pauline Sisters Bombay Society.

Chilisa, B. (2012). *Indigenous research methodologies.* Thousand Oaks, CA: SAGE.

Culler (2014). *On deconstruction: Theory and criticism after structuralism.* London: Routledge Taylor and Francis Group.

Clinton, H.R. (1996). *It takes a village: And other lessons children teach us.* New York: Simon & Schuster.

Freire, P. (1996). *Pedagogy of the oppressed.* Harmondsworth: Penguin

hooks, b. (2003). Teaching community: A pedagogy of hope. London: Routledge.

King, M.L., Jr. (1993). *I have a dream.* San Francisco: Harper.

Magano, M.D., Mostert, P., and van der Westhuizen, G. (2010). *Learning conversations: The value of interactive learning.* Johannesburg: Heinemann

Mokwena, G.K. (2016). *An auto-ethnographic life story of a black academic woman: A story of triumph in the face of adversity.* In Adeniji-Neill, D., and Anne Mungai, A. (Eds.). New York: Peter Lang, Volume 44, pp. 81-98.

Obama, M. (2009, March 11). *Remarks by the First Lady at the State Department Women of Courage Awards.* Available: https://obamawhitehouse.archives.gov/realitycheck/the-press-office/remarks-first-lady-state-department-women-courage-awards

Saunders, S., & Gowing, K. (1999). Learning from the learning conversation: Benefits and problems in developing a process to improve workplace performance. *Education Line.* Summary of presentation at the Third International Conference "Researching Vocational Education and Training," Bolton Institute, July 14-16, 1999.

Sebate, P.S. (2001). The Wisdom we lived and live by: The Setswana Question. *South African Journal of African Languages*, 3:269-279.

South Africa. (1996). *Constitution of the Republic of South Africa No. 108 of 1996: Chapter 2.* Pretoria.

Tutu, D.M. (2007). *The words and inspiration of Martin Luther King, Jr.* Cape Town: Wild Dog Press.

Vanzant, I. (1998). *Yesterday, I cried.* New York: Simon & Schuster.

CHAPTER 9

Teaching Adult Learners of Color in a Time of Struggle: The Impact on Children

Jaye Jones

BEING A BLACK Chicagoan during the era of Barack Obama was to feel like you were one of the "cool kids." His poise, intellect, and dedication to purposeful action, were a type of reflected glory on the black communities that his political run had invigorated. He was truly our president. As luck would have it, I was a doctoral student at the University of Chicago and living in Hyde Park—his old neighborhood—when he was first elected, and everywhere there were reminders of the optimism that his presence in the upper echelons of power had kindled. Not only had the 44th president nurtured the power of struggling families in Chicago through his work as a community organizer, but he had dwelled with his family *here*, eaten meals *here*, gotten his hair cut *here*.

In describing critical literacy, Paulo Freire (1987) noted that "reading the world always precedes reading the word, and reading the word implies continually reading the world" (pg. 35). In my work and research with Adult Basic Education (ABE) students at local programs in Chicago and New York during President Obama's two terms, this world was filled with promise and a sense of opportunity. Many of the learners had voted for the first time in many years. And in Chicago our discussion of Obama's memoir *Dreams from My Father*—with students who were mostly African American women—inspired a sense of connection. Indeed, despite his life of relative privilege, it was clear that many students could relate on some level to President Obama's psychic, familial, and spiritual struggles. Most were also parents or grandparents, and for perhaps the first time, it seemed possible that they could be part of a family that produced (another) potential black president of the United States.

Freire's dynamic vision suggests that learning is a process of discovery and that structural inequalities—as well as the myriad of experiences—inspiring, harrowing, complicated—that adult learners bring into the classroom must be considered. As a social worker and adult educator, I believe that this both/and (vs. either/or) vision suggests that the realities that shape the material world of adult learners—and its emotional nuances—must be made visible in the educational realm. There is no real learning without a commitment to understanding the person-in-their-environment; the various worlds in which their experiences are braided. This realm includes life in under-resourced, over-surveilled neighborhoods; making do on Supplemental Security Income payments or intermittent, low-paid work; and justified rage—often met with irritation by those who are "well meaning"—at the lack of respect with which you are treated. In this way, the "world" and "word" are not separate entities, inhabiting distinct bounded spaces. They are "read" and experienced as intertwined and interactive; they flexibly inform and impact one another. Examination of these concepts is embedded in processes that emphasize fluidity and change, action and transformation. When reflecting on her self-perception as a working mother and how that influenced what she wished for her own daughters, Michelle Obama (2015) remarked:

> For me, being a mother made me a better professional, because coming home every night to my girls reminded me what I was working for. And being a professional made me a better mother, because by pursuing my dreams, I was modeling for my girls how to pursue their dreams. (no pag.)

Parents in ABE programs are no different from Michelle Obama; they are often filled with hope and excitement as being in the classroom represents their (sometimes) first, tenuous step toward the opportunity to achieve their own academic goals and to be role models and/or better educational advocates for their children or grandchildren. They want to be able to help them with their homework, read a book to/with them, and feel confident when talking with teachers or administrators about their concerns or their child's progress. This sense of optimism, however, is almost always juxtaposed with fears of failure and humiliation, triggered by past experiences—both as students and parents—that were often undermining and demeaning. Black and Latinx women, who often make up most of the student population at ABE programs located in urban communities, are also disproportionately impacted by issues of trauma, violence, and incarceration. Consequently, they must contend with the marginalization, diminished self-esteem, and sense of powerlessness that are a residue of these experiences. The persistent racial/ethnic, gender-, and class-based oppression they experience adds another layer of pain, heightening their risk of further disconnection.

This atmosphere of oppression and marginalization has intensified since the election of Donald J. Trump in 2016. The sense of potential and progress that Obama represented has been decimated as people of color, the LGBTQ population, and other already burdened communities face increased surveillance and scrutiny. Due to more blatant and harmful attacks on their ability to make even a modest living, they develop real fears about their ability to physically survive in an increasingly hostile environment. This is a world filled with contempt, one that crushes dreams. Remaining engaged and enrolled in an educational program under these conditions is difficult.

In my current work in New York City, I have found that many adult learners are stopping or dropping out to maintain a sense of control over their lives or (appropriately) flee dangerous circumstances. For instance, heightened immigration enforcement as well as uncertainty around the status of young people protected under Deferred Action for Childhood Arrivals (DACA) has led some students to minimize the time they spend outside of their homes or neighborhoods. They may decide that going to school is too risky and opt to attend classes very erratically. In Trump's era, the joy of educating also threatens to become the routine of schooling, as content that is disengaged from what is happening on the ground and in the economy takes precedence. In ABE this is reflected in a movement toward "workforce development" that focuses on career pathways for students. Teachers are often torn—they want students to "succeed" within this paradigm, that is, students want their High School Equivalency (HSE) diploma and earning the credential does open occupational doors—but they also realize that for impoverished adult learners of color who are also struggling to raise children, this emphasis can be profoundly alienating. It doesn't necessarily focus on work in family-sustaining occupations, and it minimizes creativity and personal growth.

Adult educators must both be sensitive to these realities and recognize that we have the potential to positively impact families and young people through the work we do with the predominantly poor, female-of-color parents we serve. It is important that adult educators—and particularly educators of color—be leaders in helping students face and navigate attacks—and the attendant anguish and anger—while also acknowledging the resistance and survival strategies that repression can facilitate. Through the use of critical pedagogy, educational spaces for adults can become places where learners not only "connect their education to social change, [but] also bring to light subordinated histories, narratives, and modes of knowledge" that enhance their capacities to "both read the word and the world critically" (Giroux, 2013, p. 122).

bell hooks' (1994) notion of "engaged pedagogy" offers insights on how adult educators can begin to put into practice strategies that honor the knowledges of parents and their children. Significantly, hooks stresses the need for educators to be attuned to both their own emotional lives and that of their students. Education for transformation is linked with the complex feelings stimulated by the academic process and the relationships that are created in educational spaces. For hooks (1994) the classroom is not just a place of learning, but:

> with all its limitations, remains a location of possibility. In the field of possibility we have the opportunity to labor for freedom, to demand of ourselves and our comrades, an openness of mind and heart that allows us to face reality even as we collectively imagine ways to move beyond boundaries, to transgress. (p. 207)

Emotionally and culturally responsive instructors can play a crucial role in allowing education to be at once a source of empowerment and a weapon of resistance (Grant, 2018).

Thematic reading discussion groups can become spaces where Black and Latinx women align and integrate their own educational needs, and the sociopolitical issues impacting their families and communities. An approach I developed, Women Reading for Education, Affinity and Development (WREAD), utilizes culturally relevant texts and interactive, critical pedagogy to build learners' basic literacy skills and content knowledge, while also nurturing personal growth and supportive relationships with other women (Jones, 2012; 2014). WREAD's dialogic structure also emphasizes the links between experience, learning, and collective empowerment (Freire, 1970/1993; hooks, 1994). A commitment to exploring works that center the experiences of marginalized groups also provides a frame for exploring how the personal and political interface, and how strategies of resistance are established within oppressive environments (Brookfield, 2003; hooks, 1994).

A recent iteration of WREAD focused on *The Warmth of Other Suns* by Isabel Wilkerson, an expansive 600-page narrative of the journey to better opportunities taken by millions of African Americans from the Jim Crow South to northern and western cities from 1915 to 1970 (Wilkerson, 2010). Six ABE women of color and I read and listened to excerpts from the text, and followed the stories of three families as they made their way to Chicago, Los Angeles, and New York City. Reflecting on the aspirations exemplified by their stories, one African American student noted: "The things they [migrants] wanted…we're still them, we still want here in our lifestyle now. I want something today. I want my kids to understand me better and I want better for them. I want better for us." Her capacity to relate her ambitions for her family with those that came before her places her story within a remarkable historical context and also highlights the challenges that remain for this generation.

In *The Warmth of Other Suns,* parents were often motivated to leave their racist communities when they saw the impact this abuse had on their children; they had been forced to survive, but did not want the young people who represented their future to have to endure the same traumas. Leaving the world they knew behind seemed like a small price to pay for those used to "making a way out of no way." Similarly, the women of WREAD believed that the economic and academic struggles they confronted would allow their children to see them as authentic role models, and provide a foundation for their ability to thrive despite the obstacles they faced.

A culminating visit to the Museum of Modern Art (MOMA) to view panels chronicling the Great Migration by the artist Jacob Lawrence also encouraged an exploration of the experiential, emotional, and creative. Examining Lawrence's unpretentious but compelling tableaux led to questions about what the women would draw from their own journeys toward learning and awareness—and about what they imagined the world would look like when they attained their goals. Like Lawrence's purposeful travelers, their troubles would not end, but collectively reading, writing, listening, and dialoguing generated possibilities that took them beyond what their ancestors had realized.

As a black female adult educator and administrator, facilitating these groups has been both intensely emotional and rewarding. I have been humbled by what

I learn from students and have gained a deep appreciation for the sacrifices they make to provide for their families and attend class. Within WREAD, there is a sense of comradery as we work together and through the various texts, and the revelations they generate. It remains challenging, however, to dialogue about issues of oppression—especially those faced by impoverished women of color—outside of this space. In the places where I have worked, despite a student body that is overwhelmingly female, black, and/or Latinx, the leadership and/or teaching staff is almost always predominantly white and middle- to upper-middle-class. And despite an external commitment to issues of social justice, frank conversations about the liberal white supremacy that often undergirds these programs are nearly impossible. In a time when the white supremacist values of Donald J. Trump are ascendant, this is especially problematic. Rituals of silencing, active avoidance and diminishment reinforces organizational structures that highlight and valorize white, male-centered ways of knowing and being. The mostly white administrators also hold institutional power because they are listened to and perceived as experts, while the people of color they supervise and/or teach provide a culturally diverse, but muffled backdrop.

In a speech during his first campaign, candidate Barack Obama asserted: "Change will not come if we wait for some other person or if we wait for some other time. We are the ones we've been waiting for. We are the change that we seek" (Obama, 2008, no pag.). These words are especially poignant when they are positioned alongside those of Audre Lorde who, almost 25 years earlier, declared: "Sometimes we are blessed with being able to choose the time, and the arena, and the manner of our revolution, but more usually we must do battle where we are standing" (1988/2009, p. 140). Despite the differences in their backgrounds and politics, both Obama and Lorde make it clear that the time to stand up for change is always now and that we—educators of color and the communities we value—must be the ones to do it. Our schools, classrooms, families, and communities are the inspiration for and sites of resistance. Despite the opposition we face, we must do our work *here*.

References

Brookfield, S. (2003). Racializing criticality in adult education. *Adult Education Quarterly, 53*(3), 154-169.

Freire, P. (1970/1993). *Pedagogy of the oppressed*. New York: Continuum.

Freire, P., & Macedo, D. (1987). *Literacy: Reading the word and the world*. New York: Praeger.

Giroux, H. A. (2013). *America's education: Deficit and the war on youth*. New York: Monthly Review Press.

Grant, C. A. (2018). *Du Bois and education*. New York: Routledge.

hooks, b. (1994). *Teaching to transgress: Education as the practice of freedom*. New York: Routledge.

Jones, J. (2012). Women reading for education, affinity & development (WREAD): An evaluation of a semi-structured reading discussion group for African American female adult literacy students. *Proceedings of the Adult Education Research Conference* (AERC) (pp. 176–183). West Covina, CA: American Education Research Corporation.

Jones, J. (2014). Women reading for education, affinity and development (WREAD): Emotionally responsive learning spaces for adult learners. *Proceedings of the XI International Transformative Learning Conference* (pp. 936-941). New York: Columbia University.

Lorde, A. (1988/2009). A burst of light: Living with cancer. In R. P. Byrd, J. B. Cole, & B. Guy-Sheftall (Eds.). *I am your sister: Collected and unpublished writings of Audre Lorde* (pp. 81-152). New York: Oxford University Press.

Obama, B. (2004). *Dreams from my father: A story of race and inheritance*. New York: Broadway Books.

Obama, B. (2008). Speech to supporters after the Feb. 5 nominating contests. *New York Times*, (2008, February 5). *Barack Obama's Feb. 5 Speech*. https://www.nytimes.com/2008/02/05/us/politics/05text-obama.html

Obama, M. (2015). Remarks by the First Lady at "Let Girls Learn" event at Iikura Guest House, Tokyo, Japan.

Wilkerson, I. (2010). *The warmth of other suns: The epic story of America's Great Migration*. New York: Random House.

Chapter 10

Incivility: Experiences of a Black Widow in a Higher Education Working Environment

Sizakele M. Matlabe

Introduction: What Is Wrong with the World?

To CONTEXTUALIZE THE story of one individual who, in a most vulnerable state, persisted in completing a grueling degree as a young widow in an institution of higher education, while working as a lecturer, a brief look at the broader perspective is valuable.

Watching President Obama move into the White House with his mother-in-law led me to a deep reflection on the cruelty of African patriarchy and patriarchal academia. I could not help wondering where a man of African descent who grew up in a racist, capitalist world could have learned such a deep sense of humanity and civility. I found myself wondering why South African society could not be the same. I also wondered what my people had learned from the humility of our late and beloved president Madiba.

Angela Miles' (2002) blistering attack on capitalism in its most globalized, power-hungry form is a cry of outrage at the "destructive and still largely unquestioned neoliberal growth agenda." She points out that those who are in powerful economic positions actively assist corporate bodies to treat life and the means of life as commodities for use to further their visions of wealth and power. Individuals, life, and nature itself are expendable, despite rhetorical shows about corporate social responsibility, sustainability, and concern for citizens' welfare. The state actively participates in furthering these practices. As the well-known economist Ha-Joon Chang (2000) states:

> The state is no more assumed to be an impartial, omnipotent social guardian and is now analyzed either as a 'predator' or as a vehicle for politically-powerful groups (including the politicians and the bureaucrats themselves) to advance their sectional interests. (p. 3)

And, I would add, materialist ones, especially *in* South Africa. In this atmosphere, universities in Africa and South Africa have increasingly been pursuing a "market-oriented model of higher education" (Holland, 2009, p. 557). The market-oriented model of higher education is concerned about profit marking. Students are seen as commodities that bring in profit. The reason that students attend universities are second to the profit they bring to the institutions of learning. The moves to become Model 2 type institutions, with the typical requirement that the university finds its own research funds, has resulted in many changes in the structure, atmosphere, and ethos of universities.

The institution where I have been employed for the last nine years is no exception. I taught at a university in the North West Province (NWP) of South Africa and was employed, at the new institution, first in one of the educational departments as a temporary lecturer (2009) and then, fortunately, became permanent staff (2010). Subsequently, I transferred to another department where I am engaged in lecturing (distance mode), researching, and promoting students in a very busy schedule. If this sounds like a serene career, despite its happening in a country only recently democratized (1992), in which for some sixty years apartheid was the avowed policy of the State (circa 1948-1992), you might be surprised at the story I want to tell.

My Story: Widowhood Ordeal

Widowhood is a life-changing event that is mentally, spiritually, and physically overwhelming, especially for the individual who has lost a partner, a friend, and a soulmate. My husband died intestate in 2012.

At the time, my first draft of my doctoral dissertation was complete, but I was shattered and seemed to stop living for the next three years. I was at war with my feelings. What had happened immediately after my husband's burial was traumatizing on a deep level. Conflict frequently arises in the household of a widow when, for cultural reasons, the relatives of the deceased arrive to arrange the matters of inheritance, the funeral, the mourning rituals, and other matters seen as important to the family. My late husband's family made a concerted effort to take control of his and my estate (houses, livestock, and finances). In accordance with African cultural beliefs, without my husband, I had ceased to be a grown woman who could oversee her life and her estate. It is customary in South Africa, probably in many other African cultures as well, that after the passing away of the husband, in-laws can intestate take land away from the widow, even forcefully (Nwokoro, 2016). In some tribes, the in-laws diminish a woman's status the moment she becomes widowed. It seems as if, as the losing of her last name suggests, an African woman's social standing within the family and the community is determined through the husband (Thomas, 2008).

As a widow, the reciprocity I expected in terms of caring, kindness, mutuality, and comfort did not seem to be part of the behavior of my in-laws. I had been brought up in a family in which the concept of Ubuntu was regarded as the proper way for human beings to ensure the welfare of their own family and the broader community. Ubuntu is characterized as a "particular kind of ethic of care" (Waghid and Smeyers, 2012). Ubuntu ethics of care is characterized by sharing and taking care of each other. I believed I belonged to my in-laws' community during my marriage and expected them to be imbued with the same cultural ethic of care as I believed in. As a widow, I even felt the gossip-mongers suggesting, when I refused to give up the estate, that I was guilty of killing my late husband, to "inherit his estate." Even in this twenty-first century, *"Widows are perceived to be unclean, unholy and bearers of bad luck"* (Young, 2006, pp. 199-200) in many black South African communities. There are different rituals that widows undergo against their will, and processes that other women deem to be fit in cleansing the "black luck" that resulted in the passing away of the spouse. In some cultures, women wear black or blue cloths for a period of two years or six months. Women are also forced to shave their hair with a razor.

I fled from my in-laws to what I believed would be the sanctuary of my workplace. Being a permanent member of staff, I expected the normal civilities, such as condolences, to be extended to me. Sadly, this was done in the most inconsiderate and punishing way. In the first meeting I attended in my department, I was placed on the agenda without being consulted. It was announced that anyone who wanted to say anything such as offer condolences could do so. Ubuntu principles of communality, mutual respect, and caring were not evident in the individuals at my institution (Manala, 2015). I was treated in an inhuman way. I felt as if my colleagues were rubbing salt on the bleeding wound that I was trying to heal while I was away on leave.

To relieve my grief, as I observed in myself reactions of anger, denial, guilt, and bargaining (Kübler-Ross & Kessler, 2007; Bonanno, 2004), I decided to focus on progressing academically. After completing a doctoral dissertation, lecturers at my institution are encouraged to apply for the Vision Keeper (VK) grant. The VK grant is instrumental in the academic development of young lecturers who are in line for promotion as associate professors and wish to apply to the National Research Foundation for ratings of their research publications. This foundation rates research on a researcher's recent outputs and the impact of that work as perceived by international peer reviewers. It is a way of encouraging leaders in their fields of expertise and granting recognition to those who excel. The VK grant also enables academics to identify and visit a mentor abroad, who plays an important role in ensuring that the mentee develops rigor and excellence in research and the supervision of students. I did not apply for any other funding while I was mourning because I knew that I was going to waste the institution's resources; I thought I had acted responsibly. When I was refused the VK grant, it appeared that none of my actions had any bearing on the considerations of the vetting committee.

The impact that the disappointing outcome of my application had on me due to my age (I was forty-five and seven months, instead of just forty-five) exacerbated my sense of loss. Why could the patriarchal, capitalist, neoliberal authorities not see that I had a deep commitment to the work of teaching students and doing research? I am passionately convinced that I have strategies to help people achieve their full potential in certain communities in peri-urban districts near Pretoria. Again, I experienced anger, denial, the need to bargain, and this time I attributed all the guilt to the system at my institution. While I was in the university, in the NWP, a man without an education background was brought into my department to manage me. If the hiring had been fair, I should have been his manager, not the other way around. I felt strongly that the cause of the situation was that I was a black lecturer and a woman. I changed universities.

Women continue to suffer from limited resources and inadequate access to educational and financial opportunities (Wada & Muhammad, 2010) throughout

South Africa. Women academics at universities are often exploited, abused, discriminated against, and sidelined by their managers for exercising academic freedom. There is very little caring and no support to assist vulnerable women, such as widows, to accomplish career goals. Incivility is often expressed in the form of racism and sexism at work (Reid & Clayton, 1992). Institutional rules and policies are ignored for special individuals. Discourtesy is routine, and uncaring tendencies in behavior toward staff members at work are rife. Stewart (2007) has researched the changes faced by universities under corporate managerialism and the new roles and "new difficulties for academics, who display signs of stress and low morale" (p. 131). Stewart found out that "re-envisioning of the field of academic roles should be led by academics, involve government and university managements, acknowledging their incapacity to create an academic ethos from the top" (p. 145), which supports my argument that most of the decisions that lead to negative career lifespan of lecturers are made by management without any idea of the sacrifices and stress levels of the academic workplace.

When the time came for me to be interviewed about performance using Integrated Performance Management System (IPMS) by one of my managers, four women managers were waiting at the venue. These IPMS interviews are often used by unscrupulous managers to humiliate females who are still regarded as "emerging" scholars. Reflecting on the university policy, which clearly states that the person who is to be interviewed can write a letter and request an additional neutral person to oversee the processes of the interview, I refused to be interviewed by them. As Spivak (1988) put it "the relationship between women and silence can be plotted by women themselves; race and class differences are submerged under that charge" (p. 82). Sometimes it is not men who sabotage women at work; other women have mastered the art of suppressing their own gender species. The female managers were supposed to know about the IPMS policy before they even agreed to be part of the panel; they did not. Rather than identifying interviewees' weaknesses and assisting them to find solutions or intervention strategies, they play a power game. Therefore, I reported the matter to the Workers Union and Human Resource Department (HR). "Black female lecturers are cursed from birth!" I thought and then realized that I, having come through my grief, avoided the paralyzing depression that I could have suffered and was accepting things as they were. Even when, in May this year, I received a letter from a vetting committee notifying me and the other black female academics that our book chapters had been rejected for subsidy, I was determined to persevere, despite evidence of double standards and inconsistencies.

There are studies in abundance about the shortages of black professors in the universities of South Africa (Van Wyk, 2014; Mangcu, 2014; Ahmed, 2015) and the need for more black female lecturers (Mokhele, 2013; Mabokela, 2000). Yet, the mistreatment of black female lecturers aspiring to be professors is rampant. Ramoupi, in the *Mail and Guardian* (15 June 2017) in an article titled "Why are there so few black professors"?, shows a cartoon of a man locking the gates against blacks and there is a sign written in red "KEEP OUT." The image and the words may look and sound like a satire; however, it is the reality of most black women at universities in South Africa. In the whole of South Africa in 23 universities, there are 34 female black professors (Van Wyk, 2014).

Conclusion: Healing through Resilience

Reflecting on my story, I see a gradual strengthening in my resolve to overcome adverse circumstances and vulnerable beginnings. From the shock of the loss of my husband and his family's extreme personal discourtesy to me, to the departmental academic setbacks, the corporate neglect, and disregard for a person who had so much faith in academia, I have moved toward a determined attitude to pursue and succeed with the teaching and upliftment I believe in. This upliftment is not related to the empty promises of advancement from the state or corporations. This goes beyond "community engagement" as my institution terms it in empty phrases. It is an upliftment imbued by the resilience I saw embodied in the earliest experiences of Ubuntu. Raged against a rather hostile environment which accords value only to economics, markets, commodities, and profit, I want to reiterate the words the chapter opened with, some words of Miles (2002), "Integrative Transformative Learning, which consciously and explicitly affirms human and nonhuman life rather than profit and allies with transformative social movements, can [...] challenge rather than serve the destructive and still largely unquestioned neoliberal growth agenda" (p. 29).

Finally, I would like to end this chapter on a hopeful note that one day my daughters and other daughters of South Africa will be treated with the dignity they deserve as mothers of humanity. A society that does not treat women, widows, and orphans with humanity and compassion is a society on the path to self-destruction, and that is not what I expected from post-apartheid South Africa.

References

Ahmed, A. (2015). We need more black female lecturers. -Nzimande. *News 24*. Retrieved from https://www.news24.com/SouthAfrica/News/We-need-more-black-female-lecturers-Nzimande-20150922.

Bonanno, G.A. (2004). Loss, trauma, and human resilience: Have we underestimated the human capacity to thrive after extremely aversive events? *The American Psychologist*, 59(1):20-8.

Ha-Joon Chang (2000). An institutional perspective on the role of the state: towards an institutionalist political economy. In: L. Burlamaqui, A. C. Castro, and Chang Ha-Joon (Eds.). *Institutions and the roles of the state. By New horizons in institutional and evaluation economics*. Edward Elgar. United Kingdom. 3-38.

Holland, D. (2009). Between the practical and the academic: The relation of mode 1 and mode 2 knowledge production in a developing country. *Science, Technology & Human Values*, 34(5): 551-572.

Holton, G., & Sonnet, G. (1996). Career patterns of women and men in the sciences. *American Scientist*, 84: 63-71.

Kübler-Ross, E., & Kessler, D. (2007). *On grief and grieving: Finding the meaning of grief through the five stages of loss*. London: Simon & Schuster.

Mabokela, R.O. (2000). We cannot find qualified blacks: Faculty diversification programmes at South African universities. *Comparative Education*, 36(1): 95-112.

Manala, M. (2015). African traditional widowhood rites and their benefits and/or detrimental effects on widows in a context of African Christianity. *HTS Theological Studies*, 71(3), 1-9.

Mangcu, X. (2014). Why are there so few black professors in South Africa? *The Guardian*. Retrieved from https://www.theguardian.com/world/2014/oct/06/south-africa-race-black-professors.

Miles, A. (2002). Feminist perspectives on globalization and integrative transformative learning. In E. O'Sullivan, A. Morrell & M. O'Connor. *Expanding the boundaries of transformative learning*. New York: Palgrave. 23-33.

Mokhele, M.L. (2013). Reflections of black women academics at South African universities. *Mediterranean Journal of Social Sciences*, 14(3): 611-620.

Nwokoro. C.V. (2016). *From vulnerability to empowerment: Faith-based aid organizations, secular aid organizations and the wellbeing of rural widows in Abia State, Nigeria*. Unpublished doctoral thesis, University of Leicester.

Ogbogu. C.O. (2013). Work-family role conflict among academic women in Nigerians public universities. *West East Journal of Social Sciences*, 2 (2): 23-28.

Ramoupi, N. L. (2017, June 15). Why are there so few black professors? *Mail & Guardian.* Retrieved from https://mg.co.za/article/2017-06-15-00-why-are-there-so-few-black-professor.

Reid, T.P., & Clayton, S. (1992). Racism and sexism at work. *Social Justice Research,* 5 (3): 249-268.

Spivak, G.C. (1988). *Can the subaltern speak?* New York: Columbia University Press.

Stewart, P. (2007). *Re-envisioning the academic profession in the shadow of corporate managerialism. Journal of Higher Education in Africa,* 5(1), 131-147.

Thomas. F. 2008. Remarriage after spousal death: options facing widows and implications for livelihood security. *Gender and Development.* 16(1): 73-83.

Wada, B.T., & Muhammad, I.N. (2010). *Adult education, entrepreneurship and poverty alleviation among Kano housewives.* Retrieved from https://papers.ssrn.com/abstract=1596263.

Waghid, Y., & Smeyers, P (2012). Reconsidering Ubuntu: on the educational potential of a particular ethic of care. *Educational Philosophy and Theory,* 44: 6-20.

Van Wyk, A. (2014, August 18). How many professors are there in SA? *Africa Check.* Retrieved from https://africacheck.org/reports/how-many-professors-are-there-in-sa/.

Young, K. (2006). Widows without rights: challenging marginalisation and dispossession. *Gender and Development* 14(2): 199-209.

SECTION III
HOW BRAVE ART AFRICAN WOMEN IMMIGRANTS?

Chapter 11

Where Is Justice for Immigrants? "If You Prick Us, Do We Not Bleed? If You Tickle Us, Do We Not Laugh?"

Mary N. Ghongkedze

The Journey Twenty Years Ago

I REMEMBER LIKE yesterday, staying up all night waiting for the results of the first black president, and the results brought untold and indescribable jubilation to many people of color. This was paradise regained! To an immigrant woman, Obama's election gave me a reason to feel optimistic about the social issues and discrimination. The young, elegant, and eloquent Obama represented joys and dreams come true, and hopefulness was sensed by many immigrants, especially Africans. To see a son of a Kenyan man becoming the president of the first world gave hope to many immigrants that their hard work will pay off some day.

Watching Obama's journey through the presidency, and the hurdles he went through, brought back memories of my own immigrant experience. I remembered being bombarded with questions such as: "Where are you from?"; "Where is your accent from?"; "Why did you come here?"; "How did you come here?"; and "When are you going back?" While such questions remind us of our uniqueness, at the same time they are indicative of not being welcomed.

American people need to understand that migrating is not an exciting experience. People migrate because of various reasons, most of the time not happy ones. Some people migrate because of political issues, such as war; others because of natural calamities, such as drought and tsunamis; others because of economic reasons (Ngo, 2009). My family's decision to come to the U.S. was motivated by economic reasons. Prior to that, I never imagined what it means to leave everything you have and relocate to a different country. All of a sudden, I had to face a dilemma of what or what not to take, like what food and clothes to pack; and I started to worry about the kind of folks I would encounter. While these decisions were difficult to make, they turned out to be minor compared to the challenges I went through when I arrived in the United States of America.

Initially, despite the brutal culture shock I experienced, I was eager to enroll in graduate school. The quest for knowledge became like a vaulting ambition. I could not wait. What I did not know was the challenges with technology that lay ahead. Here I was, a new student from across the Atlantic Ocean, with no clue about computers or how to type, looking forward to making it in school. I remember how frustrated I was when an instructor asked me to type my first assignment, which I had handwritten. Technology proved to be only one out of the many problems I encountered during graduate studies. The most painful memory I have as a graduate student is that of my husband's diagnosis. While I was in the middle of the program, my spouse was suddenly diagnosed with medullary thyroid cancer. Now, in addition to school work and its own challenges, I had to make several trips driving to the hospital for my husband's treatment and take care of five children by myself. What made it worse was working with unreasonable professors who were very insensitive to personal problems. I remember one female professor who would not grant me an extension to submit my paper. I was hoping that since she was a woman she would show some compassion. Still I did not quit.

Graduation day came with mixed feelings, and I dejectedly walked across the stage. My spouse, Joseph, who could have made my day happier, was weak and debilitated. After a gruesome fifteen months, he lost the battle to the monstrous cancer at the young age of 48. Seeing a loved one degenerate right in front of my eyes, despite all the medical help given, was the most painful thing I've dealt with in life.

Lost in "Amelica" the "Wonderland"

What a slap in the face that the misfortune of losing a loved one came so soon! I couldn't make sense of it. My grandma used to call America "Amelica wonder." What a "welcome to Amelica" that had been for me! I had barely completed twenty-four months in "the land of milk and honey," and it had already turned into a land of tears and bitterness. The sun had set too soon, at noon, leaving me perplexed in the wilderness of grief. I could not imagine raising five children single-handedly. The children had formed a special bond with their dad and looked up to him for all their socio-emotional needs and support. All of that ultimately came to a miserable standstill. There was gloom, darkness, absurdness, and meaninglessness in everything around me. The period of depression, somatic pains, and dealing with the loss left me a frantic, miserable, pathetic, and desperate person.

The varied marital supports I once took for granted were gone in a flash, and my worry was how to move on in an indifferent society. As is often said, one can make lemonade out of lemons and use a bad situation to grow. Amidst my struggle, I decided to enroll in the Ph.D. program, as my husband had advised me before his death. My advisor was very understanding and helpful. He hired me as his graduate assistant, making $1,500 a month. Although useful, this stipend was not enough for me to feed my children, pay rent and bills, and take care of myself. I juggled between school and work and tried a series of low-paying jobs to make ends meet. I worked as a Certified Nurse's Aide (CNA), pulling a double shift during weekends, and substitute teaching during the week. The more I struggled with the children, the more I knew that, as a black immigrant woman, I had to rely on myself to raise my children. At one point, I thought of just packing up my stuff and going back to my cherished "S-hole" country—a country where everyone would have been sensitive to my sorrow. However, I listened to my inner voice and stayed on for the sake of the children.

The feeling of leaving and unbelongingness welled up again recently, when Donald Trump was running for president. Trump's language was a plethora of hurtful expletives to characterize immigrants, African Americans, and other minority groups. His utterances and attitude created an atmosphere of fear and hopelessness in a lot of immigrants, myself included. It was regrettably enigmatic and bothersome to hear him referring to African countries as "S-hole countries" or telling a Hispanic reporter, who was an American citizen, to "go home." As a result, immigrants took to social networks to urge each other to consider relocating or going back home. Being a resilient woman, I was not ready to go anywhere.

Post Challenges

The society's slogan of "American Dream" becomes an anecdote when someone with U.S.-earned university credentials is discriminated against because of their accent or racial identity. Upon graduation from my doctoral program, I went to countless job interviews and confidently answered all the questions. Being told they had found someone who met their qualifications always puzzled me. How trustworthy were those responses? Were they made without prejudice? I soon discovered how infected the society was with visible and invisible social injustice, racism, and partiality. A litmus test to this was when I was trying to find an apartment. Whenever I called the receptionist, I was politely told there were none available, until I asked my friend's daughter, who speaks very much like an American (i.e., with no African accent) to call the same realtor and inquire. Bingo! She was told there were vacancies. As a naive immigrant, I didn't know that discrimination was illegal or that I could sue for racial discrimination.

The apartment situation reminded me of Paulo Freire and the principle that he stood up for—to empower the disenfranchised. I reflected on the fact that I needed to make a change and be an advocate for social justice, beginning with at least speaking out and standing up for myself. I prayed to the maverick spirit of my ancestors, Nlum-nnam, to empower and strengthen me. Then, as if driven by the spirits of personal heroes—Paulo Freire and Madiba Mandela—I hurried to the apartment's main office and asked to speak to the manager about the incident and how I felt about it. What I was told blew my mind; I could not, in my faintest dream, imagine that someone would refuse to rent an apartment because of the size of a family. Though Mr. Trump had referenced that, once immigrants had seen the United States, they would never "go back to their huts" in Africa, I would have preferred the God-given huts instantly—huts that are accommodating and filled with love regardless of the number of people.

Weeping for the Paradise Lost

Obama's election was a wakeup call for equality and how dreams could come true, and he echoed this in his speeches and policies at the launch of the "Be My Brother's Keeper" Initiative (Capehart, 2014). He understood the plight and aches of the minority population. It was an era of friendliness, a feeling of belongingness, with a welcoming and refreshing atmosphere wherever one went. Abroad, even my mother in the village knew him as an elegant, family-oriented, respectable individual and was happy he was elected. There was confidence across many countries about a new era of justice, honesty, and America's leadership of the world. Obama's vision of eradicating social injustice and bridging the achievement gap was evident. He understood that separation between a mother and her child as experienced by many immigrants was problematic. He realized that immigrants were Americans in the heart, and hard working in every aspect. As a result, he sought measures to stop deportation of children and teens who had come to achieve their dreams and make immigration policy to be fair and just for all. His coming to power was very significant as a novel paradigm; not unlike John F. Kennedy, it was perceived as an embodiment of confidence, hope, youthfulness, and optimism. To kill this ecstasy, there was outcry from opponents to discredit the president's legitimacy to the office with the "birther conspiracy" perpetuated by Mr. Trump, an indication of the invisible hatred of ethnic differences in society. The issue dampened the spirit of most immigrants who have sacrificed and contributed to the society. For me personally, the victory of Mr. Trump made me fear what is to come.

A Demagogic Leadership Prevents Social Justice to Prevail

Our society's policies should focus more on inclusion and acceptance. The constant dominance of the macro culture on micro ones becomes disgusting at times. No doubt there was this premonition of a queasy feeling when Donald Trump announced his candidacy. Many people vowed it would not happen, but it ended up happening, and everyone is now bamboozled with the disrespect toward women and immigrants. It is interesting to observe that with the 45th POTUS in Washington, DC, it has become common to see on the media and in society more arrogant Americans threatening immigrants. Little did I know that I would be the target someday.

One day, on our way to a conference in Baton Rouge, my Iranian friend and I had stopped to get something to eat and use the restroom. We went into a restaurant and greeted the receptionist, but were ignored, and the shock and looks of disgust in the eyes of the customers staring at us were indescribable and sickening.

While we were still trying to process the eerie looks, we tried to order a burger and a drink, but the waiter also ignored us and gave us the look that meant "you better be out of here." The creepy and spine-chilling look dissipated the hunger in us, as we foraged for the doorknob to get out to the car. We understood later that these were anti-immigrants, white supremacists—the very people who bought into Donald Trump's slogan of making America "white again." These were the very people who, during a July 4th celebration event, bleated out, "F—ing immigrants are annoying," because two Hispanic ladies were speaking loudly to each other. In disgust, without holding myself, I retorted to the provokers' microaggression, "And if you tickled them, don't they laugh because they are immigrants?" The truth is we are all human beings, and neither ethnicity nor race should make anyone less human. A leader with a foul mouth teaches his followers that it is okay to be vile and a bully. Ultimately, Trump's (mis)leadership style has created a ubiquitous atmosphere of anxiety, gloom, and social injustice. It should be realized that enough is enough with white America's narcissistic personality disorder—that is, a pattern of behavior characterized by the dominant culture's feeling of self-importance, coupled with microaggression and indifference to others' feelings. The massive rallying of white working-class America behind Trump demonstrated that the reason why immigrants are perceived as a threat is not really because they are taking the menial jobs away from them. Much of it is fear—of losing what in their view is their beloved "white America." Fear of losing ground, fear of the browning of America, fear of having to live with people who are different and who may achieve more than they. Nonetheless, microaggression hurts and belittles, but as Michelle Obama said, "When they go low, we [should] go high."

Dare to Dream of a Better World

A vision is always what one dreams to accomplish. As an individual who, against many odds, has fought hard as a single mother, a widow, an immigrant, and a woman to be where I am today, I perceive myself as an emissary of change—change in the world's perception of immigrants, change in people's treatment of one another. Immigrants of all races have undergone untold hardships; the collective goal should be to celebrate everyone, their abilities, similarities, and differences and develop positive attitudes toward all. Being African is not a curse but a divine gift. We are endowed with the same rights and privileges as everybody else. My children today are responsible citizens of the United States. One was deployed twice during the Iraq war; the other is serving in the military abroad. They love this land and sacrifice themselves to keep it safe. I am proud of their services; thus, it is essential to recognize contributions of immigrants in society. As a mother of two men in uniform, my heart bleeds for Mr. Khizr Khan (2016) and his family, and I believe every American should empathize with him.

I dare to dream, like Martin Luther King, of a future where social injustice, bias, animosity, prejudice, bad mouthing, bigotry, and racism are a thing of the past for immigrants and their children. When Martin Luther King Jr. reminded us, about fifty years ago, that "injustice anywhere is a threat to justice everywhere," it simply meant that we should stand up and speak out for the vulnerable in society. Although born in different parts of the global village, we all have dreams. Hence, teaching toward a more inclusive social order means working toward reducing our peculiar ethnocentrism so that we can appreciate humanity in its many dimensions (Boutte, 2008). As an educator, it is my responsibility to attempt to change what is not right. Candid conversations from kindergarten to university on awareness of societal ills would help alleviate the injustices and lead to a more just society. Finally, diversity brings beauty to society through ethnic, cultural, and linguistic richness. The many shades and colors of American society take away a monotonous world and add spice to a mundane existence. Hopefully, the constant occurrence of discrimination and injustice will be eliminated or minimized if both the naïve lay people and those in positions of power who are fooling them become culturally savvy and seek to institute just and fair policies for all human beings.

References

Boutte, G. (2008). Beyond the illusion of diversity: How early childhood teachers can promote social justice. *Social Studies, 99*(4), 165-173.
Capehart, J. (2014). Obama urges nation to be 'My Brother's Keeper'. Retrieved from https://www.washingtonpost.com/blogs/post-partisan/wp/2014/02/28/obama- urges-nation-to-be-my-brothers-keeper
Khan, K. (2016, July 28). *Khizr Khan's Speech to the 2016 Democratic National Convention*. Retrieved March 25, 2018. From: https://abcnews.go.com/Politics/full-text-khizr-khans-speech-2016-democratic-national/story?id=41043609
Ngo, B. (2009). Beyond "Culture Clash"; Understandings of immigrant experiences. *Theory into Practice, 47*(1), 4-11.

Chapter 12

"Talking Some and Leaving Some"
A Community-Grounded Approach to Teaching and Sustaining African Languages in America

Esther Milu

DECEMBER 31, 2017, White Marsh, Maryland. I hosted the New Year's party for about thirty of my newly found Kenyan friends. It was my second year since moving from Michigan to work at Morgan State University. In less than three months, I had found a Kenyan community and made some good friends. I am not the best cook, so several of my closest ladies and gentlemen helped ensure the Kenyan food served was on point: *ugali, chapati, nyama choma, pilau, sukumawiki, manangu, mandazi, samosa,* and *kachumbari.*

After dinner, the kids retreated to the upstairs rooms and alternated between playing chess, UNO, Snapchatting, texting, playing on their phones, and babysitting. The women sat leisurely in the living room and let digestion take its course. They told stories and laughed. In the basement, the men listened and danced to the 1980s' and 1990s' Kenyan music, *Zilizopendwa*. The music had a nostalgic feel, which filled the entire house. Even the women agreed, *wazee hukumbuka*.

About 10 minutes to midnight, brother M. started pacing around the house with restless energy. He had asked the women and children several times to go to the basement, but everyone dragged their feet. The New Year's Ball was about to drop at Times Square. Anderson Cooper and Andy Cohen, two of my favorite people, were hosting. Before we knew it, we were in the basement doing the countdown: 5, 4, 3, 2, 1! We toasted to the new year. Hugs and cheers flew across the room. Murmurs and shouts of "Amen" were heard.

Brother M. switched off the TV. It was time to fellowship and do some speeches, and it was serious. Sister T. read a few Bible verses, and we reflected on how good God had been to us the past year. We prayed for God's love and providence as we started 2018. Brother K. started singing:

> Oh God is good...

Everyone joined in:

> Oh God God is good

Sister E. led in Swahili:

> *Mungu yu mwema...*

Everyone responded:

> *Mungu yu mwema...*

Brother K. led in Kisii:

> *Nyasae nomuya...*

Sista M. led in Kalenjin:

> *Kararan Jehovah...*

Sister T. led in Kikuyu:

> *Ngai wi mwega...*

My husband led in Kikamba:

> *Ngai ni museo...*

We repeated the hymn in endless call-and-response. I noticed the children were not singing along. They giggled as the elders alternated singing the song in different languages. The elders seemed unsure of what the children found funny. Sister T. reprimanded them in a loving but firm manner. Several elders saw this as a teaching moment and they seized it. Thus began a conversation about the importance of maintaining our Kenyan cultural and linguistic heritage in America. The children looked indifferent. We couldn't tell whether they didn't care or they were just tired. After all, it was almost 2 a.m. Sister T. told the children the church planned to start a Swahili class and they better prepare to learn the language. For another hour, the elders continued preaching and testifying about preserving our Kenyan cultural identity in America. We called it a day, or morning, around 3 a.m.

The children's behavior bothered me. I wondered about the implications of them losing their Kenyan cultural identity in a country where they will never be accepted fully as American citizens. I also thought about Kenya, where they will always be seen not as Kenyan enough because they are too Westernized and have rejected or forgotten some aspects of their culture. In the words of Gloria Anzaldúa, I began to see the children as "a synergy of two cultures," with varying degrees of Kenyanness and Americanness. As a Kenyan mother and a black language and cultural educator, I wondered what my responsibility was in helping them value and sustain their Kenyan linguistic identities even as they acculturated to American society. In other words, I started thinking of ways to help them positively deal with the "internalized borderland conflict" which, according to Gloria Anzaldúa (1999), poses the danger of one identity "cancel[ing] out the other" and, in the end, one becoming "zero, nothing, no one" (p. 43).

These fears and questions did not start in 2018. When I arrived in the United States in December of 2008, I had one dream for my children: to be Americanized, fast. A Kenyan friend who had arrived in the United States earlier than I, *God bless her heart,* advised me to discourage my kids from speaking Swahili and Kikamba. She thought this would hinder them from mastering American English and accent. I thought she was right. If not speaking Kenyan languages would make them speak like Barack Obama, why not? Little did I know Obama embodied a multilingual consciousness. His persuasive style and appeal to a range of audiences came from his ability to use both African American vernacular English and Standard American English. During his presidency, I observed how much he valued other languages as he made attempts to speak in local languages in the different countries he visited. For example, when he visited Kenya in 2015, he greeted different crowds with *Habari zenu? Wakenya mpo? Jambo! Hauwayuuni!* In these greetings, Obama valued both standard Swahili and Kenyan urban youth language, Sheng.

In fact, Obama advocated for multilingual competencies among Americans, perhaps more than any other president. Speaking at the Young African Leaders Initiative in Washington, D.C., he said, "Frankly, I wish we as Americans did a better job of learning other languages. Now, in an interconnected world, the more languages we speak, the better" (cited in Chao, 2016). As a new immigrant, I did not see the value of multilingualism, especially for my children. So, during my first year in the U.S., I did enough damage to erase my children's Kenyan linguistic identity. When we arrived, my daughter was six and my son, three. They were fluent in Swahili and spoke a little of our mother tongue, Kikamba. Within a year, the Kenyan languages were lost; well, almost. They did not seem to care about the languages anymore; they were all English, and I felt proud.

My Language About-Turn

My view of language and America took a complete 180-degree turn in spring 2010 when I enrolled in a graduate seminar entitled Language and African American Community. The course was taught by Dr. Geneva Smitherman, aka Dr. G—a language scholar-activist who has made a lifetime commitment to researching and teaching African American language. In Dr. G's class, I learned the history of African American language as we traced it back to West and Central African languages. It was an eye-opening experience to learn that, for four centuries, African Americans have maintained the linguistic and cultural baggage they brought from Africa. Their language also known as Ebonics, Black English, or African American Vernacular English has a grammatical structure very different from the dominant American English variety. We read Dr. G's book *Talkin That Talk*, which she unapologetically writes in African American language and uses African rhetorical modes to affirm and celebrate the beauty of the language.

This course got me thinking. If African Americans have for over four centuries maintained their African linguistic heritage in the U.S., where is the wisdom in me, a newcomer, facilitating the riddance of my children's heritage languages? Although African Americans were physically enslaved and trapped in America, they resisted cultural and linguistic enslavement. They have embodied the Swahili saying *mwacha mila ni mtumwa:* He who abandons his culture is a slave. To say that this course gave me an awakening is an understatement. I quickly realized the devastation I was doing to my children and myself. I realized that I was a victim of linguistic colonization and imperialism. British colonization in Kenya touted English as the language of prestige, refinement, and status and devalued indigenous languages. Today, this ideology continues to shape how we construct our linguistic identities in Kenya and wherever we find ourselves on the globe. In other words, I was suffering from a colonial mindset—a very common disease among Kenyan middle class who are brainwashed into thinking that when one speaks American- or British- accented English, it is a mark of higher social status and Westernization, as if the latter is a good thing.

My Kenyan teachers did not do a good job helping me deal with the colonial mentality. As Wangari Maathai writes in *Unbowed*:

> The trauma of the colonized is rarely examined, and steps are rarely taken to understand and redress it. Instead, the psychological damage passes from one generation to the next, until victims recognize their dilemma and work to liberate themselves from the trauma. (2007, p. 69)

Dr. G's pedagogy went beyond identifying and liberating me from the trauma; it led to my mental and linguistic decolonization. I began taking pride in my heritage languages and re-teaching my kids the same. The course also got me interested in language activism research, teaching, and service. I started theorizing and enacting writing pedagogies that transgress American monolingual ideologies while at the same time honoring, sustaining, and developing positive language experiences among my students (see de Costa et al., 2017; Milu, 2018). But more importantly, I learned to do the same for my children and other Kenyan children.

Teaching My Children: Swahili or Kikamba?

Mzika pembe ndiye mzua pembe. The one who buries an ivory is the one to dig it up. I was responsible for ridding my children of their home languages, so I was the one to help them recover it. It was a crash course in my house, as I scrambled to figure out how much damage I had done and how much could be salvaged. It was clear that they did not want to go beyond the basic greetings and polite words; they were not feeling it. Besides, it was overwhelming for them to learn two languages. I had to make a decision: was I going to teach them Kikamba or Swahili? At home, my husband and I spoke Kikamba, so we reasoned that they would pick it up as we spoke it. I decided to go with Swahili, which is Kenya's and East Africa's regional lingua franca. I reasoned Kiswahili would allow them to speak with not only members from our ethnic community, but also other communities in Kenya and Sub-Saharan Africa.

Leaving Kikamba out did not make teaching Swahili easy. The kids still resisted the effort; it was extra work for them. "Why can't we speak English like everyone else?", they asked every time I started to teach or talk to them in Swahili. But I kept doing it. Every week I made sure we learned one element of the language. Still, every day was a struggle; one day they were into it, the next day they were not. They didn't even like me speaking the language to them.

The problem has persisted till today. My strategy has been to figure out when to teach some and leave some. To talk some and leave some. Many times I have thought of giving up and letting them focus on the foreign languages they are learning in school, but I know I can't. After all, America's education system is not keen on sustaining multilingual literacies among its children.

However, my story of struggle has had some moments of triumph. One day, when my son was in fourth grade, he came home excited to tell me that he had corrected his teacher when he pronounced a Swahili word wrong. The teacher was reading a children's story which had a Swahili character called *Mzee Kobe*, and he pronounced the name *Mzee* as *Mzii*. When he asked my son how he knew it was wrong, he affirmed, "because I am a Kenyan and I speak Swahili." Another time was when my daughter shared a Swahili assignment idea for her English class. They had just finished reading the novel *The Metamorphosis* by Franz Kafka and the teacher asked them to transform into a character their peers would not expect for one class period. She decided to speak Swahili only. Another heartwarming moment was when I found out that she had changed the language in her phone from English to Swahili. Or the day she found me singing the Tanzanian Swahili pop song "Anita Wangu" by Matonya and Lady Jay Dee, and she joined in and sang it flawlessly. Reflecting on this experience of struggle and triumph, I can only say *mwanzo kokochi, mwisho nazi*. The beginning is a bud, the end is a coconut. I ain't stopping.

The Community as a Teacher: Flour Tortillas and Chapatis—What Do They Have in Common?

106 Carroll Road, Glen Burnie, Maryland. The words *Iglesia Pentecostal Jesus Fuente de Vida* in large white font contrasted the dark blue background on the electronic message board. Inside the compound, an old redbrick church spread its wings to the left and right side of the nearly 6,000-square-feet compound. In the lobby, we turned left and climbed six steps to a room a little bigger than a typical classroom. A congregation of about fifty people was singing the Swahili hymn "Ukingoni mwa Yordani" (On Jordan's Stormy Banks). When the song ended, an elder walked toward the pulpit and read a few announcements. It was the fifth time my family was fellowshipping with the Living Springs Adventist Church. Our first visit was in November 2017 when brother M. invited us to

attend their music Sabbath. It was supposed to be a one-time visit, but when we found most of the congregation was Kenyan, and half of the service was in Swahili, we decided to make it our church.

For some reason, that particular day I found myself paying extra attention to the physical space inside the church. On the front wall, the words *Iglesia Pentecostal Jesus Fuente de Vida* were repeated. On the opposite wall, the word *Eventos* in a shiny pink ribbon paper was glued on the events board. An American flag stood two feet from the pulpit stand, as if to remind us *this is America*. I asked sister A. why they had not replaced the Spanish with English or Swahili. She told me they rented the space from the Iglesia Pentecostal church, so they couldn't change anything. The worship continued in English with interludes of Swahili and Kisii hymns.

Sister A. asked me to help set up potluck lunch. They shared the kitchen and dining space with members of the Iglesia Pentecostal church. They seemed to coexist well especially because they worshiped on different days of the week. But this particular Saturday, they (or a community affiliated with the Iglesia church) were having an event on the premises, and we were sharing the kitchen space. Thankfully, most of our food was prepared from home except *ugali* and *chai*.

The Iglesia Pentecostal members' groceries were spread on the kitchen countertops and a few on the floor. A bag of wheat tortillas caught my attention. I thought about the process of making them as I cut the chapatis I had brought for our potluck into quarters. "Is it the same as that of making chapatis?" I wondered. "How can I make my chapatis less greasy like the flour tortillas?" Then I wondered about the layers of cultures, histories, and literacies in both the tortillas and chapatis.

The Hispanic congregants chopped, grated, and mixed their cooking ingredients as they conversed in Spanish. Near the stove, a Kenyan sista and brotha spoke in Swahili, sometimes sprinkling it with Kisii words, phrases, and sentences. They took turns spinning a mountain of *ugali*. I thought about the similarities between the Iglesia church members and us. Sista A. had mentioned most of them were Mexican Americans. We were Kenyan Americans. We were both minorities and immigrants in America. We had both found a safe space to worship and speak our own languages and eat our own foods, even in the dominance of English and American culture. I saw resistance. I saw resilience. I saw beauty. I saw the richness and diversity of our cultural and linguistic heritage alive and thriving in a foreign land. Even in the midst of the pressure to assimilate and insults by President Trump that Mexican immigrants are drug dealers and rapists and that we, African immigrants, are from shithole countries, I saw cultural and linguistic maintenance and sustenance for both of our communities. We were proud of who we are. We had learned where and when to talk some and leave some. We are here.

At the basement of the church building were several rooms where kids played after lunch as they waited for their parents and elders to finish their committee meetings and choir practice. I was not in any of the committees because I was new to the church and I was not an Adventist. Then I remembered Sister T.'s promise: "We will start a Swahili class at the church." I called all the children in one room. We started talking about Kenya. I asked them what they knew and liked about Kenya. Who is the current president? How many ethnic communities are there? What are the languages spoken? Surprisingly they got all the answers right. I asked them to count from one to ten in Swahili. Many of them did. Those who didn't, I taught them. Then I told everyone that their homework was to learn how to count from one to twenty in Swahili.

The following Sabbath everyone was counting and singing one to twenty. Some counted up to fifty and others up to a hundred. I was impressed by how the parents were involved in teaching them the language at home. We learned about Kenyan foods. Some even taught me some foods from their ethnic communities. Each week we focused on a Swahili language unit—*maamkizi, maneno ya adabu, majina ya wanyama, vitenzi, nyakati, sehemu za mwili, msamiati, na kadhalika*. We sang Swahili hymns and used them to learn more vocabulary. The kids had fun as they learned, but it was not a perfect class. Students ranged from the ages of one to seventeen. Their Swahili skill level, interest, and motivation varied. But I told myself *maji ukiyavulia nguo, huna budi kuyaoga*. If you take off your clothes for water, you must bathe. They had to learn by all means necessary. I used the older ones and those with stronger Swahili skills as co-teachers. I realized we could not learn Swahili discretely; we moved between English, Kikamba, Kisii, and Kalenjin and whatever other language popped up, even Spanish and French. Translation became the main approach, but food worked too. Each week I brought a sweet treat; it was unhealthy, but hey, they learned some.

References

Anzaldúa, G. (1999). *Borderlands = La frontera*. San Francisco: Aunt Lute Books.

Chao, J. (2016, October 12). "Au Revoir! As President Obama Leaves Office, We Rate His Foreign Language Skills." Retrieved from https://www.babbel.com/en/magazine/president-obama-foreign-language-skills

de Costa P., Milu, E., Canagarajah, S., Freiberg, S., Singh, J., & Wang, S. (2017). Pedagogizing translingual practice: Prospects and possibilities. *Research in the Teaching of English*, 51(4), 464-472.

Maathai, W. (2007). *Unbowed: A memoir*. New York: Anchor Books.

Milu, E. (2018). Translingualism, Kenyan Hip-Hop and emergent ethnicities: Implications for language theory and pedagogy. *International Multilingual Research Journal*, 12(2), 96-108.

CHAPTER 13

When Being Articulate Isn't Enough
The Narrative of a French-Speaking African Woman Faculty of English

Immaculée Harushimana

I WAS BORN in Burundi, a very small country located in the heart of the African continent. I grew up speaking Kirundi, my native language, except in the classroom where the school regulation required that we speak French both inside the classroom and on the playground. As a result of coercion into speaking French throughout my upper elementary and secondary school careers, I grew fond of French and had a good time speaking it to near perfection, from my non-native French speaker perspective. English, in contrast, was a non-compulsory language, which was spoken only during English lessons. I pretty much self-taught English until I became really good at it. The choice of English as my area of specialization at the university level gave me the opportunity to practice it more frequently until I qualified to come and pursue graduate studies in the United States of America in 1993. In America, I had no choice but to totally immerse myself in the English language to the point where it shifted from being my third language of literacy to being my first language of communication.

It has been a quarter of a century since I arrived in the United States of America, with the purpose of pursuing mastery in the field of applied linguistics and providing instruction about the application of English to effective reading and writing, commonly known as "literacy." In the process, I continue to work on my own English literacy skills through ongoing reading and writing both for leisure and for publication, conscious of the fact that knowledge is infinite and perfection is not of this world. The journey I am about to chronicle highlights the challenges I have gone through as an African-born, French-speaking, female faculty of English to graduate and undergraduate native-English-speaking students preparing to become teachers of English.

Since earning my doctorate in English rhetoric and linguistics in 1999, I have written dozens of articles and chapters as well as co-edited and co-authored a couple of books. With those achievements—yes, to me, they are "achievements" for someone writing in a third language—one would think that I have earned respect as an applied linguist and a competent user of the English language. Instead, students constantly question my qualifications and some colleagues still refer to me as *ESL*. Program coordinators in English language—related disciplines show reluctance in assigning me courses. They buy into students' complaints which are, for the most part, motivated by racist sentiments and fear of *my* rigor. I used to take (the white) disrespect personally until I witnessed the evil treatment that they gave to our first black president and his First Lady.

I must posit that besides the Holocaust, slavery, apartheid, and colonization are the worst evils that mankind could inflict to mankind. It is simply unfathomable that anyone, by virtue of feeling racially superior, should take the liberty to deny other people their culture, their language, their land, and even their humanity. It was most likely due to sequels of slavery and colonization that President Obama was scrutinized in every word he said and every decision he took by his opponents, many of whom had perhaps half of his intelligence. The white descendants of slave owners could not believe that someone who identified with descendants of former slaves or colonized people could postulate to become president of a white-founded country. Yes, he did; and yes, he won.

I cannot describe the fury that crossed my mind when during the 2007 campaign I watched a candidate looking at Obama from the corner of his eye and sarcastically referring to him as "articulate, bright and clean" (CNN.com, 2007). Then, as if that was not enough, his opponent's camp accused him of plagiarism (Zeleny, 2008) and forced him to apologize. "How dare they disrespect my future president?", I screamed out loud, alone, standing up from my seat. Then later, after regaining calm, I pondered the situation again and thought back about my personal encounter with *linguicism*, due to my identity as a black woman from a French-speaking African nation claiming expertise in the English language. It is then that it dawned on me that if fellow Americans can discredit one of their own, a presidential candidate with credentials from the best universities of the land, i.e., Columbia University and Harvard University, who emerged as one of the best orators that the nation has ever known, as a "plagiarist" and refer to his "articulateness" as atypical of people of his race, why would I be surprised that they would question my academic credentials in English and my right to stand in front of them and teach them about the structure of their native language? I watched with awe how Obama reacted with the grace and humility that only *he* has been gifted with. Not only did he forgive the plagiarist accusation that his opponent's camp had mounted against him and the racist innuendo from his adversary who sarcastically referred to him as *articulate*, but upon his victory, he rewarded each of them with the highest positions in his administration, by appointing them respectively as secretary of state and vice president.

I must confess that I have not been (and will never be) able to emulate Obama's decorum whenever I have felt disrespected on the basis of my skin color, accent, or country of origin (I refuse to identify myself by continent, a superficially coined concept). Instead, I have learned to brush off the overt and covert affronts from some colleagues, U.S.-born administrators and students—white, black, and Latino—who refuse to admit that a non-native speaker of English, a speaker of English as a third language, can attain mastery of English that exceeds native English speakers' mastery. I have had to learn to "keep on livin," to "... keep on lovin," and "... keep on "believing," as Stevie Wonder has suggested that we should do.

There is a saying that has proved to be true in both my experience and Obama's: "the dogs bark and the caravan goes on". Despite the hatred and sabotage that Obama has endured from his opponents and haters, he successfully completed his two terms in the White House. Similarly, despite the kicking and screaming of hostile students through protest emails and complaints, hoping to get me fired, I achieved tenure and promotion at my institution. As a result, I have learned to develop survival mechanisms to fall back on during similar crises because they will never cease.

One of the survival mechanisms that I adopted was to be my *authentic self*. Out of my eagerness to please, I used to spend time thinking about the right word to use in order to avoid students' frustrated faces. By doing so, however, I was giving them the ammunition to use against me in their claim that I was incompetent. I was also unconsciously repressing my multilingual identity instead of using it to my advantage. As soon as I became aware of this vulnerability, I decided to turn it into an asset by bringing in Kirundi or French equivalents of the English concepts that I would be trying to teach.

I remember in one instance I was trying to explain how much "deictic expressions" (words or phrases such as *this, that, these, those, here, there,* etc., that point to the time, place, or situation in which a speaker is speaking) were part of the oral discourse.

To show the students the universality of these words, and how differently they are used by oral cultures as opposed to literate cultures, I gave them the example of my own native language, which has four times more demonstrative and locative deictic expressions than there are in English (this, that, these, those, here, and there).

Compare:

English	Kirundi
This	*iki* (within one's hands' reach), *iki-i* (emphatic of *iki*)
That	*Ico* (fairly near), *ico-o* (not so near, but near enough), *kirya, kirya-a* (far, but within reach), *kiriya* (quite far), *kiriya-a* (way too far, though still within eyes' reach)
These	*ibi* (near), *ibi-i* (very near)
Those	*Ivyo* (fairly near), *birya* (not so near, but near enough), *birya-a* (far, but within reach), *biriya* (quite far), *biriya-a* (very far)
Here	*Aha* (near), *aha-a* (very near)
There	*Aho* (far, but within hands' reach), *aho-o* (not so near, but still within hands' reach), *harya* (far, yet within eyes' reach), *harya-a* (a bit farther, but still within eyes' reach), *hariya* (far, but within eyes' reach), *hariya-a* (very far, though still within eyes' reach)

It so happens that in Kirundi conversations, vowel repetition is commonly used to indicate the length of one's action (e.g., *aravu-u-u-u-ga* means he speaks too much). Similarly, the lengthening of deictics through vowel repetition may indicate the length in distance and proximity (e.g., *hariya-a-a-a-a* means way over there). As I explained these concepts, with confidence I must say, I could read on some students' faces an expression of curiosity and fascination, which gave me more confidence to keep using the *code mixing* strategy whenever I deemed it appropriate. Today, I proudly bring in my knowledge of other languages to boost my instruction, and it has served me well. In particular, doing so gives confidence to students who speak other languages than English, as they too have the opportunity to share linguistic phenomena in their own languages.

The other strategy that I use to affirm myself is the use of *poetry*. Even though my poetic expression in English is not as sophisticated or colorful as that of native speakers, I believe it is as beautiful and meaningful as anyone else's poetry. I therefore use poetry sometimes to communicate my feelings to the students, as this excerpt from a poem that I posted on Blackboard as a welcome message demonstrates,

> *Teachers-to-be or teachers-in-act,*
> *Do unto your teachers,*
> *As you would wish done*
> *Unto you!*

At times, when the classroom climate is unbearable to the point that I sense hostility in the air, I have reverted to *open speeches*. I would prepare a letter about my feelings and read it out loud to my students to invite an open and direct conversation about the situation. One such letter started as follows:

> For the past three weeks, I have observed and witnessed a lot of defiance and insubordination from some members in this class. I have read from your innuendos that you do not believe that I have a Ph.D., and some of you have gone as far as making me feel that I have deficient or no knowledge of the subject matter I am communicating to you.... I hope I have responded to your attitudes with humility, professionalism and civility...

As a survival tactic, the open speech worked, for I never had any complaints or negative attitude after that, at least with that particular cohort. We had to tolerate each other, and those who were hiding behind threats to get me to be a soft grader or reduce assignments ended up losing; their tactic had the opposite effect of hardening me. They had no choice but to do the work.

Regarding microaggressions from employers, I like to use students' notes of appreciation, rather than open letters, as my defense weapon. On one occasion, when I went on sabbatical, it came to my attention that a superior had showed a sense of relief through a mean comment that "finally, this course will be taught the right way," because the instructor who had replaced me was white. A saying in my language suggests that "instead of insulting a boss, you would rather look down on him and leave." That is what I exactly did. Since I could not confront her, I waited till the occasion presented itself and forwarded her the following email from one of my students:

> I hope all is well. I just wanted to let you know that I passed the ALST exam on my first attempt. I appreciate your feedback on my writing assignments and the work you had us do in the class. Your efforts definitely helped me achieve a passing score on the exam.

Still, when later I met the same individual in the hallway, she acknowledged the note but went on to ask me, "What about those who do not have the same appreciation?" Well, I felt like telling her, "I am not a superwoman; I cannot correct the wrongs that were done to many of our minority students by uncaring teachers who either intentionally or unintentionally cheated them of their education. All I can promise is to do my best." Again, I chose to stay silent.

One practice that I had to discontinue was giving remarks that implied I owed students an explanation (an apology) about my accent. I knew both from research and personal experience that American-born students react strongly to the accent of an instructor who is not white (Lippi-Green, 1997). So, on the first day of class, I would always dedicate the first five minutes of class to introducing myself, where I came from, which universities I had attended, and which degrees I hold from where. I would even give them time to ask me further questions, as if I was a guest speaker or having a job interview. Then, one day, a student brought up to me the practice and suggested that I stop doing it since it gave the impression that I felt that I owed my students an explanation. I immediately realized that the student had a point and followed her advice. Through the student's remark, I was reminded of the wise words of Marianne Williamson and decided to constantly remind myself that

> [My] playing small does not serve the world. There is nothing enlightened about shrinking so that other people won't feel insecure

> around you. We are all meant to shine, as children do. . . . And as we let our own light shine, we unconsciously give other people permission to do the same. As we are liberated from our own fear, our presence automatically liberates others. (1992, n. pag.)

Today, the only detail about me that I insist on in class is the correct pronunciation of my name, for I have noticed that while American people may be offended when someone mispronounces their names, they make no effort to say unfamiliar names correctly. I make a point to demonstrate to them how to pronounce my French name, and discourage them from using my family name, *Harushimana*, which they find too long and enjoy mispronouncing as *Hiroshima*.

I should also acknowledge that my boost in confidence came from my ability *to spot weaknesses* in the writing of most students, who think of themselves as native English speakers and English experts. As I always mention in class, no writing is perfect. Most native English speaking students do not understand Jim Cummins' (2008) famous distinction between basic interpersonal communication skills (BICS) and cognitive academic language proficiency (CALP). They do not know that BICS tend to develop naturally among native speakers, whereas CALP is formally taught and acquired by both native and nonnative speakers. In fact, I argue that academic language is nobody's native language; its mastery depends on the amount of effort put into learning its elements, such as grammar, academic vocabulary, and syntax, and practicing them in context. At times, I get the feeling that my white students do not expect me to find mistakes in their writing, and they look shocked when I do. I am a skilled editor, whether they like it or not.

In one instance a student confidently (and perhaps defiantly) approached me to find out what mistake was in this sentence taken from his narrative, "The students' statement did not reflect any respect for teachers." I could see in the student's face that he was confident that he had "got me." I reread the sentence in silence and reaffirmed to him that indeed there was an error, without identifying it. Finally, he found it and sighed, "Ah! The '-s'!" Yes, the missing plural "s" in "statement" was the problem, even though to me the entire sentence was weak and did not meet my expectation from a native speaker of English pursuing a master's in teaching English.

Native English speaking teacher candidates of English seem to take lightly their responsibility to serve as role models for their students, especially those who speak and write dialect versions (i.e., nonstandard, slang, or Creole English). Many tend to equate the English discipline with English literature, yet there is more to teaching a language as a discipline than just focusing on literature. The linguistic, phonetic, semantic, lexical, and social aspects of the language matter equally. Moreover, just because the students' level of English may be too low should not give teachers an excuse to not polish their modeling of the language for the students. As Lisa Delpit (1986) rightly argues, minority students who did not grow up in literacy-rich families, unlike many of their white, middle-class teachers, need to be taught how to write well-formed and grammatically correct sentences.

It is about time that native English speaking people come to terms with the fact that English is no longer a panacea, even if it is still the lingua franca of scientific research and technology (Graddol, 2000). Many intellectuals from non-English-speaking countries have conquered the English language to the point of writing it far better than well-educated native English speaking writers. Nobody can deny the fact that two Nigeria-born authors, i.e., Wole Soyinka and Ben Okri, respectively and deservedly won the 1986 Nobel Prize in literature and the 1991 Man Booker Prize for fiction. In-service and pre-service teacher candidates, especially those in the English field, need to humble themselves and accept the fact that a non-native-English-speaking faculty with the right credentials has the intellect and ability to teach them English as an academic subject. Good writing, whether academic or non-academic, requires careful practice and can benefit from explicit instruction; that is why there are courses in academic writing, creative writing, business writing, report writing, etc. May the most articulate writer win!

References

CNN.com. (2007, Feb. 9). Biden's description of Obama draws scrutiny. Retrieved: http://www.cnn.com/2007/POLITICS/01/31/biden.obama/

Cummins, Jim. (2008). BICS and CALP: Empirical and theoretical status of distinction. In Street, B., & Hornberger, N. H. (Eds.). (2008). *Encyclopedia of*

Language and Education, 2nd Edition, Volume 2: Literacy. (pp. 71-83). New York: Springer Science + Business Media LLC.

Delpit, L. (1986). Skills and other dilemmas of a progressive black educator. *Harvard Educational Review, 56*(4), 379-386.

Graddol, D. (2000). *The future of English*. London: The British Council.

Lippi-Green, R. (1997) *Language, ideology, and discrimination in the United States*. London: Routledge.

Williamson, M. (1992). *A return to love: Reflections on the principles of A Course in Miracles*. Harper Collins.

Zeleny, J, (2008, Feb. 19). Clinton camp says Obama plagiarized in speech. Retrieved: https://www.nytimes.com/2008/02/19/us/politics/19campaign.html

Chapter 14

Can You Get It If You Really Want?
A Jamaican-Born Science Educator Reflects on Success Attainability

Ellie Williamson

> You can get it if you really want;
> You can get it if you really want;
> You can get it if you really want;
> But you must try, try and try, try and try;
> You'll succeed at last, mmh, yeah!
>
> *Jimmy Cliff*

BARACK OBAMA ONCE said, "The future rewards those who press on. I don't have time to feel sorry for myself. I don't have time to complain. I'm going to press on" (Associated Press, 2011, n. pag.). My journey to professionalism in science education is a result of "pressing on."

The Beginning

I grew up in the parish of St. Andrew in Jamaica. I am the youngest of four children born to my parents. Since my siblings were considerably older than I, I would rely on myself to entertain myself. We grew up in a comfortable home in a respectable neighborhood. Some of my fondest childhood memories were when we would sit together and eat a delicious Jamaican Sunday dinner that my mother lovingly prepared for us. We never bolted from the table at the end of the meal because that was when my father would share his stories about his childhood. He was and still is a great storyteller, and he always shared the funniest stories, even if the stories were about difficult times. His parents and his siblings would find the humor behind the situation, thereby easing the difficulties. I remember laughing so much and learning his underlying lessons of family always supporting each other, always being persistent, working hard and never grudging someone for what they have. These lessons have had an impact on my life and have shaped how I perceive myself as an educator.

As a child, I took myself very seriously. As the baby of the family, sometimes I was teased or laughed at when something embarrassing that happened to me was caused by my older siblings; it was never done maliciously—all in good fun. My usual response was to cry, sulk, and withdraw. One day after everyone had a good laugh at my expense, my mom said to me, "Ellie, you need to learn to laugh at yourself." I still hear her saying that to this day, and it has helped me to consider the situation from the viewpoint of the individuals who are looking on. As a result, I have been able to move on very quickly and laugh either out loud or in my mind when something embarrassing happens to me.

I was an average student in my elementary and secondary school years. But my sister was an amazing role model. She had the greatest influence over me, especially in my high school years. In my country, all students took a series of Caribbean exams. These exams were scheduled over the month of June, usually during the 11th grade. I had a total of 22 exams to take for eight subjects—no pressure on a 16-year-old, it's all good. I was determined to take the exams at the General level not at the Basic level, since that was not enough to move on to grades 12 and 13, pre-university. Fortunately, I successfully passed those exams and I was promoted to the next levels. I tried during those senior years, but I was not as successful on those exams as I was in the previous exams. Still my efforts were enough to get me into the only university on the island at that time, the University of the West Indies. I felt like I went through the fire at that university; my tenure there was four years instead of three. Most of the classes were large, and the delivery and reception of the content mostly impersonal. Each semester I only had one shot at demonstrating mastery of the content, and it was through a final laboratory and a theoretical exam. We completed labs twice a week, but the work did not contribute to the final grade.

Learning from Failure

I failed miserably during my first and second year. However, those were hard lessons, especially when I saw members of my cohort being able to graduate on time when my graduation was delayed for a year. During my third and final years at the university, I made the decision to study and to be a better student. Upon my graduation, I applied to graduate school with the sole intention to study with a professor whose courses and teaching methods I had enjoyed. After that, I decided not to enroll for any classes, thereby dropping out of the program. After all, it was not my intention to pursue graduate studies in science, at least not at that time.

Sink or Swim

After graduation, I was at home for four months, without a job or attending school. Then someone in my family told me about a traditional high school for boys that needed a science teacher to cover for a teacher who took a leave of absence. I applied, interviewed, and was selected to teach seventh- and eighth-grade general science and ninth-grade chemistry. Looking back, I was not fully equipped for the job. I had taken a lot of biology courses but no education courses. I had the content, but I was not trained in how to deliver it. My work was poor because of my lack of training. I remember crying many times, feeling very insecure because I had no clue what I was doing. To make matters worse, I was very timid and unsure of myself. There were many times when I wanted to quit but never did; maybe it was my pride, but I hated not seeing things through to the end. "I really wanted to get it," as Jimmy Cliff's song taught me. I think that he would be so proud of me persisting despite my insecurities and challenges.

Be the Best in Your Field

Although being at the all-boys' school was very challenging, I remember a particular day when alumni were invited to share their experiences with the boys and offer advice for the future. One of the visitors was an accountant, and he shared something that resonated and remained with me. He said, "Essentially, whatever field you decide to pursue, ensure that you are the best in that field." For him it meant that he had certifications to practice in the United Kingdom, the United States of America, and Jamaica. Those certifications provided him with options, and more doors could open for him. For some reason when I moved to America I remembered that advice, and it has influenced the decisions that I have made and the paths that I have taken over the years.

I endured another year at the school. During that time, I listened closely to the head of the department as well as other senior teachers and learned what I could from them. I did my best, but it was not enough. Eventually, I was asked to leave that job because I was often late. Fortunately for me, at that time, my best friend who also had no teacher training was working at her alma mater. She told me that there was an opening for a biology and general science teacher.

The school was also a traditional high school; however, it was only for girls. I interviewed and was hired. This time, I was determined *not* to make the mistakes that I made at the other school; I was never late. However, because I still lacked the training, the way I delivered the content was very teacher-centered. At the time, my metaphor for teaching was that I viewed my students as "empty vessels." I remember speaking with other teachers in my department to get ideas for lessons and activities, especially prior to being evaluated. Those discussions were very helpful, and they stirred in me a desire to seek teacher training.

The Re-Education of Ellie

It so happened that later in the spring of that year, my sister who was a lecturer at the second university on the island told me and my best friend that the university had an accelerated summer teacher training program. Initially the program was conceived as an in-house program geared toward training their professors, but they decided to open it to individuals who had no formal teacher training. This appealed to me, even if it meant giving up my summer for school. It also meant that I would not have to attend classes while I was teaching during the school year. My friend and I quickly applied to the program and were accepted. Those two summers were very intense and grueling, but they were the most fulfilling and revealing times for me. I felt that I had grown up—I no longer saw myself as a youth because it was the first time that I truly felt valued and had a voice. I believe that the maturity level and professional experience of my cohort made a major contribution to the way that I felt.

Unlike during my undergraduate years, my professors at this university were colleagues of most of the members of the cohort, and they ended up treating the rest of the cohort as such. It was such an intimate setting where I got to know my professors, and where there was mutual respect—an environment in which I was able to learn about myself and thrive. My peers had a range of experience and wealth of knowledge. Most of them were lecturers at the university; some had their master's degree, others Ph.D.s. Some were high school teachers with teacher training certificates who wanted to get additional training. Bottom line, most of the program participants were established in their fields. They stood out to me because they were confident people with a very strong sense of self who knew what they wanted. That was the persona that I wanted to emulate. I believed that they had these traits because they were disciplined and highly educated. I believed that it was thanks to the training that they had received from their education that they were brave and open to different and/or new situations. For example, one of my peers went to a country where he did not know the language or anyone, but he came back with a degree, certifications, and skill sets that he would not have gained if he had just stayed at home.

Perhaps the reason I learned so much about myself was that I had a new beginning and was in an environment in which I could thrive. Although I was surrounded by people who were older and more experienced than I was, they still wanted to hear what I had to say during discussions and presentations. My voice mattered, and I had not experienced that until then. Because I felt valued, I worked harder than I ever had before. I made the decision to not settle for less than my best by setting high expectations for myself. My new motto was to always give and do my best. Not just "to try and try" as Jimmy Cliff's song suggested, but to finally succeed in my own eyes. I also worked very hard because I wanted to be able to relate to my peers and show them that I could contribute relevant and meaningful insights during conversations. I realized that would only happen once I increased my knowledge, which meant reading more and learning to think critically about things, by considering conjectures and thinking about other viewpoints.

Where the Streets Are Paved in Gold: Lessons Learned in New York City

I left the island for Canada with the hopes of continuing my career as a teacher. Unfortunately, my qualifications and experience were not enough to teach with the Ontario public schools. Disappointed, I attended a job fair where the members of personnel from New York City Department of Education were recruiting educators to teach in New York City public schools. I signed the necessary paperwork, obtained my H-1B visa, and arrived in the city after the 2003-2004 school year had started. It took some time for me to be placed in a school permanently; I was in two schools before I finally landed in a school in Williamsburg, some time in March. The students' unruliness made me feel as if I had been placed in the school depicted in the movie *Dangerous Minds*. I was shocked at the norms and the behavior of some of the students. I had much to learn. I was assigned to teach ninth-grade students who had been without a teacher for at least one month—how delightful—*not*! I have never counted down until the end of the school year as often as I did during that time. Even though I was English proficient, I felt as if I had a language barrier since some of the things that the students said I either did not understand or misinterpreted as them being rude. I remember one incident when a student told me, "Let me see that pencil"; I felt offended because I thought that he was demanding my pencil, as if I had stolen it from him or something. You never knew with those students. It turned out that it was his way of asking for the pencil. It wasn't until my fifth year in the system, when I was at my current school, a high school in Manhattan, that I began to have a better understanding of the New York City public school culture. I had to make the decision to learn their language and expressions and open up myself so that they could get to know me as I got to know them. I am still learning their evolving language.

Be a Chameleon without Losing Yourself

As I continue to work on myself, I am reminded of the words of Michelle Obama when she said, "One of the lessons that I grew up with was to stay true to yourself and never let what somebody else says distract you from your goals" (Pfetten, 2009, n. pag.). Five years ago my principal partnered me with an instructional coach. I did not take offense to the decision; I was open to the idea of having someone watch my lesson delivery. We would share our ideas about how the lesson went, she would give me feedback on the strengths and weaknesses, and we would make plans for the next lesson based on her feedback and my thoughts. I was fortunate that year to teach courses that did not culminate in a standardized exam. I had complete freedom with my curriculum. I could teach what I thought truly mattered within the framework of the courses. I could boldly go where I had never gone before in my teaching career, like incorporating Socratic seminars with my students, replacing traditional final exams with panel discussions, and going deeper into topics rather than having a superficial approach. This time was significant; I grew because I had made the decision to be receptive to critical and constructive feedback, and I bravely experimented with new and different ways to deliver content to my students. I was able to follow through with these decisions because, like Michelle Obama, I remained true to my personal expectations of not doing less than my best, and this is also something that I expected of my students. One of the rewards of the changes and growth that had occurred was being accepted into Math for America, a competitive yet rewarding Math and Science Teacher fellowship.

Mentorship as a Two-Way Street

My utmost conviction that all students can learn science drives me, beyond planning instruction, to find my own mentors from whom to learn how to improve my pedagogy. My mentors hail from local and prestigious universities such as Lehman College and Harvard University. These mentors are visionary, creative, and active researchers in their fields. Through their research, I have become aware of current research as it relates to teaching and learning science. They have become my very good friends who support my work in and outside of the classroom. Through their support, I have been able to accomplish various things such as planning and implementing action research in my classes and to facilitating adult learning in collegiate settings.

Having received so much support and gained much insight as a teacher, it is imperative that I give back to the profession. For five years, I have been working as a cooperating teacher for pre-service teachers. My co-workers have asked me, "Where do you find time to do all of these activities?" I make the time for the love of the students; I believe that it is important that students are provided with educators who not only know the content but who can also deliver the material in ways that pique students' curiosity. Those convictions have become my strength and a legacy that must be passed on to the next generation of teachers.

Mentoring is mutual. Pre-service teachers whom I mentor gain from me as I gain from them. I have learned much and have become a better teacher through my interactions with these pre-service teachers because they challenge me when they share perspectives that I might not have considered, particularly when they are framed around things that they may have noticed after I missed mentioning them in the class.

Final Thoughts

I may have held the title of master teacher from various professional organizations, but I do not view myself as a master. Rather, I see myself as a master teacher in progress, for there are aspects of my practice in which I excel and areas in which I need to grow. I realize that growth happens when I make the most of all my encounters, whether it is with a student or an adult, or inside or out of the classroom. Growth also happens when you are open to critical and constructive feedback. I am constantly inspired by how wise Barack Obama was when he listened to individuals who did not necessarily share his viewpoints; doing so enabled him to consider multiple viewpoints when making decisions. I try to be wise by being receptive to critical feedback. Furthermore, like Obama says, I don't waste time indulging in self-pity or complaining; rather I choose to be persistent in my endeavors. Although it is reaffirming to be heard, meaningful changes and progress are made when we acknowledge our weaknesses. As educators, we are called to be brave, not afraid to reinvent ourselves and try new things, but rather remain true to our teacher tenets—courage and actions—not titles. As for me, I will follow Jimmy Cliff's advice to "keep trying" to care and inspire, for our students, as a whole, have the ability to succeed. What I try to give them, which they need more of, is support and encouragement from caring educators who keep reminding them that they will "succeed at last."

References

Associated Press. (2011). *Obama at Black Caucus Dinner: "I Need Your Help."* https://www.cbsnews.com/news/obama-at-black-caucus-dinner-i-need-your-help/

Cliff, J. (n.d.). "You Can Get It If You Really Want." Available: https://www.stlyrics.com/lyrics/hardertheycome/youcangetitifyoureallywant.htm

Pfetten, V., von (2009). *Words of Wisdom: Michelle Obama's Most Inspirational Quotes.* Available: https://www.huffpost.com/entry/michelle-obamas-most-insp_n_172485

Chapter 15

Beware of False Consciousness: A Letter to My Son

Shirley Mthethwa-Sommers

Mr. Barack Obama represented hope for all of us, including you, my dear son. I saw how you watched his speeches with awe and ease. Awe for his ascension to the highest office in the U.S. He inspired you to set your eyes on Harvard as the only college you want to attend. You felt at ease with him as the president because he made you feel good in your skin. Obama was a symbol of strength and empowerment for you. I am so glad you have had a person like him to look up to.

Like you, Obama is biracial.

Like you, Obama has roots both on the continent of Africa and the United States.

I know that you admired him. While I know that your sense of pride in him was different from mine when Nelson Mandela became the first apartheid-free president, I know that you were proud to have had him as your role model during your formative years.

Son, our lives may be different, yet race is a constant defining feature. You were born in South Africa as a "born-free," a term ascribed to people born post-apartheid. I was born in apartheid South Africa. In our discussions I have always wondered what it would have been like to be born in a free and democratic society. Unlike you, I grew up in a township—an area designated for Africans with permits to work in the city. I grew up in a house made of asbestos roofing, a deliberate act of the apartheid government to truncate our lives. You know my home in the township—a place inspired by hate that my parents turned into a haven, a place of love and growth. You have become fond of this place. The asbestos is now covered but it is still there. We live with it. You have visited it. With you I have made sure that both homes you have had here in the U.S. and in South Africa are free of environmental hazards. When you get headaches, I speculate about the environmental contribution of your headaches. Environmental pollution and hazards were used as a weapon against my survival. Even in the U.S. most environmental hazards and pollution are in black and brown neighborhoods. Nevertheless, you, my son, grew up with Obama as your president, a president who understood the importance of the environment and the negative impact it can have on our lives. Obama acknowledged environmental racism, and the dangers of environmental pollution and hazards. You were 12 years old when Obama took an oath to work toward ensuring a future without environmental hazards brought by climate change. The oath that he and leaders of other polluting countries took was to be known as the Paris Agreement. On that day, Obama said,

> I believe, in the words of Dr. Martin Luther King Jr., that there is such a thing as being too late. And when it comes to climate change, that hour is almost upon us. But if we act here, if we act now, if we place our own short-term interests behind the air that our young people will breathe, and the food that they will eat, and the water that they will drink, and the hopes and dreams that sustain their lives, then we won't be too late for them. (Obama, October 5, 2016)

While the South African apartheid government intentionally poisoned me, you grew up with a black president who wanted to protect your health and your future by curbing climate change. I want you to know this truth: the oath that President Obama took has been rescinded by his successor. I also want you to know that laws, oaths, and policies that politicians make have a direct impact on people. When Obama's successor annulled the oath, he was not only undermining Obama's legacy; he was also indirectly telling youth like you that he is not concerned about the air you will breathe, the food you will eat, and the water you will drink. My dear son, when we care about people, we care about the environment in which they live.

I remember the first day you went to kindergarten here in America. You were eager to go. I was worried. My worries stemmed from many factors. I am a teacher-educator; I speculated on whether your most likely white teachers would know how precious you are to me, to us as a family. Will they treat you the way they disparagingly talk about black kids and black boys? Would they know how intelligent you are, or will they assume you incompetent based on your skin color? It is the same worry that I still have today, as you are getting older. The presumption of deficit and incompetence based on skin color is something that I did not experience under apartheid South Africa. Under apartheid South Africa, races were segregated in all aspects and spheres of life from housing to schooling, to public transport, to restaurants, to movie theaters, to even the beaches. Note that born-frees are still confounded by the segregation of beaches. This segregation, which was grossly unequal, meant that I was educated by fellow black people and only interacted with black people in all institutions. The inadvertent benefit of that was to grow up free of the psychological harm engendered by living in a society that promotes the myth of white supremacy. I grew up with people who shielded me from the deleterious ideology of white supremacy. In the U.S., it is different. The myth of white supremacy is perpetuated in all facets of society, especially schools. Yes, my education in apartheid South Africa was an education to further oppress me, but my teachers would always say, "What we are teaching you about yourselves is not true; we are required to teach it." In other words, it was an education aimed at oppressing us, but teachers made sure we knew that reality. Here in the U.S., an education steeped in the myth of white supremacy is paraded as neutral and democratic.

My dearest son, I hope you know the falsehood of white supremacy and the fabrication of black incompetence and un-intelligence. Your schools and teachers will speak of the achievement gap between black and white students. They will hardly note that the concept of the achievement gap only existed after integration. Prior to integration, the concept did not exist because black kids, and black boys like you, were excelling and doing well under the tutelage of teachers who valued them and did not doubt their intelligence.

My son, you are intelligent and capable. I am very proud of your academic and athletic achievements. You have been on the honor roll for your entire schooling career. You have received academic distinctions. I have observed with pride how Ivy-League universities and top colleges in the country are already recruiting you, at 10th grade. I hope you never believe the invention of your intellectual incapacity. I wish you continuance of your academic excellence. I am sorry that I cannot shield you from the deleterious effects that books you read in school such as *To Kill a Mockingbird, Huckleberry Finn,* and other books that are supposed to be classics which actually reinforce marginalization and perpetuation of the myth of black inferiority and incompetence. You have had Obama as a president; you know he has undermined this myth. But you are so bombarded by this myth of black inferiority and white supremacy from all aspects of society that you might start to believe it.

Son, this is called *false consciousness*, when we internalize and believe the myths and stereotypes that are meant to oppress us. I cannot shield you from the myths and negative stereotypes about who are, but I can only provide you with the armor that my black teachers in apartheid South Africa provided me, "What [they] are teaching you about yourself is not true, [they] are required to teach it," and beware of false consciousness. The irony is that we live in a country with government policies that are far different than apartheid South Africa, we live in a country that holds equity and racial justice as an ideal, yet the practices are oddly similar.

My dearest son, I would like to tell you about the importance of activism and fighting for your rights. Did you know that when Obama's presidency ended, he and Michelle Obama started a foundation that focuses on activism, particularly of young people like you? The Obamas know that activism is one way to move the country forward in its policies and practices. When I was your age I was an activist against the apartheid regime. I attended Chesterville High School in the Chesterville township in the mid-1980s. The apartheid regime was extremely brutal and uncontrollably violent toward dissent and subversion. I was a member of the Congress of South African Students or COSAS, as we called it. My generation was called the generation of *fire-eaters*. We wanted the apartheid system to end with us, and it did, but not without sacrifice, not without bloodshed, not without indelible trauma.

When I was your age, my son, we, the students of COSAS, decided to join in protesting the apartheid government's assassination of Ms. Victoria Mxenge, an anti-apartheid activist from one of the townships in Durban. She was assassinated in front of her children as she came home. Two years earlier, the apartheid government had assassinated her husband, Griffith Mxenge, also an anti-apartheid activist (my late nephew Mlungisi Griffith was named after him). We took to the streets in protest of the brutal killing of Ms. Mxenge. Many of my fellow students were arrested. Again, we took to the streets in protest; we demanded their release before we could go back to school.

The apartheid government responded by sending the military to Chesterville. The township was under siege. The air was constantly cloudy with teargas, and the roads and pathways were constantly peppered with blood. The school was shut down. COSAS was banned. My schoolmates were murdered. We continued to fight against what seemed to be the mighty apartheid system that was financially supported by the U.S. government. We continued to take to the streets protesting against the brutality of the system, shouting, "An injury to one is an injury to all." I did not attend school for two years. Chesterville became a place of pogrom, with the apartheid government infiltrating those of us who were fighting against it with informants and executioners who called themselves the *A-team*. These were our neighbors, our schoolmates, our classmates who were so steeped in false consciousness that they chose to kill their brothers and sisters for a stipend from the apartheid government. The military became a permanent fixture in the township. We lived under what the apartheid government called the *state of emergency*. This meant they could imprison people without trials; the murdering and maiming of people happened day in, day out. I buried many of my school- and classmates who were brutally murdered by the apartheid regime. It is important to remember that a lot of people died in order, as we would say, to nourish and cultivate the tree of freedom.

And I got to admire Winnie Madikizela Mandela. Winnie Madikizela Mandela was an indomitable leader in our fight against apartheid. Remember, son, that other leaders such as Nelson Mandela were imprisoned. Others such as Oliver Tambo were in exile. It was in the 1980s and it was the unrelenting struggle in which we engaged that contributed to the release of Nelson Mandela and other leaders in 1990. It was our intentional activism to be ungovernable which contributed to the unbanning of the African National Congress, COSAS, and the return of the exiles. My three brothers whom you know also returned home after over 25 years of living in exile because of their anti-apartheid activism. It was activism that ended apartheid and ushered in democracy in South Africa in 1994. The lesson that I hope you are gleaning, son, is that there is no substantive change without a fight; there is no childbirth without labor, or as Frederick Douglass put it, there is no rain without lightning and thunder. Activism is the precursor of any social change; one does not have to be extraordinary, although you are, to engage in activism. Obama reminds us that "ordinary people can do extraordinary things" (Kenning, 2017, p. 4).

My dearest son, you are growing up in the age of *Black Lives Matter (BLM)*, a movement that continues the work of all of us who have fought for freedom, here in the United States and on the continent. I had hoped that in 2018 it would be a given that Black Lives Do Matter, but clearly it is not the case. Please don't be steeped in false consciousness of believing that your life is worth less than your white peers' lives. Your life matters, a lot. Lives of all black children matter. This is what Nelson Mandela and thousands of South Africans who defiantly said Black Lives Matter were imprisoned for. Your grandmother, my mother, was among those detained for standing their ground and maintaining that Black Lives Matter. Engaging in activism is part of our family history and a history of all freedom-loving people from Harriet Tubman to Frederick Douglass to Rosa Parks to Lillian Ngoyi to Winnie Madikizela Mandela.

I hope you continue this tradition whenever you witness an injustice. Join other young people like you in fighting against injustices. The former president Obama conceptualized the My Brother's Keeper program in 2014 to show that lives of black and brown young men matter. The program works in partnership with community organizations and businesses to mentor and uplift young men of color. The significance of this program, my son, is that you are not alone; there are other men, young and old, in society who care for you and are invested in your success. I urge you to join a local My Brother's Keeper chapter and experience brotherhood. Brotherhood is what former president Obama envisioned when he conceptualized the program. You know, like you, he grew up just being him and his sister, even though he had brothers on the continent of Africa. Developing brotherhood with young men, who are like you, is your assertion to the world that you and every young man of color matter.

I am sad to have to tell you that racial marginalization reproduces itself in many ways. It morphs and manifests itself in the policies aimed to "clean up" Israel, policies that target immigrants of African descent. It manifests itself in the vulgar language used to refer to African countries as *shitholes* by the present president of the U.S. It evinces itself in young men like Trayvon Martin, Mike Brown, Oscar Grant, Tamir Rice being gunned down for being "suspicious." You are experiencing different forms of racial marginalization; please know that you have agency. I want you to know that you can walk with your head held up high.

You do not have to live in the state of nervousness and dis-ease in your skin. Your intellect and humanity exist independent of the Western and Northern ideas and pontifications about people who look like you. When announcing the My Brother's Keeper program, Obama said that if he had a son, he would

> ... want my son to feel a sense of boundless possibility. [I] want him to have independence and confidence. I want him to have empathy and compassion. [I] want him to have a sense of diligence and compassion for himself, the tools to succeed that he would need. (Obama, 2014, n. pag.)

I wish and want the same for you, my son. Please have pride in your background as a young man of African descent. Remember that phenomenal women and men have paved the path for you to soar to the stars and contribute to the advancement of humanity.

Remember, my son, this message I just shared with you is not just for you alone. Go tell it on the mountain. Go share it with your friends, classmates and schoolmates of color, for they share your destiny. The black race and maleness bind you together. Therefore, be each other's brother's keeper. Amandla Awethu! Aluta Continua! Ngothando!

References

Kenning, C. (October, 2017). *Obama Seeks to Spark Civic Activism with Chicago Event.* Reuters. https://www.reuters.com/...obama/obama-seeks-to-spark-u-s-civic-activism-with-chica...

Obama, B. (2014, February 27). *My Brother's Keeper.* Available https://www.cnn.com/2014/02/27/.../obama-brothers-keeper-transcript/index.html

Obama, B. (2016, October 5). *Remarks by the President on the Paris Agreement.* https://obamawhitehouse.archives.gov/the-press.../remarks-president-paris-agreement

SECTION IV
BLACK SELF-AFFIRMATION

CHAPTER 16

Standing with Barack Obama:
The Need for Black Scientists in STEM Education

Diane Price Banks

> *One of the things that I've been focused on as president is how we create an all-hands-on-deck approach to science, technology, engineering, and math... We need to make this a priority to train an army of new teachers in these subject areas, and to make sure that all of us as a country are lifting up these subjects for the respect that they deserve. (Obama White House, 2013)*

Blacks Can Be Scientists, Too—and Presidents!

THE LEADERSHIP OF Barack Obama has brought white hatred toward the black race back to the forefront. Inasmuch as his antagonists opposed his agenda, President Obama made major accomplishments during his term (Glastris & Letourneau, 2017). With every initiative introduced, Obama faced opposition despite his policies being robust and likely to positively impact the majority of American citizens. None of his accomplishments came easy, and barely any of them were hailed. The problem was not because his proposals were weak, but rather due to the color of his skin. Just as Eurocentric textbooks silence the contributions of blacks in microbiology, so did the mainstream media outlets silence the contributions of our first black president. The Eurocentric perspective, in academia, results in the detachment between the student and historical relevance. Black students are led to believe that all great scientists were European or descendants of Europeans. It is Obama's commitment to the advancement of science education that resonated with me the most, as a woman and a science educator. I know from experience that students tend to have a sense of onus to education when they learn that someone who looks like them has created something useful to the world.

In microbiology, for example, textbooks used to help educate nurses, physician assistants, nutritionists, and medical laboratory technicians exclusively highlight European scientists and bacteriologists. To give a few examples, *Antonie Van Leeuwenhoek*, who developed the single-lens microscope and was the first man to see bacteria, is Dutch; *Robert Hooke*, the first person to view and coin the term "cells" under a microscope, is British; whereas *Louis Pasteur* who discovered the principles of vaccination and the process of pasteurization, is French. The list goes on. In contrast, the books neglect to even state that the medium used to grow microorganisms was created in collaboration with a black woman named *Jane Hinton*. Mueller-Hinton, not Jane Hinton, is credited with the agar used in antibiotic susceptibility testing and the isolation of Neisseria and Moraxella species. It is on this premise that we as black educators must challenge societal norms and push back against the silencing of our people. This chapter focuses on the need to expose the biases of Western-dominated media and science textbook authors who deliberately choose to ignore the contributions of black scientists to the proliferation of scientific knowledge. A section of the chapter will look at President Obama's stance on education and equity. Another aspect of this essay will consist of a self-reflection over my choice to pursue the field of science. The implications section shares thoughts on how black science educators can supplement the Eurocentric science curriculum with materials and resources that highlight the achievements of black scientists.

President Obama's Legacy on STEM and Education

The 44th president of the United States of America, Mr. Barack Obama, will be remembered as a legendary, progressive, forward-thinking, innovative leader, and a catalyst for decreasing the perpetual achievement gaps instituted by racist policies that historically denied or hindered the advancement of people of color in this country.

In 2016, during his commencement speech at Benjamin Banneker Academy High School in D.C., Obama commended the institution for being a model school that the entire country should use as a template. Banneker High's student population is 99% minority. Despite being an urban institution, the school gives students access to quality education. Due to its leader's strong vision and support and access to viable academic resources, the school's graduation and college admission rates for 2016 were 100%. Students at Banneker High exceeded the national average (510) scores, in Reading (551) and Math (541) (About BBAHS, n.d.). If all urban public schools throughout the country would model themselves after Banneker, formerly developing nations, like China and India, which have caught up with and outpaced the USA in math and science, would be second to us. Worse still, due to existing and permeating racial inequities in this country, black and brown students significantly lag behind their white classmates and trail the rest of the world (McFarland et al., 2018).

Obama acknowledged that, in our global economy, graduates from the United States are not only competing with fellow Americans but also with graduates from around the world. He worried that as technology and the internet expand their reach, jobs will become more and more global, and the best jobs will go to those with the best education regardless of geographic boundaries.

To minimize the existing trend of outsourcing American jobs, throughout his tenure, President Obama increased access to high-quality preschool education by adding 60,000 children to Head Start programs. This initiative increased the national rates for preschool enrollments from 38% to 46% by 2016 (Obama White House, 2016) and paved the way for black and brown youth to gain access to quality education at an early age. He also funded high-speed internet for schools and libraries across the nation, thus granting access to the internet to 20 million students. Initiatives of this caliber led to the record national graduation rate of 84% in 2016, primarily due to the increase in graduation rates among black students, from 66% in 2013 to 73% in 2016 (Aud et al., 2013; Kena et al., 2016). Obama also invested in getting people of color, low-income students, and young women and girls in the fields of science, technology, engineering, and mathematics (STEM) (Hendelsman & Smith, 2016; Obama White House, 2013). Lastly, and certainly not least, to promote his education agenda, Obama enacted the Race to the Top law (to fix No Child Left Behind) that gives teachers more flexibility to teach creatively rather than just teaching to the test. Needless to say, Obama worked aggressively to put forth an education agenda that was inclusive of all Americans, specifically black and brown youth. I am proud to join his cause.

Joining the Call: My Untold Passion for the Field of Science

I am a child of the '80s, the era when the crack and HIV epidemics commonly referred to as "planned shrinkage" plagued the Bronx (Wallace, 1988 & Wallace, 1990). My generation came right after the government repressions of black political leaders which led to the assassinations of influential leaders of theCivil Rights Movement (Price Banks, 2017). This era was followed by those in power intentionally slashing minority neighborhood resources, which perpetuated the spread of HIV, drugs, and the destruction of housing by fires due to lack of fire stations (Wallace, 1990). Family circumstances and the cultural climate during the '80s led me to my present career as a scientist.

The HIV epidemic was the catalyst for me pursuing a career in science and public health education. I was passionate about finding cures to defeat incurable diseases that plagued my community. I faced conflicts about being a medical doctor versus a healthcare professional. My indecisiveness led me to a high school in the Bronx that specialized in health careers. Still unsure of my trajectory in life, I decided to pursue a bachelor's degree in biology. I knew that I wanted to work in the laboratory to discover novel approaches to curing diseases, but that career choice was unknown to me. Then an older relative, who attended a local community college studying to be a medical laboratory technician, reached out to me and told me about the field of epidemiology. I felt a huge weight lifted off of me. In the absence of the internet, to research this newfound career, I went to the library. The more I read, the more I felt I had finally found myself. As soon as I determined my education pathway, I geared my academic studies toward the master of public health degree in epidemiology. To further solidify my career trajectory, one of the nuns at the college secured me a microbiology internship at a local hospital in Yonkers.

I still deplore the fact that during the late '80s to early '90s, the primary and secondary curriculum did not include scientists who looked like me, so the work of black scientists was not influential to my pursuit of a career in the field of science. This injustice must stop. Curricular reform is direly needed to make sure that minority scientists are recognized.

The Need to Supplement the Eurocentric Science Curriculum

Democratic principles should require that at all levels of education in America, from elementary school to academia, students of color should be taught the role that their ancestors played in the making of this great country. Despite the dark past that includes kidnapping and human trafficking of African people to a foreign land for enslavement, notwithstanding other atrocities that led to constant rebellious attempts at freedom (Aptheker, 1937), blacks in America have proven that we are a resilient people (Price Banks, 2017). Out of the darkness emerged black scholars who defied all odds and became doctors, politicians, and other types of influential intellectuals. These illustrious people need to figure in the science curriculum. Going forward, the Eurocentric curriculum must change to include culturally relevant pedagogy (Ladson-Billings, 1995). Giving students access to materials published by all races in America is not only inclusive pedagogy; it "improves the promotion and protection of human rights in relation to cultural diversity" (Donders, 2010).

The science curriculum must improve and include minority scientists like Drs. William and Jane Hinton and Charles Drew, to name a few. Dr. William Augustus Hinton is a phenomenal African American who did great work to improve the field of science as it relates to the diagnosis and treatment of syphilis in the late 1920s. Dr. Hinton, like Obama, had to defy many odds. He was born in the late 1800s to emancipated slaves during the time of Jim Crow laws that segregated blacks from whites. The environment was very hostile to black Americans, who were often the victims of brutality and did not have access to quality education. Despite adversity, he persevered and triumphantly graduated from high school at the ripe age of 16 (Cave, 1975). In 1912 he earned his doctorate from Harvard Medical School and wrote a book about the diagnosis and treatment of syphilis, becoming the first African American to publish a medical textbook. His was the leading text in the field and helped doctors to better treat patients with the disease. Sadly, despite having a medical degree from Harvard, Boston hospitals refused to hire him because of the color of his skin. Turning lemons into lemonade, Dr. Hinton worked in the Wassermann Laboratory that eventually became the Massachusetts State Department of Public Health Lab, where he became the director and developed the Hinton test (Cave, 1975) that helped to diagnose syphilis. In spite of his scientific contributions, there is no mention of Dr. Hinton in contemporary science textbooks that discuss the dynamics of the disease. The implementation of culturally relevant pedagogy would ensure that Dr. Hinton's biography, and others like him, is made available to students alongside Antonie Van Leeuwenhoek and Louis Pasteur.

For the sake of gender equality, Dr. Hinton's daughter, Jane Hinton, is also a prominent figure in the evolution of science in America. One of the first African American females to graduate from the University of Pennsylvania with a doctorate in veterinary medicine, Jane Hinton teamed up with J. Howard Mueller at Harvard Medical School to develop the Mueller-Hinton Agar. This agar was initially designed to support the growth of meningococcus and gonococcus bacterium (Mueller & Hinton, 1941). The usage over time also evolved to include the determination of antibiotic susceptibility (Nizet, 2017). Including this key fact in contemporary science textbooks will address the need for gender justice and racial fairness in urban schools, and may increase the potential to inspire girls and boys of color to pursue a career in bacteriology.

Another African American scientist, Dr. Charles Drew, was a blood banking pioneer, and his initiatives paved the way for the development of the American Red Cross blood bank. Born of African American parents in Washington, D.C., Dr. Drew earned his medical degree from McGill University in Montreal, Canada, after being rejected from Howard University's Medical College and being waitlisted at Harvard. In 1940, Dr. Drew became the director of the Blood Britain project mainly because hospitals would not hire African American doctors in fear that white patients would refuse treatment from a black man. As director, Dr. Drew created bloodmobiles which allowed blood to be donated and transported. Paradoxically, due to racism and ignorance, blacks were prevented from giving blood, including Dr. Drew. He became an advocate for the inclusion of African Americans as viable blood donors during World War II, stating that the restrictive policies were unscientific and insulting (U.S. National Library of Medicine, n.d.). Including Dr. Drew's scientific contributions in science textbooks will show minority students the power of resilience and unlimited possibility.

In closing, as we continue to push forward, we must be aware of those who will continue to push back with the primary goal to dampen our successes. It is the rightful thing for black educators, including science educators, to come together and rewrite textbooks from the black perspective or at the very least push for the inclusion of the black perspective in contemporary and future textbooks.

> *The greatest success will come from all of us being committed to each other's success; when we understand that no matter what you look like or where you come from, what your faith is, or your gender, that regardless, we should all have great opportunities to succeed.* (Obama White House, 2016)

References

About BBAHS. (n.d.). *About Benjamin Banneker Academic High School*. About us. Accessed May 31, 2018. http://www.benjaminbanneker.org/apps/pages/index.jsp?uREC_ID=261776&type=d.

Aptheker, H. (1937). American negro slave revolts. *Science & Society* 1(4), 512-538.

Aud, S., et al. (2013, May). The condition of education 2013, NCES2013-037, p. 241. https://nces.ed.gov/pubs2013/2013037.pdf

Bailyn, B. (2012). *The barbarous years: The peopling of British North America-the conflict of civilizations, 1600-1675*. 1st edition. New York: Vintage

Cave, V. G. (1975, Jan.). A Tribute to William Augustus Hinton, M.D. *Briefs* 67(1), 181–182.

Donders, Y. (2010). Do cultural diversity and human rights make a good match? *International Social Science Journal*, 61(199), 15-35.

Glastris, P., and LeTourneau, N. (2017). *Washington Monthly | Obama's Top 50 Accomplishments, Revisited*. Accessed May 31, 2018. https://washingtonmonthly.com/magazine/januaryfebruary-2017/obamas-top-50-accomplishments-revisited/.

Handelsman, J., and Smith, M. (n.d.). "STEM for All." whitehouse.gov, February 11, 2016. https://obamawhitehouse.archives.gov/blog/2016/02/11/stem-all.

Kena, G., Hussar, W., McFarland, J., de Brey, C., Musu-Gillette, L., Wang, X., & Barmer, A. (2016). The condition of education 2016. NCES 2016-144. *National Center for Education Statistics*, p. 347.

Ladson-Billings, G. (1995). Toward a theory of culturally relevant pedagogy. *American Educational Research Journal* 32 (3), p. 465. https://doi.org/10.2307/1163320

McFarland, J., Hussar, B., Wang, X., Xiaolei Wang, Zhan J., Wang, Ke, Rathbun, A., B., et al. (n.d.). The Condition of education 2018. NCES 2018-144. Eric Document ED 583502. Available: https://files.eric.ed.gov/fulltext/ED583502.pdf p. 384.

Mueller, J. H., and Hinton, J. (1941). A protein-free medium for primary isolation of the gonococcus and meningococcus. *Proceedings of the Society for Experimental Biology and Medicine* 48 (1), 330-333.

Nizet, V. T. (2017, July 4). The accidental orthodoxy of Drs. Mueller and Hinton. *EBioMedicine* (22) 26–27. https://doi.org/10.1016/j.ebiom.2017.07.002.

Obama White House. (2013, April). Third Annual White House Science Fair. https://obamawhitehouse.archives.gov/the-press-office/2013/04/22/remarks-president-2013-white-house-science-fair

Obama White House. (2016, Oct. 17). *Remarks by the President on Education*. whitehouse.gov, October 17, 2016. https://obamawhitehouse.archives.gov/the-press-office/ 2016/10/17/remarks-president-education

Price Banks, D. (2017, Mar. 20). "Black History in America: An Authentic Look at a Historically Rebellious People." Theory, Research, and Action in Urban Education, no. Special Issue #BlackLivesMatter (March 20, 2017). https://blmtraue.commons.gc.cuny.edu/2017/03/20/black-history-in-america-an-authentic-look-at-historically-rebellious-people-b/

U.S. National Library of Medicine. (n.d.). The Charles R. Drew Papers: Biographical Information. Accessed May 31, 2018. https://profiles.nlm.nih.gov/ps/retrieve/Narrative/BG/p-nid/336

Wallace, R. (1988). A synergism of plagues: "planned shrinkage," contagious housing destruction, and AIDS in the Bronx. *Environmental research*, 47(1), 1-33.

Wallace, R. (1990, January). Urban desertification, public health and public order: "Planned shrinkage," violent death, substance abuse and AIDS in the Bronx. *Social Science & Medicine* 31(7): 801–813. https://doi.org/10.1016/0277-9536(90)90175-R

Chapter 17

"Yes, I Can; Yes, We Can!"
Reflections of a Caribbean Immigrant Sistah in the Struggle with a Legacy of Determination, Strength, and Empowerment

Mary V. Alfred

> *True, I am a woman and I am Black. I ask you to take a painful journey with me. The waters are high and the treasures are buried deep. What are those precious treasures that I long to find and labor for in the walls of our ivory institutions? They are the forgotten achievements of Black women. When I find them, where will I place them, back in the stacks of forgotten records or will they be placed on a shelf where explorers such as I can easily capture the beauty of the Black woman's experience in higher education? (Payton, 1981, p. 223)*

I BEGIN THIS reflection with the words of L. Payton, who in 1981 articulated the struggles, determination, and plight of black women in U.S. higher education. Payton spoke of black women in general and, particularly, those native to the United States. I would argue that foreign-born black women, some of whom President Donald Trump referred to as coming from a "shithole" country, have a particular angle of vision from which to view and articulate our experiences in U.S. academia and the wider society. In higher education, black, immigrant women are often rendered invisible, yet we contribute significantly to the academic mission of teaching, research, service, and leadership. Commenting on Caribbean immigrant women's invisibility, Paule Marshall (1994) observed:

> If African Americans have suffered from a kind of invisibility, and if the Black foreigner has been treated to a double invisibility, then

> the West Indian female immigrant suffers from a triple invisibility as a Black, a foreigner, and a woman. She simply is not seen, nor has her experience been dealt with in any substantial way in the social science literature. (p. 81)

Making our lives visible is the purpose of this chapter, calling for us to tell our stories and place them among those of other black women of the diaspora. While we join our native-born sistahs in the struggle as a collective, we recognize that the additional identity of "immigrant with an accent" makes us more vulnerable to discrimination, alienation, and marginalization. Yet, through sheer hope, inner strength, resilience, and a strong sense of self, we persevered to realize the dream with which we came—the dream of creating a more sustainable life for us and our families, both in the United States and our home countries. Barack Obama's election in 2008 as the president and commander in chief of this great nation rekindled that dream and gave renewed hope to a nation of immigrants. In his victory speech, with conviction and passion, he said:

> This is our moment. This is our time, to put the people back to work and open doors of opportunity to our kids; to restore prosperity and promote the cause of peace; to reclaim the American dream and reaffirm that fundamental truth, that, out of many, we are one; that while we breathe, we hope. And where we are met with cynicism and doubts and [to] those who tell us that we can't, we will respond with that timeless creed that sums up the spirit of a people: Yes, we can. (CNN Politics, 2008)

While the story presented here is that of one black female immigrant, many professional immigrants will find excerpts of their experiences within my story, and together we join President Obama in dispelling cynicism and doubt and professing the spirit of "Yes, I can; yes, we can!"

A Snapshot of the Early Years

When I reflect on my past and examine my present, I am energized to share some aspects of my history with the hope that it will be an inspiration to others along their journeys. You see, during my early socialization, influenced by parents, family, extended community, and particularly teachers, no one ever told me that I couldn't. Hence, I grew up with the belief that "Yes, I can," to borrow President Obama's legacy of hope. His legacy reaffirmed the messages I received and which continue to guide my personal and professional development—a journey that has led me to my position as full professor and administrator at a predominantly white institution of higher education. Judging from my early beginnings, the odds were against my being here—in this space and place that represent my life career. This elusive career began in St. Lucia, the place I first called home.

Born to parents who were sharecroppers, I came into this world in the 1950s, the second of three girls. Unable to read and write, my father continued to sharecrop on the same land as his parents until his death in 1976; he was 66 years old. My mother, with a fourth-grade education, toiled with my father until her death in 1972; she was 55 years old. I could have gone down a very different and less promising path with the loss of my parents at a young age, especially that of my mother who was diagnosed with diabetes and glaucoma when I was 15 years old. However, my parents, my grandmother, and other significant adults had set the foundation for us to build our lives. Precious were the ancestral messages they left us through frequent stories they told depicting humility, perseverance, hard work, excellence, respect for self and others, and financial responsibility, among others. These messages, or ancestral legacies as I call them, have sustained me through my professional and personal development journeys, particularly in the U.S. where the odds are stacked heavily against those who are black, female, and immigrant, who speak with a foreign accent.

President Obama and his wife, Michelle, left the nation with the legacy of family and family values. The love for other people's children, despite their social position in society, was evidenced by First Lady Michelle Obama through her interactions with them in and out of the White House. The symbol of family in its many forms and manifestations (I am referring to all forms of family composition) is paramount to the development of one who will later say and believe, "Yes, I can!"

Today it is disheartening to see the current president, 45, through his policies and directives, destroy children and families. Separating children from their parents and placing them apart, in what look like concentration camps, is far removed from the images the nation has from President Obama's tenure in the White House. For me, growing up in St. Lucia, the conviction that *we could* was made possible with messages about the value and support for education.

My most vivid recollection of my educational experience started with fourth grade (referred to in the Caribbean as Standard One). It was then that, I, the sharecropper's daughter, was discovered to be a bright student. The principal of my new, all-girls' Catholic school saw great potential in me as well as 12 other girls and pulled us out of our regular class to form a special class under her tutelage. My teacher's interest did not stop in the classroom. She kept in touch with our parents and encouraged them to remain involved in our educational life. Although my father could not speak the official English language, he was empowered to communicate in his Creole/Patois dialect because my teacher/principal met him in his space and place and communicated with him in his language.

When I look back on the events that have shaped my life, this one stands out as the most significant. Everything that happened and continues to happen is a result of this teacher's intervention in my life, starting at nine years old. As I reflect on paradise gains and losses, I have concluded that while there were some losses, the gains overwhelmingly surpassed the losses and they armored me with the necessary tool kit for the next chapters of the journey. After high school, at the age of 16, I spent two years as a probationary assistant teacher in an elementary school and was awarded a scholarship from the Ministry of Education to attend teachers' college. As one of the three youngest students to attend teachers' college at the time, I graduated at age 20 and became an interim school principal at 22.

When I reflect on that period of my life, I often wonder why I never questioned my ability to take on such responsibilities. Perhaps it is because I never received the message that I couldn't. Such a legacy of self and others' affirmation that "I can" has been a major factor in my approach to challenges and opportunities in my adult life. Ella Bell (2010) emphasized the importance of self-knowledge or self-awareness as critical to a woman's success. As she explained, part of knowing yourself is being sure of who you are, and such knowledge is a major contributor to the development of self-confidence. I credit the individuals who contributed to my early socialization, on my tiny island of St. Lucia, for my sense of self and the can-do attitude that I now embrace. My humble beginnings did not determine my destiny; the ancestral messages I received from the many networks of adults, both formal and informal, had a powerful influence in shaping my future direction to a positive life career. According to Jack Mezirow (1991):

> As adult learners, we are caught in our own histories. However good we are at making sense of our experiences, we all have to start with what we have been given and operate within horizons set by ways of seeing and understanding that we have acquired through prior learning. This formative learning occurs in childhood both through socialization (informal or tacit learning of norms from parents, friends, and mentors that allow us to fit into society) and through our schooling. (p. 1)

The knowledge acquired from my early socialization and educational systems were paradise gains that became critical to my survival and further development upon becoming an immigrant in the United States—a country that I now call "home."

Coming to America: From Temporary Immigrant to Naturalized Citizen

Coming to America at age 24 was, indeed, a major, life-transforming event. I went from someone who was highly visible in my country to one who became totally invisible within American society. In particular, my career as an educator and as a community activist helped define my place and my identity in the old world. Without these identifiers in the new world, the perceptions of self and belonging were in question. I was faced with a discontinuation of a life known and the beginning of another yet unknown. However, Mary Catherine Bateson (2004) reminds us that much of coping with discontinuity has to do with discovering threads of continuity. She suggests one cannot adjust to change unless one can recognize some analogy between the old and the new situation. That analogy, she argues, is critical to the transfer of learning, the application of skills, and the recognition of problems that have been previously solved, though under a different guise. It was important to recognize these prior experiences as critical to the transfer of learning and perspective transformation in my new geographical and cultural spaces.

Before I delve into the discussion of life in the United States, I will first provide the context of my arrival and situate that within the current immigration discourse. My husband was serving in the U.S. military while I remained in St. Lucia for two years after we were married. We decided it would be quicker for me to travel to the United States on a temporary visa and apply for permanent residency from the United States than to apply from St. Lucia, which could take up to five years. Upon arrival, I was given a three-month stay and immediately applied for a permanent visa. During that time, I became pregnant with our first child. At the end of the three months, we went to the U.S. immigration office in Texas, discussed our situation, and I was granted a three-month extension, at the end of which we were granted another extension. At that time, I was toward the term of the pregnancy and unable to travel. My visa was finalized during that last extension, and I became a permanent resident of the United States and a naturalized citizen five years later.

Many professional immigrants can relate to my experience of first arriving on a temporary visa, either as a visitor, international student, or employee, to later transitioning to a permanent resident. When I analyze and reflect on today's immigration policies and practices, I am convinced that my life would have been vastly different from what it is today, under President Trump's administration. I fear I would not have had the ease of securing residency because I am from one of those "shithole" countries that were disdainfully referred to. While St. Lucia was not a direct mention, it is reasonable to assume that as a majority-black nation, we belong with Haiti and other African nations. Fast-forward to this immigration landscape, anything is possible under the current administration. As Margie McHugh explained:

> After riding a wave of populist anger to victory, almost immediately upon assuming office, President Trump made good on many of his campaign promises to clamp down on U.S. immigration and refugee policies. Among his earliest actions were the signing of executive orders seeking, for example, a reduction in refugee admissions, construction of a border wall between the United States

and Mexico, significant expansions in the types of noncitizens targeted for deportation and a ban—at least temporarily—on entry of immigrants from seven countries alleged to pose a danger of sending terrorists to the United States. (2018, p. 1)

Most disturbing of President Trump's actions are decisions to terminate the Deferred Action for Childhood Arrivals (DACA) program advanced by President Obama and the temporary protected status (TPS) for large numbers of migrants/refugees from Haiti and San Salvador who have lived in this country for a very long time. It is well understood and accepted by those who both support and oppose immigration that this country was built on the backs of immigrants, both authorized and unauthorized. Yet their contributions to this great nation and the excellence they have achieved are often discounted and rendered invisible.

... every day tens of millions of immigrants, most of whom have established deep roots in the United States, in communities across the country. Their success in joining the mainstream of the country's economic and civic life is arguably the most consequential—and the most often overlooked—question in national immigration policy debates. (McHugh, 2018, p. 1)

My journey exemplifies that of many who came to this country, and despite the condition of entry, have contributed immensely to building this great nation of the United States of America. Contrary to President Trump's slogan to "Make America Great Again," America has always been a great nation with contributions from a long history of immigrant people from many nations and diverse identities.

America the Great: A Black Female Immigrant's Contribution

Upon receiving permanent residency status, my first goal was to acquire job skills since I was not qualified to teach in the United States with my teaching credentials from St. Lucia Teachers' College, an affiliate of the University of the West Indies. I completed an associates degree in office education and, two years later, I completed an undergraduate degree in occupational education and business administration. With that degree, I was employed at the same community college where I started as a student. I was a faculty member and later became coordinator of four workforce development programs. During my employment at that institution, I completed my graduate degree and eight years later applied and was accepted to the number-one public research university in the state of Texas to complete the doctoral degree. I spent 18 years at the community college, and four years after receiving my Ph.D., I left and started my career as a university professor in 1999.

That phase of my career started at the University of Wisconsin-Milwaukee, then Florida International University in Miami, and currently I am employed at Texas A&M University (TAMU) in the College of Education and Human Development, where I have been since 2006. In my second year at TAMU, I was made associate head of my department; two years later, I was appointed interim department head when the current head vacated the position. Later that year, I became an associate dean and two years later I was appointed executive associate dean. It is important to note that I never applied for a leadership role at a university setting. These appointments came as those in higher administration observed my work ethic and quality of work. As part of my inherited work ethic, I try to demonstrate resourcefulness, creativity, innovation, and a sense of independence while working interdependently with others. My most noteworthy accomplishment was my induction into the International Adult and Continuing Education Hall of Fame, an international recognition of premier individuals worldwide who have contributed significantly to leadership, scholarship, teaching, and service to the profession. Most recently, I was nominated and elected to serve as president-elect of my national association, the American Association for Adult and Continuing Education. I will serve in that capacity for one year and take on the presidency in 2019. Taking on that leadership role will provide another opportunity to contribute to this great nation as a black female immigrant, the daughter of sharecroppers from the small British island of St. Lucia.

On final reflection, I draw on President Obama's victory speech when he said:

> If there is anyone out there who still doubts that America is a place where all things are possible, who still wonders if the dream of our

founders is alive in our time, who still questions the power of our democracy, tonight is your answer. (CNN Politics, 2008)

My story and that of many others yet untold is testament that America is a place where all things are possible. To heed the words of Payton (1981), as black women, we must continue to tell our stories to chronicle the achievements of black immigrant women in U.S. higher education.

References

Bateson, M. C. (2004). *Willing to learn: Passages of personal discovery*. Hanover, NH: Steerforth Press.

Bell, E. L. (2010). *Career GPS: Strategies for women navigating the new corporate landscape*. New York: HarperCollins Publishers.

CNN Politics. (2008). *Transcript: 'This is your victory,' says Obama*. Election Center, 2008. Available at http://edition.cnn.com/2008/POLITICS/11/04/obama.transcript/

Marshall, P. (1994). Black immigrant women in brown girl brownstones. In C. R. Sutton & E.M. Chaney (Eds.). *Caribbean life in New York City* (pp. 81-95). New York: Center for Migration Studies.

McHugh, M. (2018). *In the age of Trump: Populist backlash and progressive resistance create divergent state immigrant integration contexts*. Washington, DC: Migration Policy Institute, Transatlantic Council on Immigration. Available at file:///C:/Users/malfred/Downloads/TCM-StateLocalResponses_Final.pdf

Mezirow, J. (1991). *Transformative dimensions of adult learning*. San Francisco: Jossey Bass.

Payton, L. R. (1981). Black women in higher education: Power, commitment and leadership. In G. L. Mims (Ed.). *The minority administrator in higher education* (pp. 221-233). Cambridge: Schenkman Publishing.

Chapter 18

Writing Ourselves into History
Examining a World of Black Imaginings and Possibility

Tracy Cook-Person, with Djenaba Dekkatu and Quincy Merrill

> "Roast me! Hang me! Do whatever you please," said Brer Rabbit. "Only please, Brer Fox, please don't throw me into the briar patch."
>
> "The briar patch, eh?" said Brer Fox. "What a wonderful idea! You'll be torn into little pieces!"
>
> Grabbing up the tar-covered rabbit, Brer Fox swung him around and around and then flung him head over heels into the briar patch. Brer Rabbit let out such a scream as he fell that all of Brer Fox's fur stood straight up. Brer Rabbit fell into the briar bushes with a crash and a mighty thump. Then there was silence.
>
> Brer Fox cocked one ear toward the briar patch, listening for whimpers of pain. But he heard nothing. Brer Fox cocked the other ear toward the briar patch, listening for Brer Rabbit's death rattle. He heard nothing.
>
> Then Brer Fox heard someone calling his name. He turned around and looked up the hill. Brer Rabbit was sitting on a log combing the tar out of his fur with a wood chip and looking smug.
>
> "I was bred and born in the briar patch, Brer Fox," he called. "Born and bred in the briar patch."
>
> And Brer Rabbit skipped away as merry as a cricket while Brer Fox ground his teeth in rage and went home.
>
> (Abridged excerpt from "Br'er Rabbit and the Tar Baby"—African American Folktale)

Obama as a Talisman of Success

The Br'er Rabbit folktales always represented to me the ways in which the peoples of the African diaspora have developed brilliant ways to survive and thrive. In the deepest snare, Br'er Rabbit had the ability to think beyond the snares that were set for him and prosper in the face of adversity.

I am fascinated by narrative and the power that it has to transport us and take us to another level. The stories that we tell ourselves inform who we believe we are and help us to understand who it is we believe we can be.

Reflecting on the impact of the Obama candidacy and presidency, I think of how I felt the night of the presidential election. Obama's candidacy shook the nation. On Election Day—as I stood inside the voting booth with my two-year-old daughter in her stroller and one of my young sons, his hand beneath mine so that we could pull the lever together—I thought about what might change. I hoped the change would be real and everlasting. My husband stood in another booth with our other son poised to help make history as well. He was a black man, voting with his son, for another black man.

I thought about all my elders, known and unknown, who had toiled and struggled, never dreaming this day might come. The elders of my family had passed on a responsibility to me to excel beyond limitations and take others with me. Obama's election that night was not a message for me that black people had arrived. Rather, it was a call for me to push myself further so that I could make a path for others, stretching boundaries so that they too might achieve.

Story Is My Family's Tool and Legacy

I come from a long line of storytellers and from a culture of storytelling people who used the spoken word and narrative to teach and inspire. My extended family on both sides has many storytellers and jokesters. The gift of story as a motivating tool is the legacy of my southern roots on both sides.

I have always loved stories. As the child of academics, words both spoken and written were important in my household. I was an early reader. My mother told me that I was reading at the age of three, and that an early reading child meant a child who asked lots of questions. Each time my family meets, the same stories are trotted out again. Each time the stories are told, they grow. From the legacy of American slavery, my family has forged itself into a family that excels. The stories of how my ancestors have achieved excellence are told and passed down to my children, who can look back and understand who they are and will be within this society.

My family has used stories both spoken and written interchangeably to create for ourselves a vision of hope born of my ancestors on both sides who dreamt of freedom.

> *They went to the ceiling and Ntikuma said the magic words,*
> *"Let-it-be-full-and-eat."*
> *The pot became full with groundnut soup, meat and fufu which they ate.*
> *He repeated the words several times and each time the pot became full.*
> —"The Pot and the Whip" (Excerpted from *12 Great Ananse Stories*)

Learning to Dream Big: Lessons My Parents Taught Me

Manifesting our abundance is something that people of the African Diaspora have believed in historically. "Making a way out of no way" is just another way to talk about dreaming big. My parents were the first few in their families to gain a college education. The promise of the Civil Rights Movement gave my parents a platform of possibility allowing them to create a vision of excellence and forward motion that they shared with both their children and their surrounding community. They shared this vision first as community workers and then as educators. What they could envision, what they could dream, they could manifest. Their thoughts became actions, and their actions made their desires concrete.

As a child, when I watched television or read books, I rarely saw myself reflected in the media or in popular culture. Each new black figure who entered the world of politics, entertainment, or sports was a big achievement that preoccupied my friends and myself endlessly. Initially, popular culture for me was a place where those who looked like me were largely absent. In many ways, this absence acted as a catalyst, along with my parents' supplemental information, for me to dream big about what those fictional worlds would be like if I, or someone like me, were present in them.

I felt compelled to reconfigure the worlds of fiction and popular culture, writing stories about myself, pretending to host shows starring myself, and giving commentary on the world from my point of view. It was a sweet narcissism that I now know was necessary for building my strong self-concept. When I was not constructing my own fictions, I spent time re-writing the endings to novels for adolescents by authors like Carolyn Keene. I was convinced that the novelist had somehow missed something by not including me in her work. I re-wrote endings to the Nancy Drew mystery stories, introducing myself as a character. While I did have access to resources and my parents were well educated, Nancy Drew and her friends had the level of agency that I wished to have. They spoke their minds and were listened to, and their escapades formed in me a desire to travel the world and have the type of adventures like those in the novels.

> *We are climbing Jacob's Ladder*
> *We are climbing Jacob's Ladder*
> *We are climbing Jacob's Ladder, soldiers of the cross*
>
> *Ev'ry round goes higher, higher*
> *Ev'ry round goes higher, higher*
> *Ev'ry round goes higher, higher, soldiers of the cross*
>
> —Negro spiritual c. 1825

Teaching Others to Dream Bigger:
Educating Black Children during the Obama Era

When I became an ELA teacher in the New York City public school system in the early 2000s, I became acutely aware of the narrow scope of my black and brown students' imagination. Although many of my students did well in their studies, they seemed to lack an expansiveness of thought that allowed them to imagine themselves to be successful in diverse settings. When challenged, they gave up easily and they didn't hunger to try new things. Out-of-the-ordinary experiences to them were weird or meant for white people only.

Some of my students were the children of parents who were recent immigrants to the country. Their parents came to give their children access to the "American dream." It was difficult for some of them to navigate the rules of social mobility in this country. They struggled to help their children gain the agency needed to become assertive about creating their own success. The pathways they created for their children were narrow and usually only about making money in practical ways. Some of my students came from families that had suffered from generational oppression. They struggled with a kind of learned helplessness that caused them to believe that advancement was impossible and working toward advancement was futile. In a country where people are encouraged to live out their dreams, where was the space for my black and brown students to do just that?

Unlike in my youth where we struggled to see ourselves mirrored in the media, my students were inundated with images of blackness in the media. Many of the images they received were either far outside the scope of their own life experiences and felt unobtainable to them; others mirrored the hopelessness and helplessness of their lived experiences, reinforcing the notion that they shouldn't try hard to excel.

Obama's candidacy, and subsequent presidency, influenced both mine and my students' lives dramatically from the very beginning. Just the thought that a black man could win the presidency in this country, a country still unwilling to have deep soul-cleansing dialogues about racism, was enough to stir up my students. It spurred me to open my own boundaries as a teacher, and the curriculum I created from that point on was filled with themes meant to spur the activism of my students and to promote student voice. Obama showed himself to be the epitome of intellectual class and calm. He was someone whom my students could look up to, but they could also relate to him. He had grown up without his father; he had struggled with his identity and had improved his status in life through education, becoming first a lawyer and, later, the consummate politician.

Most of the students whom I taught during this time-period have done well in their careers and in their lives. Many of them have become educators in their own rights. Here, two of my students share their feelings about how they were inspired to dream bigger by the Obama era and by me. They also share how they are inspiring their post-Obama-generation students to dream bigger in a time where we may be losing ground.

It Takes a Village to Raise a Child: Obama Yes, but the Village Makes It Happen

Tracy Cook-Person, with Djenaba Dekattu

Djenaba Dekattu is a 29-year-old NYC public school teacher. When I first knew her as a vibrant 13-year-old girl in my 9th-grade English class, I saw the seeds of the life-changing educator she has become. Supporting her through the tragic loss of her mother and continuing to mentor her, as she mentors others, has taught me that the power of helping others manifest their greatness comes with the infinite reward of lasting connection.

Djenaba Dekattu: Teachers are as essential as parents in the village that raises children. Teachers also create safe havens for children who are suffering physically, verbally, and emotionally at home. I was a teenager during the beginning of the Obama administration and I had no idea how important and impactful that time period or the relationship between a teacher and myself could be until tragedy struck my life. Tracy, as my English honors teacher, took me under her wing and helped shape the person I am today. She nurtured me emotionally, showing me how to use poetry as an outlet to express my feelings and to carry out the political activism first taught to me by the mother I lost in my adolescence.

To this day I model myself after her; I aspire to be for my students what she was to me. I allow my students to express themselves free of judgment and encourage them to question everything, including my teaching. The Obama administration taught us that many things were possible. I empower my students not to allow their circumstances and situations to dictate who they are and who they can become, much as Tracy taught me during that specific time in my life.

Pushing beyond Capacity

TRACY COOK-PERSON, WITH QUINCY MERRILL

Quincy Merrill was the young black man whom we often label a "statistic." Coming from a challenging home life, poorly skilled, and possessing a cavalier attitude about both his school work and his future, he was the epitome of the type of student the system gives up on. His narrative below illustrates not only the power of pushing students beyond their perceived capacities, but also the power of the individual, once he believes he can change himself to effect change in others.

Quincy Merrill: Tracy was my high school English teacher, mentor, and mother figure. She not only pushed me beyond what I believed to be my full potential; she also made me believe in myself with confidence that I had the ability to do anything that I put my mind to. I went from being in a remedial English class, reading below my grade level, to doing work on a college level, and I progressed quickly within one year. I went from having a GPA of a 2.0 to a 3.4! Tracy told me, "Quincy, it is more than okay to dream BIG!" I dreamed about going to a college but never thought that I could go. I had little money and no blueprint. She pushed me beyond my boundaries and gave me confidence in myself to push to the highest peaks. In my senior year, I was accepted to Morehouse College with multiple scholarships to help pay 75% of my tuition, a miracle within itself.

The election of President Barack Obama happened during my sophomore year in college and it was a point where we saw something that many of us never thought would happen. Seeing an African American as the leader of our country for the first time in American history, and being a college student at an HBCU, created so many other possibilities in our minds that the floodgates opened for young African American scholars to not only chase our dreams, but to also know that there aren't any limitations. To see so many young first-time voters, and myself being one of them, at the age of 19, meant a lot. My first voting experience was for a president who looked like me, who won! Who would have thought? Seeing President Obama win lit a fire in all of us that I continue to see in my former classmates as we push the limits, earning higher degrees. We are pushing for higher career positions and opening doors for others.

I became a teacher right after graduating from college. I taught 5th grade through 12th and, in those years of teaching, I made sure to put my students first while tending to their needs and their strengths; I gave them the power to believe and build their confidence from years of not loving to learn, facing multiple struggles in the classroom and with little celebration of success. I gave them everything that was given to me and more. I am paying for those who came before me and made it possible for me to dream BIG— made it possible for me to become the person I am today and provide others the opportunity to dream. Today, my students truly believe they have a future, the same way I was taught to believe I had one.

Visioning the Future Post-Obama Era

Obama's election was a watershed moment in American history and for people of the African diaspora. After eight years of an administration that was complex and gave hope to many African Americans' dreams for achievement and recognition in this country, we are now experiencing a political and social shift backward with the current administration. As our current administration moves us further away from the advances of the Obama era, Americans should ask as a nation, and African Americans should ask as a people, what it all meant.

What does the future hold for black people? The question of how we are continuing to dream big and move forward with intention is more important now than ever. Beyond dreaming, how is the current generation of black educators aiding young people in analyzing the present climate and preparing for the future?

During my second year of teaching, I dreamed that the students in my care were like drops of rain in a river. As each student hit the pool of water, their impact had a ripple effect that spread. Suddenly, the landscape of the dream changed, and the students whom I was teaching became teachers of their own accord, and these students moved forward to teach when I was old and no longer in the classroom. The dream felt so real at the time that I still remember it vividly the feel of its impact. Years later, it has come to pass, and I am no longer in the public school classroom. I am an educator of teachers, and the dream is being enacted. Many of the children whom I pushed to dream bigger are teaching, expanding the world for those in their care. The toxic social climate has become dangerous at times for black people. The Obama era gave us a picture of success that we hadn't expected, but ultimately, we can decide individually how to continue that momentum. In his autobiography, Malcolm X states:

> It's a crime, the lie that has been told to generations of black men and white men both. Little innocent black children, born of parents who believed that their race had no history. Little black children seeing, before they could talk, that their parents considered themselves inferior. Innocent black children growing up, living out their lives, dying of old age—and all of their lives ashamed of being black. But the truth is pouring out of the bag now. (History Is A Weapon, n.d., n. pag.)

Therefore, it is imperative that **we** continue to keep telling our stories and push forward to write ourselves into history.

References

Ankrah, G.N.D. (2007). *12 great Ananse stories.* Accra: GhanaSam Wood-Ltd.

History Is A Weapon. (n.d.). *Excerpts from the Autobiography of Malcolm X.* Available: http://www.historyisaweapon.com/defcon1/malcolmeduc.html

Scholsser, S.E. (2004). *Spooky South: Tales of hauntings, strange happenings, and other lore.* Guilford, CT: Globe Pequot Press.

CHAPTER 19

On Being a Biracial Woman of Black and Puerto Rican Descent
A Mother Reflects on a Mother-Daughter Conversation

Patricia Isaac

IN A SPEECH delivered at the Philadelphia Constitutional Center on March 18, 2008, Senator Barack Obama stated:

> I am the son of a black man from Kenya and a white woman from Kansas. I was raised with the help of a white grandfather who survived a Depression to serve in Patton's Army during World War II and a white grandmother who worked on a bomber assembly line at Fort Leavenworth while he was overseas. I've gone to some of the best schools in America and lived in one of the world's poorest nations. I am married to a black American who carries within her the blood of slaves and slaveowners — an inheritance we pass on to our two precious daughters. I have brothers, sisters, nieces, nephews, uncles and cousins of every race and every hue, scattered across three continents, and for as long as I live, I will never forget that in no other country on Earth is my story even possible. (Talk of the Nation, 2008, n. p.)

Although he does not use the word biracial in the above excerpt, Barack Obama is conscious of his biracial identity. Even though he self-identifies as a black man—African American, his biracial identity, as half black and half white, played an important role both during his electoral campaign and throughout his presidency. For some blacks, he was not black enough, whereas for some whites he was black as black could be. Obama is not the only biracial personality of African descent to identify himself as a black man. Biracial celebrities of white-African descent, such as Alicia Keys, Colin Kaepernick, Don Lemon, etc., also identify themselves as African Americans. The identification of biracial black people as black has been attributed to "the legacy of racist laws that relied on the so-called 'one-drop rule,' which dictated that even a tiny amount of black ancestry meant a person was considered black" (Kellogg Insights, 2017, n.p.). Whereas biracial blacks of white-African descent seem to have a historical context to draw upon to self-identify as either "black" or "African American," to date, no historical explanation has been advanced to either classify or identify other multiracial children (i.e., born from unions of black and Latin Americans, black and Middle Easterners, blacks and Eastern Europeans, Black and Asian parents, etc.). As an African American woman and mother of a biracial child of black and Latin American ancestries, I frequently find myself pondering how my daughter and other children like her, i.e., from a union of black and non-white ethnic/non-black parents, (1) perceive their racial identity, and (2) are treated by peers and society. For this chapter, I am offering to share from an interview I had with my biracial daughter of African American and Puerto Rican descent. My hope is that parents in a similar situation and educators can gain some insight into how these children's educational experiences shape their racial and professional identities.

Background

I wish to welcome the reader to a conversation I had with my daughter, Melissa, as she and I explored her struggles, her joys, and her journey in general as a biracial woman growing up in America. I have always been a single mother and raised my two biracial children. However, it hadn't occurred to me to tell this story, as I first thought it was too personal. It was during the deeper conversation I had with my daughter that I gained a new perspective on her life as a biracial "African AmeRícan," to borrow Tato Laviera's (2014) AmeRícan concept and felt that sharing it might help children who share her background to achieve self-understanding and acceptance.

I always thought our struggles as women of color would be similar, but after listening to my daughter I realized how dissimilar our experiences with racial identity were because she was raised and walked in two worlds—mine and her father's. Her self-identity is not only shaped by her self-perceptions, but also by society's perceptions of her. I see my daughter's life as a personal journey, a "personal diaspora" in spreading, extending her life beyond society's perceptions to be the woman who she is and has become, i.e., an African AmeRícan who:

> salutes all folklores,
> European, Indian, Black, Spanish
> and anything else compatible.
>
> (excerpted from Tato Laviera, 2014, AmeRícan, n.p.)

It was just a few months after the triumphant exit of the 44th president that Melissa and I had an interview and a candid discussion by phone, since we are bi-coastal. She lives in Oregon, where she went from being a chef to working in human resources. I live in Upstate New York. As a mother of two biracial children, I was concerned about how they were perceived both by the American society and themselves. For more than 30 years, I lived in New Mexico and Arizona, but our larger family resides in different boroughs of New York City.

The Study's Structure

This chapter explores my daughter's life experiences as a black and Puerto Rican woman in America. Initially it was to be presented in a non-intrusive dialogue-interview format. This format was deemed suitable because it would have allowed her to take ownership of her story. In the end, it was agreed upon that the findings would be presented in summary form to respect the interviewee's request. A condensed "Mother's thoughts" summary, which comprises reflections on her daughter's accounts, follows each summary of findings. Some of the issues we discussed include: where our lives differ as women of color, how my being African American and her being African American and Puerto Rican were different, the places where our life experiences intersected, and what she learned from her mother on being a woman of color. Principles from grounded theory, critical race theory, and critical discourse analysis guided the data analysis and interpretation.

Mother-Daughter Conversation

On racially self-identifying. Melissa states that in her early years she was able to embrace her biracial/bi-cultural identity as a black and Puerto Rican woman, which she attributed to her New York experience. In her adult life, however, perhaps due to change in geographic location, that innocent perception changed. She remarked that when asked about her race, on surveys, which restricted someone to choosing between black or non-Hispanic, she puts "other," instead, to hold onto both sides of her family and keep her identity alive. Among her earliest memories of diversity was the time when "Mother dyed my Raggedy Ann doll brown"; she could not understand why Mom dyed her doll brown. Moreover, she noted the fact that Mom bought books with black children characters. In hindsight, she appreciated the fact that Mom did the best she could at the time for her to see someone like her. She interpreted Mom's act as "her" wish to have black dolls—dolls that look liked her. Melissa affirmed to "still have that Raggedy Ann doll."

Mother's thoughts: Melissa seemed frustrated that she should be asked to self-identify as "other" on census-survey forms. It annoyed her that while there was "multiracial" category, there was no "biracial" category (e.g., African American-Non-Hispanic or African-American-Hispanic). As I reflected more in-depth about her concern, it dawned on me that both Latinos and African Americans have multiracial identities (i.e., comprised of white, black and Native American heritage for blacks, and white, black and indigenous people of the Americas for Latinos). Her discussion of dolls reminded me of the look of surprise on her face when I was dying the doll brown. She was three years old, but that look still stays in my memory, and she still remembers.

On being a black and Puerto Rican child and woman. Melissa's understanding of black Puerto Rican woman or Afro-Latina identity is that of someone who "has interaction in that world—someone who lives in that world, can speak Spanish and embodies a lot of different parts of her culture." Having lived in Portland for almost 20 years, she does not feel that she completely fits into the Afro-Latina world; she feels a little more on the outside even though her Puerto Rican family has embraced her and helped her want to keep that part of her alive. As a result, she finds her Puerto Rican identity important.

Mother's thoughts: I can understand Melissa's position. My family and her father's family grew up together in the projects in Bedford-Stuyvesant, Brooklyn. I'm proud that she has such a warm connection to her Puerto Rican family and heritage. I respect her choice and decision to construct her own identity. She is who she is.

On how society has made her feel about her identity. For some reason, this prompt brought up in Melissa's memory the TV show *90210*, which featured white, rich teenagers. This kind of misportrayal of ethnicity made it difficult for her to self-identify until *In Living Color* aired and made it a little easier for her to identify with characters of color who were successful.

Mother's thoughts: I understand her taking issue with the framing of people of color in movies and TV shows as unsuccessful. I agree with her observation that successful people of color are not acknowledged enough in the mainstream discourse.

On schooling as a teenage girl. This seemed to be a sensitive period for Melissa. She recalled that it was a period of lots of insecurities and challenges of being a teenager, with most girls getting pregnant in high school. She recalled how the busing practice of African American and Mexican children to a predominantly white high school contributed to a lot of racial fighting among girls and made her not want to identify with being black. Because she had a mixed group of friends, i.e., both in high school and the trailer park kids, she did not want to take sides, unlike her biracial black-white friend who did not want to identify with being African American.

Mother's thoughts: Melissa reveals some of the reasons why she does not self-identify as black. It is mainly because of the experiences that she had in school, watching fights. Although she was not alone to feel that way, she did not view blackness as a negative thing, which is a good thing.

Words of wisdom for biracial girls. Melissa's message to biracial children is to keep moving forward and not allow others to dictate abilities of what they can or cannot do based on their race or cultural heritage.

Mother's thoughts: Melissa has grown to be her own person, beyond her ethnic makeup. It is a quality that minority parents should instill in their children. At no time should racial identity be used as an excuse for what a child can or cannot achieve.

On misconceptions in the workplace. Melissa claims that experience has taught her to try to be comfortable in her own skin. She remarks, "If I internalized people's prejudices, I would have shriveled up and been unable to survive." She learned to go beyond the culinary industry's stereotypical expectation of African American women as being light and jovial and, therefore, being the right type of person for the business. Well aware that being upset feeds into the stereotype, she opts to comport herself in an assertive manner.

Mother's thoughts: Melissa raises an important point; black women are forced to pay attention to society's expectations of their demeanor and performance. I find her "don't care" attitude to be a good way to handle societal pressure.

On working as a chef in the culinary world. Melissa acknowledged that being a *woman* was the biggest challenge she has had when it came to her career. She attributed her strength of character to her maternal grandmother, who taught her that there was a certain way to behave in society. Thanks to her grandmother's teachings, she has learned "to be proud of who you are and what you are putting across without being superficial. If you can't accept all of me, then you don't need to be with me." Having worked as a chef in a kitchen where women are not well regarded, she vows to do all in her power to be successful, no matter what people may think or say. She remarked that the culinary world was fraught with more female/gender issues than ethnic identity issues, in particular being Afro-Latina. She remarked that she had to grow a thick skin and learn to brush off, from within, the misogynistic attitude of men who worked under her orders. Her message to them was clear: either "deal with me or leave"; she was well aware that in the kitchen, she had to adopt an "I don't have time to deal with you" attitude.

Mother's thoughts: Melissa's attitude toward workplace space has been influenced by the misogyny she observed in the culinary world. However, her response to that has been shaped by values and lessons she learned from her grandmother—my mother. This is a true testament to the importance of family values.

On acceptance in family and community. Melissa has retained great memories of love and acceptance by members within her direct family, but not so outside of her family. On the one hand, she remembered her aunt once saying that she and her brother had such lovely accents. On the other hand, she did not seem to forget the kids in the black community who did not embrace her as much as she would have liked because she "did not talk like them" and therefore called her "geek" and "weird." Growing up in an environment where guys minimized girls with darker skin, she learned to *not* view her having "nice hair and light skin" in a positive light. Instead, it made her feel uncomfortable. She associated life in her Brooklyn neighborhood with bittersweet memories.

Mother's thoughts: It is unfortunate that her experience in the Brooklyn community was not always positive so that she could feel proud of her blackness. It is comforting that her family was there to reinforce love and acceptance.

On Obama's identity as biracial. Surprisingly, Obama's history-making presidential victory did not strike her as the victory of biracial people, but rather minority people being able "to do this, to go this far!"

Mother's thoughts: Although Melissa may not identify as either black, Puerto Rican, or biracial, she at least identified with Obama as a racial minority who made history and made her proud.

Insights and Takeaway

There were several things I learned from the interview-dialogue I had with my daughter. First and foremost, I never realized that society perceived my daughter differently than it perceived me. I did not realize that her Puerto Rican side was viewed differently by society. While she comes through as a woman of color, her biracial makeup subjected her to a different treatment from me. I could not relate to her checking the "other" box on job applications and census surveys, for example. I could not relate to her frustration when people, due to ignorance, assigned her a different ethnic identity such as Mexican or Middle Easterner because of the color of her skin or the texture of her hair. She was treated differently as a child by neighborhood kids in Brooklyn because she did not act like them, as if she was not expected to be friendly and open to new people. In high school, she was bullied by black kids because she did not look or speak like them.

In reflecting on the interview, it also became clear that I had not fully understood her life. I did not and could not prepare her for the different worlds she encountered because, as much as she shared my blood, I was ethnically different from her. Additionally, she grew up in different family environments and was exposed to different cultural models—Puerto Rican and African American. I cannot claim that I am the sole person who prepared her for life as a woman of color. My mother, as she constantly refers to her grandmother, and other women in my family and her father's side of the family, certainly contributed to giving her life's foundation.

Another unanticipated realization that came to light was that Melissa's greatest battle was fought along the lines of gender. Since she worked in the culinary industry, which is a male-dominant business, she had to stand up for herself and command respect. That strong spirit and sense of self were learned from the women in her life. Just as she credits her maternal grandmother for teaching her to carry herself in public with confidence, so does she cherish her Puerto Rican family and retain a warm and welcoming connection with them.

Conclusions, Implications, and Recommendations

Through this mother-daughter dialogue, Melissa affirms that family is essential in helping a (biracial) child feel accepted in society. Despite the mixed messages given by society, what the child becomes is a result of his or her processing of the tips and clues from family members. Therefore, it is important that parents and relatives, especially, mothers, grandmothers, and aunts, in the case of girls' upbringing, take role modeling seriously. For as the famous poem by Dorothy Nolte (1976) highlights, children do learn what they live.

> Where she encountered criticism
> Melissa learned to condemn.
> Where she experienced hostility,
> Melissa learned to fight.
> When ridiculed
> she learned to be shy.

> When she received encouragement,
> she learned to be confident.
> And when she felt accepted,
> she learned to love.
> (Adapted from Dorothy Nolte's poem "Children Learn What They Live")

Parents of biracial children need to allow their children to explore all sides of their heritage, particularly during adolescence when they go through stages of identity confusion as they are trying to find their place in society.

Educators need to be vigilant and not assume that biracial children have no acceptance issues. According to Bellamy-Walker (2015), citing a Clemson University report (Limber, 2013), *Status of Bullying in School*, of 160,000 students who are bullied every day, 31% are multiracial. It is noted that multiracial and biracial students are victims of racial slurs, cyberbullying, and harassment.

Educators and policy makers need to create a classroom environment that is safe and inclusive by allowing for multiple opportunities for students of all racial backgrounds to explore their own and each other's heritage through culturally responsive activities, such as project-based learning on genealogy and family history.

There is power in self-identifying. Just like former president Barack Obama and other black-white children have the flexibility to self-identify as African Americans, biracial and multiracial children of black-non-white makeup need to be afforded the same right. The strength of character starts with identity affirmation. Biracial children of color ought to know and be proud of who they are if we are to teach them to dream big and reach high like our first-ever black first family, Barack and Michelle Obama.

References

Bellamy-Walker, T. (2015, October 8). Multiracial girls open up about getting bullied. *We*.news. Retrieved from: https://womensenews.org/2015/10/multi-racial-girls-open-up-about-getting-bullied/

Kellogg Insights. (2017, Dec. 6). How are black-white biracial people perceived in terms of race? Available: https://insight.kellogg.northwestern.edu/article/how-are-black-white-biracial-people-are-perceived-in-terms-of-race

Laviera, T. (2014). AmeRícan. In Laviera, T. *Bendición: The complete poetry of Tato Laviera.* Houston, TX: Arte Público Press. https://www.poetryfoundation.org/poems/58197/american

Limber, S. P. (2013). *Bullying in US Schools: 2012 Status Report.* Hazelden Foundation. Available: http://citeseerx.ist.psu.edu/viewdoc/download?doi=10.1.1.641.9457&rep=rep1&type=pdf

Madden, M., Lenhart, A., Duggan, M., Cortesi, S., & Gasser, U. (2013). Teens and bullying in US schools: 2013 Status report. Clemson University: Hazelden Foundation.

Nolte, D. L. (1976). Children learn what they live. In Anfield, J., & Wells, H. C. (eds.), *100 ways to enhance self-concept in the classroom: A handbook for teachers and parents.* Boston: Allyn & Bacon.

Talk of the Nation. (2008). *Obama and the politics of being biracial.* National Public Radio. Retrieved from https://www.npr.org/templates/story/story.php?storyId=98455533

Chapter 20

To Dream the Impossible Dream

Lindamichelle Baron

ON NOVEMBER 22, 1963, I was in my junior high school math class, when the loudspeaker interrupted the lesson with the sound of a TV news personality. I don't remember the school principal framing what we were about to hear. I only remember the solemn voice of the newscaster, reporting that at 12:30 pm President John F. Kennedy had been shot in Dallas, Texas. Our class of 12- and 13-year-olds was stunned. Our president had been assassinated.

John F. Kennedy was a president many of us in the class felt we knew and whom we even felt we loved. He was young for a president of the United States and seemed younger than our parents. He had a beautiful, stylish wife and two young children. At church, luncheons, and other such occasions, many of the ladies, our mothers and others, wore pillbox hats, popularized by the First Lady, Jackie Kennedy. There was even a song parody that most of us knew as written by a seven-year-old singer, Jo Anne Morse, from the perspective of one of his children, Caroline. The song made the president seem even more connected to us.

> *My daddy is president.*
> *What does your daddy do?*
> *We live in a big white house on Pennsylvania Avenue.*
> *I always play beneath the desk in Daddy's den,*
> *When I play hide-and-seek with Secret Service men.*
> (Presidential History Geeks, 2015)

I felt another connection as a young black girl. The president had a relationship to the issues of black people, who were called *Negro*s at that time. We believed he supported our cause, the Civil Rights Movement and its motto that "black and white together, we shall overcome someday." We saw him consult with Reverend Martin Luther King Jr. about the terrors of race hatred and segregation in the South. Many of our parents spoke of him in glowing terms. It was as if we believed he was our "great white hope."

Yes, we were devastated over the news of his assassination. The only break in our trance was the disconnected voice of our math teacher asking us something about the time difference between Texas and New York. I don't believe this could be described as a teachable moment. This was not the right time to change the discourse to something so insignificant in the wake of such devastating news. But this was a time in history in which there were many teachable moments. There was the uproar throughout black and white America, when a charismatic black Muslim, Malcolm X, took the announcement of President Kennedy's assassination as an opportunity to chastise the country, announcing, "The chickens were coming home to roost." There was the surprise when President Lyndon Johnson, a southerner, supported and signed the Civil Rights Act. There were sides drawn in an escalating conflict between the philosophies of non-violence, and militancy. A few years later, President Kennedy's brother, Bobby (Robert) Kennedy, as attorney general, made a prediction that seemed absurd at the time. "There's no question about it," he said; "in the next 40 years a Negro can achieve the same position that my brother had." As we now know, his prophecy became reality in 2008.

But at the time those words were spoken, Bobby Kennedy's statement seemed more like the perfunctory impossibility we often wrote in our essays, or heard our teachers recite to us, that all of us could become the president of the United States. No need to say black and brown children. We knew who we were and discounted those words as less than fiction. It meant as much to us as saying one day I'll become a millionaire.

Reverend Dr. Martin Luther King Jr. had a dream rather than a prediction that his "four children will one day live in a nation where they will not be judged by the color of their skin but by the content of their character." Dr. King's dream seemed aspirational, something we could aim toward. That dream resonated. Made sense. Seemed at least remotely possible. Many of us believed that if we spoke articulately enough, dressed professionally enough, wore our hair straight enough, were educated enough, and maybe even lightened our skins enough, America, white America, would do as Langston Hughes espoused in his poem—that we would be invited to join the whites at the table as a true American. I, too, shared that sentiment.

Tomorrow,
I'll be at the table
When company comes
Nobody'll say "eat in the kitchen."
Then.

Besides
They'll see how beautiful I am
And be ashamed—
I, too, am America.
(excerpted from Langston Hughes' poem, "I Too Am America" (2004)

There were others of us who believed we did not have to sit at the table. During this period, militancy and racial separation were considered options to a civil rights agenda of integration through non-violent activism. One expression of this sentiment was the Black Panther Party, which emerged under the direction of Huey P. Newton and Bobby Seale. Another expression to the options contrary to the Civil Rights agenda of non-violence was the Black Muslims, under the Honorable Elijah Muhammad, which prescribed separation from what they considered the "white devil." Malcolm X, then a Black Muslim minister, extolled "the right to be a human being, to be respected as a human being in this society, on this earth, which we intend to bring into existence," and he ended the sentence with "by any means necessary." During this same period Stokely Carmichael of the political civil rights group SNCC (The Student Non-Violent Coordinating Committee) used a phrase that exemplified Black Nationalism, in which he called for "Black Power." And many newly minted revolutionaries responded with "Right on!" and "Power to the People."

Ironically, this was also a period of black self-imposed limitations. As we fought for freedom so that we could become "free at last, free at last" some of us determined we would be in charge of our ethnic identity, reframing and renaming Negro to black. There were those of us of African descent who believed in *the Black Aesthetic*, a movement based on the cultural politics of Black Nationalism. This movement defined and identified what it meant to be black with acceptable belief systems, hairstyles, clothing, and even childnaming practices. African and Muslim names were preferred in place of those considered "slave names."

Even sports, music, housing, and any number of other preferences seemed to be rated in terms of degrees of blackness. Song lyrics even questioned, "Am I black enough for you?"

I wore Afro-centric attire, which usually included a head wrap called a "gele." Under my gele was a short natural hairstyle. Yet, I refused to change my name. Instead, I used linguistic subterfuge. I wrote my name Lindamichellebaron, rather than Linda Michelle Baron. I knew I would be assumed to have an African name, because as much as African names were in style, few had tolerance for sounding out multisyllabic names, so mine was often assumed to be from the continent. My poetry reverberated in themes from the Black Arts Movement. I was also an activist—and I still am. I wrote poetry about black identity, white racism, and black introspection. My poetry included the perfunctory epithets; the only way you and your art could be taken seriously was by spicing it up with curse words. In fact, according to the Encyclopedia Britannica, the Black Arts Movement adhered to the belief system and practice in which the literature of the movement was generally written in Black English vernacular and confrontational in tone, addressing such issues as interracial tension, sociopolitical awareness, and the relevance of African history and culture to blacks in the United States.

Much of my poetry from the late '60s through much of the '70s was embraced by my peers, because it fit the guidelines of the times. But at the same time, I was conflicted. The movement, the aesthetic seemed inhibiting. I wanted to write, and I wanted my writing to represent the many views and perspectives that I embraced. For example, I embraced the Harlem Renaissance. I was not just one section of the compendium of who I was as a person and an author; I was multifaceted as a black woman in this era. One of my poems, written in the '70s, speaks to this questioning and desire not to be constrained by racial identity.

I Wish I knew how it would feel to Be Black

I wish I knew how it would feel to be black.
Not act like or be like—just be black.
Some puppet show, no go!
Black with no strings attached.
Black without having to prove black.

I wish I knew how it would feel to be black.

So black—I wouldn't have to be beautiful.
So black—I could hide my pride.
So black—I could be anti or pro
whatever I feel.
So black—I could believe I am
black for real.

Excerpted from *Rhythm & Dues* by Lindamichellebaron (Baron, 2007, p. 18)

"So I would know, and know I knew how it feels . . . really feels to be me." How can we know which me, when we have called ourselves and been called so many things throughout our history? I, like so many of us of African descent, search and have been searching for our identity.

I remember I was comfortably colored and Negro, spelled with a capital "N." In fact, in the early 1960s my family and I flew to Jamaica, West Indies, to visit my grandmother. Before we landed, we were given a form to complete, indicating basic information including our nationality. In answer to the question of "nationality," I wrote "Negro." We were Negroes then. But that was not the answer required. For the purpose of international travel, the right answer was, "American."

Even though we knew we were Americans, and said the "Pledge of Allegiance" every morning in school, followed by "My country tis of thee, sweet land of liberty of thee I sing...," we knew that on many levels we weren't truly considered Americans. The Civil Rights Movement was designed to affirm our rights, even as the response to us by segments of society denounced those affirmations and proclaimed us "less than." In response we believed, at least many of us believed, we needed to prove ourselves "human" and "equal."

The Negro National Anthem, written by James Weldon Johnson, proclaimed our American history.

Sing a song full of the hope that the dark past has taught us.
Sing a song full of the faith that the present has brought us.

(Poetry Foundation, 2019)

That song announced our American heritage. Our dreams, our faith, our hopes are passionately embedded in the words. And yet, so much of this country's history cast us on the sidelines of America, despite all proof to the contrary.

Our dreams have been awakened and dashed, realized and destroyed by swings of the pendulum, over time . . . yay, then nay; ying, then yang. Yes, the amazing sense of unity when President Kennedy was assassinated. We seemed to come together as a nation. We then, again, felt a collective American spirit, even more powerfully, after September 11th, 2001. The horror of the "terrorist" attack linked us together. It was as if we all were united as one. We all bonded together in deep ways, except, of course, for the overreaction against Muslims, whether American or not, whether from a country from which some of the terrorists originated or not. The religion itself, and anyone who practiced it, were framed as terror-based. But black people who were not misidentified as Muslim, or who did not practice the faith, embraced America, land of the free and the home of the brave.

A few years later, the dream was shattered, again. We of African descent returned to the virtual back of the bus, back to the race-based underpinnings upon which this country was conceived. A horrific act of nature returned us to a status of less than. The victims of the hurricane (Katrina) became "predators," "villains," "thieves" and "murderers." American citizens, mainly black citizens, crying out for help, were described as "refugees." How did that happen? How deep was the disrespect, the devaluing of people of African descent, for Americans who were cast out of their city by a horrific act of nature to be called interlopers in their own land . . . losing their citizenship on every news report? Each of us was assaulted with the click of the remote. As Langston Hughes wrote:

> What happens to a dream deferred?
> Does it . . . like a heavy load
> Or does it explode?
>
> Excerpted from the poem "A Dream Deferred" (2004)

Some of us of African descent have exploded during various periods in our history, but not during the 2008 election cycle. Instead, American voters seemed to act out the American creed. The best person for the job won, judged by the content of his character, charisma, and wisdom. A dream we didn't dare to dream was realized. We felt empowered as Americans, again . . . the impossible dream had been manifested.

A man whose name extolled African and Muslim roots, Barack Hussein Obama, a first-generation descendant from the continent of Africa, became the 44th president of the United States of America. The ugliness of racism reared its head through verbal and visual assaults during both his candidacy and his presidency. It continued through the first administration as we approached the possibility of a second term. The ugly America, with the racism hidden on the surface and in the creases of the nation, continued exposing itself.

A seemingly arrogant, bigoted, white real estate developer began his introduction into the world of national politics by initiating a "birther" movement. His so-called campaign platform was built upon the false premise that President Obama was actually born out of the country, in Africa. His qualification to question any aspect of President Obama's presidency was the fact that he had his last name emblazoned on buildings that he owned or had owned; had access to large amounts of money, even after being bankrupted multiple times; and had coined a phrase, "You're fired," in the entertainment world. That race-based premise would make the president's election illegitimate. The taunts would not stop even after the president showed the country his actual birth certificate.

I sang a song full of the hope and the faith that our history has taught and brought us. At the same time, I felt the disappointment of one who recognized that this was the same hate, the same disrespect for the leader of the "free world," because of his ethnicity. There were many supporters of President Obama, but serious hate-filled individuals, including judges and politicians who attempted to end our 44th president's legacy by blaming him for the inability to walk on water. If he had been able to do so, they would have criticized him for not being able to swim.

The viciousness continued during President Obama's run for a second term. A news show scanned signs of some who picketed against him. One sign read, "Vote. Don't Re-nig!"

Who would have thought that America could take what was proclaimed to be the postracial/racist era, with the two-term election of a scholarly, insightful, classy president and beautiful family, and create an electorate who voted into power a man who presents himself as a classless denier of truth, justice, and the

American way? Yes, a classless denier of truth, justice, and the American way is (mis)leading America when an amazing prepared contender, a woman of virtue, ready to take the job was left to wonder how it happened.

I have agonized over the loss of the election by the eminently prepared presidential candidate, Hillary Rodham Clinton. I continue to ask God to bless America, the land that I love. But there is a pain. There is a pain stuck in my skin that continues to make me bleed when I least expect it. The pain of subliminal and blatant attacks pokes and sticks my American spirit. And yet, I continue to sing a song full of the hope and the faith that has taught and brought us. Adam Clayton Powell encouraged us to "keep the faith, baby!" I will (and I) continue to pray for the presidency and for our country (United States House of Representatives, n.d.).

Although I do not consider myself political, I do vote in every election. Voting is more than a right; I see it as my responsibility. There were too many lost lives and horrific interactions during the fight for that right. I will not relinquish my right to vote under any circumstance. I had a visceral response when I heard a young black man who was part of the Black Lives Matter movement say, during the 2012 election, "I won't vote until black lives matter." He was oblivious to his history, to our history. I realize I must ensure that our young people are made aware of the sacrifices that give us this opportunity that so many Americans take for granted.

I must also make donations and sign petitions for candidates I believe in, regardless of the party. My most recent unconditional support was for the "two termed" president of the United States, Obama, and for Hillary Rodham Clinton.

There is something else I'm expected to do. The expectation was presented to me by a prestigious politician in our community who "sought me out" at an event. She did not want to discuss politics. Instead, she recounted a dream she had that included me.

The dream was compelling. According to her, both she and I were at a large body of water where children were drowning a long way from the shore. She said that in her dream I was far into the massive water, near the children, grabbing them and handing them over to her. Together we were saving the children.

The dream must have been real, if we can describe a dream as reality. Most politicians would not recount a dream with someone other than themselves as the hero. They would more likely cast themselves as the activist pulling the children in to safety. Instead, the dream as she described it has me as the risk-taker, saving the children with her assisting.

I do believe that dreams hold meaning. Does the dream foretell a path I need to follow in order to make a more significant impact on our children? Is this my call to action above and beyond what I can see for myself? The dream particularly resonated with me because my life has always involved children. All of my summers from late high school through college I have worked with young people as a counselor, group leader, or teacher. I taught for years in an elementary school and am now a performing author and professional developer in my own business. I am also in academia now. I have been a chairperson and a faculty member in the Department of Teacher Education, responsible for educating future teachers, who will have the lives of the children in their hands. I embrace the challenge of growing educators who will make a difference in the lives of children. So, to be envisioned in a dream saving children is consistent with my sense of purpose.

Dr. James Comer (1997), well-known psychologist and educational activist, cites a parable in his book *Waiting for a Miracle*. He tells of a ship's captain in the ocean where he sees a child drowning. He calls his first mate to help him use a life preserver to bring the young person to safety. Just as the child is pulled aboard, another child is sighted, then another and another. To the first mate's horror, the captain orders him to stop trying to save the children by pulling them on board the ship. The captain answers by saying, and I paraphrase, "We can't save all these children. We need to take the boat to the shore and see who is pushing them in." Unlike the captain, I feel the imperative to save our children in deep and profound ways. I don't know whether the politician's dream or the psychologist's parable holds the answer to how I must expand my capacity to make the necessary difference for our children. But I am certain that I am ready to do so "by any means necessary."

References

Baron, L. (2007). I wish I knew how it would feel. In *Rhythm & dues*. p. 18. New York: Harlin Jacque Publications.

Comer, J. (1997). *Waiting for a miracle: Schools are not our problem*. Boston: Dutton.

Editors of the Encyclopedia Britannica. *The Black Art Movement*. Available: https://www.britannica.com/event/Black-Arts-movement

Hughes, L. (2004). I, too. In Arnold Rampersad (Ed.). *The collected poems of Langston Hughes*. New York: Vintage Books.

Poetry Foundation. (2019). Lift every voice and sing. Retrieved from https://www.poetryfoundation.org/poems/46549/lift-every-voice-and-sing

Presidential History Geeks. (2015, August 14). Presidents in parody: My daddy is president. *Live Journal*. Available: https://potus-geeks.livejournal.com/625677.html

United States House of Representatives. (n.d.). Powell, Adam Clayton, Jr. Retrieved from https://history.house.gov/People/Listing/P/POWELL,-Adam-Clayton,-Jr--(P000477)/

SECTION V
CAN A BLACK MALE CHILD DREAM BIG IN A MELANIN-PHOBIC WORLD?

Chapter 21

Hope: President Barack Obama's Legacy to Black Children

Eleanor T. Campbell

THE 2008 ELECTION year was filled with excitement. The possibility of a black president of the U.S. would be a major feat and a great accomplishment. Our country was moving forward in so many positive ways, and the election of Barack Obama would be the pinnacle of Dr. King's "I Have a Dream" speech. A fully integrated United States where people would be judged by their character and not their skin color or religion would finally be realized. After all, we had experienced General Colin Powell as chairman of the Joint Chiefs of Staff, and Condoleezza Rice, secretary of state. On the streets of Harlem, I heard young black males say with pride that they would like to have a conversation with Obama—just to *"hang out with the brother."* The church sisters had prayer circles for him and young black men and women were wearing the coveted campaign slogan "Hope" buttons, volunteering for voter registration. I too did my part to register voters and to encourage my students to get out and vote no matter what candidate and exercise their rights as citizens. There was positive energy in the air, and it was a joy to experience. In fall 2008 the voting polls in my community of mostly black and brown people had long lines and yet there were smiles on the faces of everyone there. This year there was a real candidate to vote for, someone who looked like us and would hear our voices. There was a chance, a hope that change was coming. Looking forward this is the hope that we must instill in our youth for they are our future. Looking back is understanding our personal journey and how we got to where we are today.

My Story

My personal story like so many other African Americans is one of a history of hope from enslaved Africans to emancipation and reconstructing our lives from servant class to leadership status. It includes institutional racism and power struggles, terrorism and setbacks, Jim Crow laws, segregation, constitutional amendments and achievements, integration and black pride. Throughout it all we never lost hope and continued to experience positive changes. We are a resilient people.

Now I am a college professor of nursing with a bachelor's, two master's, and a doctoral degree. My journey here was borne out of the hope of my parents who each had only a high school education but dreams for their two daughters to be more than they were, both educationally and economically. We did achieve that dream through their constant encouragement, support, expectations, and hope. Both of my parents had the ability and drive to achieve but were hindered by the Jim Crow laws in the South where they were born and raised. Along with other African Americans they were a part of the Great Migration north to New York. They had hopes of having a better life free from the restrictions on voting, employment, education, etc., that southern laws enforced. Although they faced other forms of discrimination in New York City, their survival, dignity, and daily lives were not imperiled as in the South. They and their siblings who migrated north enjoyed different freedoms and developed black communities that supported their hopes. They married and had children who they hoped would have still greater advantages than they had.

As a young girl I was told of my worth, my inner beauty even though there were few positive media images like me on television, in magazines or movies. My parents and relatives instilled black pride in me and were my role models. During post-holiday meals my elders shared oral histories where I learned black history by first hearing about my own family history and came to understand myself. Knowing our history may mean learning what is not taught in school but in the home. Reading our authors who write about our past and present. Whatever our hope for our children we must work to instill that in them. My parents made sure that I had the resources to achieve academically and to compete with other children within and outside of my immediate neighborhood in a Harlem housing project—NYCHA despite the limited plans that mainstream America had for me.

The first positive image of a black women on television in the late 1960s was a nurse portrayed by Diahann Carroll. In the TV series she portrayed a nonstereotypical role, the widow of a Vietnam veteran raising her young son alone in middle-class white society. The message in the program was one of struggle and integration while claiming the right to live anywhere one chooses. Fast-forward a few years and off I went to study to become a nurse at a white college campus. Here as the only black in my nursing class, I learned to claim my right to be a student like everyone else there. I knew that I belonged because my parents had prepared me for this. Their hope was for me to earn a college education and advance economically. My hope was not to disappoint them in the process.

After completing my basic college education, I started my professional nursing career, and continued my education, teaching nursing students, and caring for sick children and families. I've travelled across the U.S. and around the world using my education and profession as a vehicle for many of these experiences. I've learned about the culture, policies, and politics of the places I visited, which has shaped my understanding of health care and life in general. I've become a citizen of the world experiencing things far beyond my expectations. My mother's words still guide me: "prepare yourself, you never know what opportunities will be available to you" as you move through life.

Today there are many black images in the media. They are a mixture of positive, negative, successful, and defeated—the complexity of black lives is now depicted in many ways as we tell our own stories. The success of the movie *Black Panther*, the black comic superhero, is just one example of the hunger we still have to see ourselves shown in positive ways. Seeing positive and diverse images like ourselves inspires hope for what we can accomplish and is so critical for our youth.

The Legacy

As we look back on the eight years of President Obama's tenure in office, we must examine the legacy that he left for all Americans and especially for black and brown parents and children. I believe that his first term in office while still challenging offered examples of his tenacity to get the economy back on track, to sign legislation that helped women receive equal pay for work, creating jobs for minorities, re-establishing a diplomatic relationship with Cuba, laying the foundation for Deferred Action for Childhood Arrivals (DACA), and the Affordable Care Act (ACA), which would eventually be actualized during his second term as president. In the face of declining congressional support by a Republican Congress and weakening Democratic base Obama never gave up on the American people even as many gave up on him. He was true to his supportive base and did not forget the marginalized men and women. The first sitting president to visit a maximum-security prison that houses more people of color, he gave hope and inspiration to these individuals as being recognized and valued. He appreciated the need for our American youth to be prepared to compete and lead the world in this century through education—something that families around the world covet and sacrifice for their own children. During his tenure, President Obama continued to request congressional support for research into new energy sources, charter schools, and STEM programs.

In his presidential acceptance speech, Obama said that *"change has come to America."* What he meant was that a new era of hope had been actualized. In the words of Abraham Lincoln (1863) *"...a new birth of freedom..."* Hope for changes in dominance by the wealthy and powerful. The challenges he faced were economic depression, poor access to healthcare for many Americans, climate changes affecting our environment, a housing foreclosure crisis, and the continued threat of terrorism from international forces. The hope was for change in these conditions with social policies and government support and oversight. He and Mrs. Obama put the power back into the hands of the people—*"government of the people, by the people and for the people"* (Lincoln, 1863). In his speeches he let Americans know that we also could aspire to high public office, and Mrs. Obama as First Lady often spoke of the White House as *"the people's house."* Government and the White House were to be seen as accessible, unlimited to the public, and belonging to us. Their message also included a level of public responsibility to not only look toward government for help but to be actively engaged in politics and government for our individual and collective success.

The message to young men and women is that we must have hopes for ourselves and to see that hope actualized. We must be actively engaged and not just criticize and sit on the sidelines. We must be active in the political process in order for our hopes to be realized into the changes we want to see. We must be different, creative in our approach to these desired changes.

So, in the end what virtues did President Obama teach our youth? That life is a continuous growth process. Now, he is the epitome of intelligence, grace, and style. He's also a common man with a wife and two daughters. But he was not always this way. The son of black and white parents and raised by white grandparents, Obama had to search for his identity and experimented with various roles along his journey. From being Barry in Hawaii to emerging as Barack in college, President Obama learned to apply his life experiences into the development of an academic scholar, community organizer, assemblyman, senator, and president.

While our own children may not want to be president of the U.S. they now know that it is possible; it is something that they can achieve if they want it. No one can tell them that they do not belong anywhere or cannot become anyone that they choose. They have their own stories to tell and as parents to help shape them into the successful adults that you want them to become and they want to be. First one must have a vision of what personal success looks like. What are the hopes that you and your children have for their lives? Success and hope may look different at various stages of life. It may be narrowly focused and very specific at the start—*I want to pass my final exams and graduate from high school,* or broad and general—*I want to be a lawyer and make a lot of money.* Our hopes have to be put into a plan of action in order to be achieved or they wither on the vine and later in life become regrets. It begins with knowledge, which is a powerful tool.

Virtues

These virtues are a start of a few characteristics that successful people practice.

> *Above all be true to yourself.* Know who you are and be comfortable in your own skin. Love and respect yourself, your family, and close friends. Choose your friends wisely and know who has your back.

> *Respect* your associates and demand the same in return. Insults and bullying are the tools of the weak and fearful who are often victims of incivility themselves. Don't let anyone weaken your self-esteem and self-worth.

> *Listen* more than you speak, and when you do, have something intelligent and meaningful to say. Be unapologetic about your *beliefs and values* yet *flexible* enough to listen and understand those of others

who are also willing to hear your message. We can all learn something from someone else.

Be *open to criticism* and able to defend your position at the negotiation table. Have valid supporting information to give weight to your position. There is a lot of "*fake*" information in the world, and you have to learn to be selective in your choices.

Be cool under pressure and know when, where, and how to let off steam. President Obama never let them see him sweat, though they tried often. He used his intelligence and sometimes humor to get his point across.

Have a *sense of humor* and laugh at yourself once in a while; it's good for one's soul. Being human means that we make mistakes: "*to err is human*" (Pope, 1711). Although you may have a great title, power, and prestige, never let your ego be so large that you do not have *humility* for great and small things in life. Getting angry and throwing temper tantrums means you have no self-control, which translates into tyranny. Tyrants are overthrown by their governments and fearful "supporters."

Conclusion

Here, in paradise, a new nation was born—one that is made of indigenous peoples, Europeans who conquered and exploited the indigenous peoples and became land owners, as well as indentured servants escaping prison and poverty. This paradise brought captured Africans who were enslaved and forced to till the soil to grow new crops, build mansions including the White House. Later, Asians from China were brought over to build railroads. Later, the ancestors of enslaved Africans from Caribbean islands and Africans from various parts of the Motherland came to paradise—all those seeking political, religious freedom, fortune, and adventure, economic and educational opportunities. These black and brown peoples speak many languages and have unique cultures that sometimes have clashed due to a lack of understanding and political undermining. These peoples learned that we are all the same with a shared history and are now beginning to learn and understand and appreciate one another. Like every parent, these black and brown peoples have high hopes for children. We want success. We want our children to know that they are valued, they are intelligent, they belong and can be anywhere and anyone they choose to be. They can even be president of the United States—in this paradise.

References

Lincoln, A. (1863). *The Gettysburg Address.* Abraham Lincoln online. http://www.abrahamlincolnonline.org/lincoln/speeches/gettysburg.htm

Pope. A. (1711). *An essay in criticism, part II.* In The Phrase Finder. https://www.phrases.org.uk/meanings/to-err-is-human.html

CHAPTER 22

Dreams for My Son: Dreaming Big in America

Faith N. Muturia

Isaac, My Dear Son,

The 2009 inauguration of President Barack Obama in Washington, DC, was phenomenal and I wish I was there, on Pennsylvania Avenue, in person with you, to witness it. I am glad that I followed it live on TV like millions of television viewers. I was up that night when the announcement was made, when I joined millions of viewers in crying happily, trying to let the reality sink in: President Obama, son of a Luo man, was the 44th president of the United States of America; his wife, Michelle, was now the First Lady; and his daughters, Malia and Sasha, were the first daughters and, together with granny, Mrs. Robinson, the president's mother-in-law, they would live in the *White* House. This day had come! For me, this was a truly once-in a lifetime event. What was the collective reaction among President Obama's supporters? Celebration of many kinds: dancing, crying for joy, and singing. As I watched the emotions, one song clearly came to my mind: "This is the day that the Lord has made, let us rejoice and be glad in it."

Tears of Joy

Yes, I cried; and many people cried tears of joy. Why? Because President Barack Obama represented great change, and triumph; because he heralded hope; because I was alive to share in the joy when so many others who had dreamed of such a day were no longer present to be part of this history-making event. Most importantly for me, and for many African people living in America, I cried because I saw myself in him—a Kenyan son—a son of a Luo man. I cried because you, my son, also a Kenyan son, were not yet born to witness history being made, to feel the audacity of hope of "a skinny kid with a funny name who believes that America has a place for him, too!" My colleague and co-author of this book, who is also from Africa, shared with me how blessed she felt when she watched it with her two sons. She told me how she had her son read to her Obama's autobiography, *The Audacity of Hope* (2006), just like I am reading to you *Dreams from My Father* (2007/1995), his earlier autobiography.

Writing Is Power

You know, there is power in the written word. Do not grow up to hate writing, or reading for that matter, as I will revisit this topic later. Writing is power. The pen is mightier than the sword. If you were the age of my colleague's sons, we would have celebrated the victorious moment together. I wished you were that age, so we would have discussed what the odds were, the odds of a black man of African roots getting elected president. They were steep, and there was no precedent. They were so steep that an obsessed competitor started a conspiracy theory to sabotage his candidacy. The theory, which is now known as *the birther movement*, posited that Obama was born in Kenya, that as a Kenyan man, he was ineligible to become a candidate for president of the United States. He had to post his birth certificate on the World Wide Web for all to see; yet, he was qualified in every sense of the word. In fact, one could argue that he was overqualified to be president on many accounts. Which other president had his portfolio? We are talking of a young, handsome black man, born to two intellectual parents, who graduated from two Ivy League institutions, one of which gave him expertise in constitutional law, and who married a woman with similar credentials. A young man who had published his own book before becoming president! Son, the man was prepared to handle the duties of president from day one.

Play It Safe

Was he fortunate to be the 44th president of the United States? One would say yes. Other men and women of color have unsuccessfully attempted a run at the presidency, with Reverends Jesse Jackson and Al Sharpton being some notable ones. Was it a case of the "right person at the right time in the right place for the job"? I encourage you to find out the answer to this question for yourself; find out how Barack Obama, the son of Barack Obama Sr., a Kenyan-born economist and lawyer, ascended to the presidency of the United States of America. Find out how a young *black* man, who was mostly raised by a single mother, grew up with an absent father, and struggled with his racial identity, became president and not another "statistic." Issues of our black sons, like all black sons in this country, are issues of high concern to my colleague and me as mothers of black sons in this country. The sad tragedies of Amadou Diallo, Trayvon Martin, Michael Brown, and the list goes on, concerns us very much. Like most mothers of black men, we worry that our sons may be the next statistic. Amadou Diallo, in particular, was an innocent, unarmed young man from Guinea, who was shot 40 times only for reaching in his pocket to show his wallet. He did not deserve that unfair death. It is therefore legitimate to ask the question, "Do black lives matter"?

Seek the Truth

The best thing you can do for yourself is to abide by the law and get an education. I advise you to find out how a young Obama, who was not always an innocent man, by the way, turned his life around and ended up attending Ivy League schools: Columbia University and Harvard Law School. Find out when and why he received the Nobel Peace Prize. Find out how he became an affable, beloved and admired, husband, father, commander-in-chief, and world leader. Please find out for yourself who Barack Obama is, for I can only tell you so much. You must find out so that you can "own your knowledge."

Sure enough, President Obama's journey is well documented: Books have been written, movies and documentaries have been made, and magazine articles about him, and his wife Michelle and their family, have filled and will continue to fill magazines and weblogs. In other words, my son, there will be no shortage of information about Obama; my only advice is that you seek this information for yourself, scrutinize your sources carefully, and arrive at your conclusions, while all along avoiding being misled by some who choose to only portray him in a negative light. Let me give you a hint about where you can begin your exploration on this subject: make a point to read President Obama's two best-selling, autobiographical books—*Dreams from My Father* (2007/1995) and *The Audacity of Hope* (2006). From the former, you will find out about his longing to know about the birthplace of his father and his inherited Africanness, like in this excerpt:

> "How does the saying go?" 'When two locusts fight, it is always the crow that feasts.' "Is that a Luo expression?" I asked. Sayid's face broke into a

bashful smile. "We have a similar expression in Luo," he said, "but actually I must admit that I read this particular expression in a book by Chinua Achebe. The Nigerian writer. I like his books very much. He speaks the truth about Africa's predicament. the Nigerian, the Kenyan—it is the same. We share more than divides us."

Excerpted from *Dreams from My Father* (2007)

Like Obama, it is important that you know about your heritage; know about your country and your continent. There is something good about having an identity, even if it may not be well respected in the world. At least you will know who your great-grandfather is, if you so choose to. As you read and learn from Obama's writings, I hope you come away not only inspired, but energized to grow, to learn more about your roots and to serve steadfastly, while all along "standing on the shoulders of giants."

From his second book, *The Audacity of Hope*, you will learn all about his educational, activist, and political journey. If you dream big and see the sky as the limit, I strongly encourage you to read that book as many times as it will take you to understand it.

We do not know how long it will be before we get the next person of color or female president to run this country. What we know is that not too long ago, after 200 years of the existence of the USA as a country, one young black man gave a shot at the presidency of the United States and, against all odds, he emerged the winner, not once, but twice. Whatever his failings or shortcomings or those of his administration and his party might be, no one can take the double victory, the two-term presidency, away from him, ever. He inspired a generation, and he will always inspire; the hope he gave to every black and brown boy and girl is still alive and well. The triumph of his election was celebrated across the globe; the news reverberated for days, weeks, months. The acclaimed Desmond Tutu, Archbishop Emeritus of Cape Town, South Africa, wrote eloquently about President Obama's election victory: "Today Africans walk taller than they did a week ago—just as they did when Nelson Mandela became South Africa's first black president in 1994" (Tutu, 2008).

Seek to know Obama's story, his real story, and don't ever forget it. There is much that has been and will be written about him, but not everything written about him is good or true; don't fall for fake news. Not only did he win the presidency, but he also "pulled up" many other qualified people to govern with him, especially members of minority groups, including women. All of a sudden there were plenty of women of color serving in the White House: UN Ambassador Susan Rice; Attorney General Loretta Lynch; and Senior Advisor to the President, Valerie Jarrett; to name but a few. You might ask yourself: "Where were these people before? Why were they not nominated before?" Perhaps it is that simply no one asked whether they were there, or no one cared to know if they were there or to give them the opportunity to serve at the highest level of government, period. There still are many narrow-minded people in this country who believe that only one race should govern it while the rest take orders.

Dare to Dream Big

As you grow up, you may also wonder: "Why would anyone want to get into the rough-and-tumble of politics, with no assurances of success, while also possibly tarnishing one's name?" I ask you, "Why shouldn't you?" Indeed, you will find that President Obama was not immune to that. He was tested and grilled on the campaign trail and in the presidential debates. He was called "liar" in public, and his wife "an ape in heels." During a joint session of Congress, Representative Joe Wilson of South Carolina shouted "you lie" to him; Newt Gingrich called him a "food-stamp president." You will not be surprised to find out that black teachers will be called derogatory names by your peers; just never partake in that petty practice. You will no doubt find out plenty of information about this as well, about the negativities and disrespect he endured that were not the case for his predecessors. However, despite all these challenges and tests, President Obama persisted and withstood negativity of unbelievable proportion, demonstrating in action one of the favorite mottos of his wife, Michelle: "When they go low, we go high." After all, as the great philosopher Martin Heidegger once wrote, "The grandeur of man is measured according to what he seeks and according to the urgency by which he remains a seeker" (1994). President Obama will be remembered for his quest for justice and equality. As history will tell, some people, in particular his successor, have tried and continue to try to destroy his legacy or to nullify his achievements, but no one should ever make you forget that a black man once ruled the greatest country in the world, and that he stirred pride in all of us. My colleague and I wish, as Louis Pasteur stated, that "the grandeur of your acts should be measured by the inspiration from which they spring," in your case, from Barack Obama.

No Future without Reading

What best advice do we have for you, our sons, and for all young black and brown boys and girls growing up in the United States and in all countries of the world? You must read, not only about President Obama and other notable public figures of this generation, but about many more individuals and historical movements like the Civil Rights Movement. You must read because books are windows to the world. Always remember this comment that Obama made in his 2008 acceptance speech, that "If there's a child on the south side of Chicago who can't read, that matters to me, even if it's not my child." Ignorance is *not* bliss. You must read to learn about many others who came before you, who paved the way, who made sacrifices so that you can enjoy the freedoms that you have today: men like Malcolm X, and women like Rosa Parks. Listen to Rev. Dr. Martin Luther King's "I Have a Dream" speech. Find out about slavery abolitionists, such as Frederick Douglass and Harriet Tubman. Read about world-renowned peace and justice fighters, such as Mahatma Gandhi. Find out how these great men and women, who were once ordinary boys and girls, were able to hold their heads up in the face of opposition and make a difference. Most of all, do not forget about the heroes of African independences starting with the Baba of Kenya, Mzee Jomo Kenyatta, and his contemporaries in other countries such as Kwame N'krumah, Mwalimu Julius Nyerere, Kenneth Kaunda, Patrice Lumumba, Robert Mugabe, and the great Nelson Mandela. The West may misrepresent these men as tyrants; I suggest you read about their deeds and misdeeds from all angles and learn the truth for yourself. Always remember, perfection is not of this earth; every human makes mistakes. The truth is those heroes liberated Africa from colonialism, and that is what should matter to you.

Love Seeking Knowledge

While reading on your own is important; it is also very important that you should go to school and love to learn, so that you can develop the basic, but vital, tools that open the world to you: the three Rs, as I still like to call them (reading, writing, and arithmetic), in order to understand and address real issues. Always remember this quote from the great Mandela (1994) about education:

> Education is the great engine of personal development. It is through education that the daughter of a peasant can become a doctor, that

the son of a mineworker can become the head of the mines, that a child of farm workers can become president of a great nation.

Please cultivate character, associate with diverse people, and work hard and smart.

As you grow up, I hope you join the rest of the family as we read, watch, and analyze the news, not to become riled up or for the sake of passing time, but to understand the issues of the day, and to try to understand how people from different groups, parties, and ideologies sell their opinions, values, and mindsets, and seek to understand why. I want you to grow up hearing "keywords" like politics, economics, geography, taxes, slavery, war, government, immigration, law, and development and to learn how they are interconnected and how they affect you in a very real way. I want you to ask questions and to be knowledgeable, beyond what you learn at school. Remember the African proverbs which claim that "knowledge comes from asking," and "one who grows up without asking ages without knowing." I don't want to overburden you, but I want you to be aware that we don't live in a vacuum.

Love the World

You will learn that no man or woman can do it all alone; you will learn that we are all fallible; but above all, you will learn that although enemies are there, always trying to pull you down, you will have family and friends supporting you. Indeed, as Hillary Clinton noted when she quoted an African proverb, "It takes a village to raise a child." This said, keep in mind that "here as immigrants, we do not have a village; we have our small family." We must be willing to support each other and to count on each other. At the same time, always try to make friends, not enemies. Do not discriminate against anybody on the basis of anything—gender, sexual orientation, looks, nation of origin, or race.

Be Yourself

On a final note, be yourself. As you still are too early in your journey to manhood, I don't know what shape your life will take, or what the path ahead for you looks like. You never know who you might become or what you might accomplish someday. Whatever it is, I want you to be you, the best version of you. Embrace the timeless values of love, and service and character. Strive high and be well prepared so that when you hear the call to service (to teach, to preach, to lead, to cure or create the cure, to profess the law, to be an entrepreneur, to be a singer or performer, to be a travel guide or a sports coach, or to be president), you will be ready to serve to the highest standards and to offer the best version of yourself.

Unlike us, your parents, you my son, are Kenyan-born and American; embrace that identity wholeheartedly and be yourself. Hear me again: Be strong. Dream big. Speak up. Study in school. Ask questions. Laugh often. Carry a book often and read it, really read; read widely and voraciously. Serve others. Pave the way for others. Be kindhearted. Give a lot, and expect no payback. Learn from this excerpt from *Dreams from My Father* (2007):

> I remember there was an old man living next door who seemed to share my disposition. He lived alone, a gaunt, stooped figure who wore a heavy black overcoat and a misshapen fedora on those rare occasions when he left his apartment. Once in a while I'd run into him on his way back from the store, and I would offer to carry his groceries up the long flight of stairs. He would look at me and shrug, and we would begin our ascent, stopping at each landing so that he could catch his breath. When we finally arrived at his apartment, I'd carefully set the bags down on the floor and he would offer a courtly nod of acknowledgment before shuffling inside and closing the latch. Not a single word would pass between us, and not once did he ever thank me for my efforts. (p. 4)

Whereas the English proverb states that "a good deed deserves another," always remember President Obama's attitude. Even though the people to whom you do the good may not acknowledge you or thank you, keep doing good anyway. Learn from the Kirundi proverb which states, "The good you do will await you ahead" (*ukora iciza ukagisanga imbere*). Likewise, Aesop, the great fabulist of all times, is credited with saying that "No act of kindness, no matter how small, is ever wasted"; always invest in doing the good whenever you can, and you will make me, your father, and your ancestors' home PROUD.

References

Heidegger, M. (1994). *Basic questions of philosophy: Selected "problems" of "logic."* Bloomington: Indiana University Press.
Mandela, N. (1994). *Long walk to freedom*. UK: Little Brown. (R. Rojcewicz & A. Schuwer, Trans).
Obama, B. (2006). *The audacity of hope: Thoughts on reclaiming the American Dream.* New York: Three Rivers Press.
Obama, B. (2007/1995). *Dreams from my father: A story of race and inheritance.* UK: Canongate Books.
Tutu, D. (2008, November 9). What Obama means . . . for America's global village. *Washington Post*. Retrieved from: http://www.washingtonpost.com/wp-dyn/content/article/2008/11/07/AR2008110702896.html

Chapter 23

Dreams Shattered and Restored
President Barack Obama Confronting the Shadow of Absent Fatherhood and the Pursuit of a Healthy Relationship

Faith Maina

Introduction

A FEW WEEKS after my 28-year-old son graduated with a master's degree from an American university, he called me from Kenya. He sounded almost giddy with excitement and conspiratorial, if you may, because he had not informed me of the impending trip and he triumphantly had arrived in Kenya to live with his father. You see, it was supposed to be a surprise and a final stab for divorcing "the best father" in the world. My divorce decree arrived via a New York court on Valentine's Day 2003. My son was 15 years old but the marriage had shattered as early as 2000 when his father relocated to another country to pursue higher education before returning to Kenya for good. As they say, all men live under the shadows of their fathers and the more distant the father, the deeper the shadow. My son idolized his father. I remember eavesdropping on one conversation when he was about seven years old and his sister was about five years old. He had asked his sister, "Who do you think is the brightest in our family?" He had gone on to answer his own question that his father was the brightest, followed by himself and then his mom came third and his sister was the "dumbest." At the time of this conversation, I was about to complete my doctoral degree at a prestigious institution of higher learning in Canada, and the father had dropped out of college back in Kenya. Call it childhood naiveté but it dawned on me, at that particular moment, that the colorful stories of his father's brilliance had dominated his psyche and this is the image he had to live up to.

My son's returning to Kenya as an adult to live with a father who abandoned him as a teenager did not surprise me. I had encountered the same story earlier when I read President Obama's 1995 autobiography titled *Dreams from My Father: A Story of Race and Inheritance*. In this book, President Obama vividly describes what he calls "an honest account of a particular province of my life, a boy's search for his father" (p. xvii). Obama's father, a student from Kenya, had met his mother at a college in Hawaii. The short-lived marriage ended when Obama's father left Hawaii when Obama was two years old to study at the prestigious Harvard University. Obama met his dad again only one time when he was 10 years old. All he knew about his father was through the colorful stories regaled by his mother and the grandparents who helped raise him. But it was not until Obama visited Kenya as an adult that he was finally able to confront the shadow of the absent father, who unfortunately at the time had passed away. It is through his relatives that he learned about his father's drinking habits, his arrogance, and his decline from a successful academic to an object of pity. His psychological odyssey, fraught with many conflicting emotions, was a kind of catharsis and exorcism born of the will to transcend. It is not a wonder that Obama expressed remorse that "had I known she [Mother] would not survive her illness, I might have written a different book—less a meditation on the absent parent, more a celebration of the one who was the single constant in my life" (p. xii).

The story of President Obama growing up with an absent father is not unique. Indeed, there are millions of children in this country and beyond who grow up in homes with absent fathers for many reasons, such as death, divorce, and so forth. What is unique about this story is that he defied the odds and grew up to become the president of United States of America, successfully completed two presidential terms, winning a Nobel Prize in the process: an achievement beyond comprehension which contradicts the existing theories of absent fatherhood. The question to ask then is how Obama overcame the challenges of absent fatherhood and what lessons are there for us single mothers raising children, and especially sons.

Growing Up in an Absent Father Household

Obama senior left his young wife and child to pursue a Ph.D. at Harvard University as a way to enhance his career. It is generally believed that such a move, disruptive as it may be, is a small sacrifice in regard to the financial stability and status the completion of a doctoral degree would bestow on the family. Indeed, in the household in which President Obama grew, his father was a legend. He remembers vividly the stories that were told by his grandfather (Gramps) who clearly admired Obama senior. One such story is how Obama senior had dangerously dangled another African student over the railing of a cliff to retrieve a pipe he had dropped accidentally. While this story would be seen by many as sheer bullying and cruelty toward a fellow human being, to Gramps, it was an act of "chivalry"! A quality so admirable according to Gramps, "your dad had this deep baritone, see, and this British accent" (p. 6) and therefore, could do no wrong. "I only wanted to teach the chap a lesson about the proper care of other people's property" (p. 7) was Obama senior's response to this act of cruelty. This admirable "chivalrous" quality is reinforced by Anna (Obama's mother), who clearly objects to this kind of behavior and explains it away as "a bit domineering," but it is just that "he is basically a very honest person. That makes him uncompromising sometimes" (p. 8). These stories told by Gramps, Toot (Obama's grandmother), or Anna to the young Obama over and over had one moral message: to make him proud of his absent father, and emulate him. The stories are replete with moral messages such as *versatility*—"Your dad could handle just about any situation, and that made everybody like him"; *confidence*—"Now there's something you can learn from your dad, *confidence*, the secret to a man's success"; and most importantly, the *brilliance*—"But your brains, your character, you got from him" (p. 50).

Hearing these stories over and over from the trusted adults in his life, President Obama idealizes and worships his absent father and creates a fantasy of what he wishes his father would be. In fact, his fantasy father is a prince, "he will take over after my grandfather dies" (p. 63), and as he told this fantasy story to his grade school friends, a part of him began to believe it but "another part of me knew that what I was telling them was a lie, something I had constructed from the scraps of information I'd picked from my mother" (p. 63). The ordinariness of his father struck him the one and only time he remembers meeting him at the age of 10. At the time, Obama senior had returned to Hawaii in the hopes that he would bring the young Obama and his mother back to Kenya after his third wife had left him and he had been involved in a car crash. The harshness experienced by the young Obama, such as of the father refusing to let him watch a television show during Christmas because he should be studying, provides a small glimpse of what the presence of his father would entail: a disciplinarian. "Go in your room and study now, and let the adults talk" (p. 67). Nonetheless, Anna is there to explain away this harshness when she tells him the following: "You shouldn't be mad at your father, Bar [short for Barack]. He loves you very much. He's just a little stubborn sometimes" (p. 68). Even though this visit was filled with tension, when his father was invited to speak in his class about Kenya, the admiration from teachers—"You've got a pretty impressive father"—and students alike—"your dad is pretty cool" (p. 70)—makes amends for all the suffering the young Obama had endured growing up in an absent father household.

Nonetheless, it is the resiliency of President Obama, even at a young age, that is impressive. When they moved to Indonesia to live with the man his mother had married later, he had acculturated very quickly and "made me relatively self-sufficient, undemanding on a tight budget and extremely well-mannered when compared to other American children" (p. 47). What is intriguing about this move is that his mother supplemented his Indonesian schooling with lessons from a U.S. correspondence course. His mother would wake him up in the morning at 4 a.m., force-feed him breakfast, and proceed to teach him English for three hours before he left for school. This did not occur without a struggle; he would find every available excuse not to study, but his mother would not hear of it.

Raising a child, especially a son with an absent father, is not easy. The son may find it difficult to develop a healthy sense of identity and, like President Obama, suffer moments of shame and stigma. And not to forget the poverty associated with one-parent households which affects the child psychologically that could lead to the adoption of destructive behavior such as drug abuse, low-level educational attainment, and ultimately incarceration. Indeed, President Obama remembers living in a two-bedroom apartment with his mom and sister Maya when they returned from Indonesia. His mother was receiving welfare checks at the time.

Lessons Learned

President Obama was able to overcome the challenges of growing up in an absent father household and become a role model for millions of children across this nation and beyond. There are many lessons we can learn from the way President Obama was raised. The circumstances of his father leaving them to pursue a doctoral degree at Harvard exempt him from a selfless act;

he had received two scholarship offers. One was to The New School in New York that would have paid for everything "room and board, a job on campus, enough to support all three of us" (p. 126); the other was to Harvard, which just agreed to pay tuition: "but Barack was such a stubborn bastard, he had to go to Harvard" (p. 126). Even though this was indeed a selfish act, Anna did not find it necessary to fill her son with negativity about his father. Instead, she made a lot of effort to help her son relate to his absent father in different and preferred ways. She took every opportunity to remind her son of the positive qualities of his absent father: "how he grew up poor in a poor country in a poor continent" (p. 50) but did not cut corners. "He was diligent and honest, no matter what it cost him. He had led his life according to principles that demanded a different kind of toughness, principles that promised a higher form of power" (p. 50). It is "therefore" not a surprise when the young Obama concludes after a vivid dream that "even in his absence his strong image had given me some kind of bulwark on which to grow up, an image to live up to, or disappoint" (p. 129).

It helps also that Obama's mother received consistent support from her parents. Gramps and Toot are a constant presence in President Obama's life. They provided the material and emotional support that helped Obama's mother maintain a positive relationship with her son. It helps even more that the grandparents admired the qualities espoused by the absent father and reminded the young Obama the qualities he needed to emulate from his absent father.

President Obama's parents had met when they were both attending the University of Hawaii. This means that Anna herself was adequately educated and even if the father was absent and she suffered moments of debilitating poverty, she did not internalize it. At some point, she lived in a two-bedroom apartment with her two children on welfare. According to some studies, that could have been a recipe for the children engaging in self-destructive behavior such as drug abuse, dropping out of school, and even incarceration. Anna's determination, possibly sheltered by the material and emotional support from her extended family, ultimately earned her a doctoral degree and landed her a prestigious position at a world organization. In the end, it is President Obama's resilience and courage to confront the shadow of his absent father that have set him free.

Epilogue

On July 16, 2018, President Obama returned to Kogelo, the village in which his father's remains are buried. This time, it was to open the Barack Hussein Obama Sr. Sports and Vocational Training Facility (Daily Nation, July 16, 2018). Even though the facility belongs to Sauti Kuu, a foundation started by Auma Obama, clearly, this facility was built as a commemoration of the lasting legacy President Obama would like his father to be remembered by.

You may be wondering what happened to my son once he returned to live with his father in Kenya. For a few months, it was all good. He lived in his father's house with his stepmother and two brothers. He obtained a job and moved to his own apartment. I'm not quite sure how the relationship with his father can be characterized at this point. I would say it is cordial but strained. A sad realization for my son has been that the man he idealized as a child was just ordinary and human in the eyes of an adult child. He has no choice but to accept his father's human foibles no matter how painful and, like President Obama, cultivate the resiliency and courage to confront the shadow of his absent father and transcend it to pursue a healthy relationship.

References

Daily Nation. (July 16, 2018). Obama open's youth center in Kogelo. Retrieved on September 1, 2018 from https://www.nation.co.ke/news/Obama-leaves-Nairobi-for-Kogelo/1056-4665098-lpvplo/index.html

Obama, B. (1995). *Dreams from my father*. New York: Broadway Paperbacks.

Chapter 24

The Black Male as World Citizen and Cultural Ambassador
Embracing Multiple Identities

Rasheeda Ahmad

Introduction: A Short-Lived Dream Come True

(FORMER) PRESIDENT OBAMA's presidency stands in stark contrast to that of his successor, President Trump. It was an extraordinary milestone in American history, which saw the son of a black Kenyan father and white mother, from Kansas, elected to the highest office. Forever etched in our collective consciousness, who can forget the images of unified Americans from all walks of life, colors and hues galvanized around the political vision of the first black president of the United States? Despite inheriting the worst financial crisis since the Great Depression, and extreme partisan politics, Obama embraced his new responsibility with a great deal of optimism and achieved a lot under the difficult circumstances in which he governed. His major accomplishment included providing universal health care and moving the Justice Department to address critical social justice issues. He also made sure that his cabinet represented diverse, competent individuals from various backgrounds. Although he encountered obstacles and disrespect, his presidency reflected elegance, civility, and intellect. Elected twice, he gave the impression that the United States was getting closer than ever to Dr. Martin Luther King's dream of equality and justice for all.

Inauspiciously, the cultural landscape of the United States shifted dramatically with the election of President Trump. It catapulted an unheralded flux of explicit open racist attitudes and actions toward vulnerable diverse groups in the United States (Muslims, immigrants with and without legal status, individuals with disabilities, LGBT, etc.). Trump's campaign speeches in which he refers to Mexicans as rapists, along with the multitude of racially insensitive comments, are now supported by policies and practices. Daily reports of immigration reform that forcibly separates families from their children with images of children being detained in "cages" leaves even the strongest heart weak.

Attorney General Jeff Sessions' oversight of these inhumane policies as he continued to roll back civil rights gains made during the Obama administration to address the school-to-prison pipeline and issues related to policing practices (racial profiling, gender bias, sexual assault, etc.) is not unexpected. Mrs. Coretta Scott King's prophetic letter to the members of the Judiciary Committee against the appointment of Jeff Sessions as a federal judge, three decades ago, sheds a troubling light on an individual in charge of protecting the rights of all Americans. In the letter, Mrs. King testified:

> Mr. Sessions sought to punish older black civil rights activists, advisors and colleagues of my husband, who had been key figures in the civil rights movement in the 1960s. These were persons who, realizing the potential of the absentee vote among Blacks, had learned to use the process within the bounds of legality and had taught others to do the same. The only sin they committed was being too successful in gaining votes. (McCann, 2017)

Not surprisingly, President Trump's racist ideas can also be traced back to the 1970s and '80s. Whether it's refusing to rent to African Americans, or sponsoring an ad urging the death penalty for five innocent minority males (later exonerated with DNA evidence) falsely accused of raping a white woman in Central Park, the Trump-Sessions leadership calls into question their legacy, which will adversely affect the safety of America for decades to come.

Given that stereotypical negative perceptions of African American men are deeply rooted in the fabric of American society, they are particularly at risk in the Trump era. It is imperative that young black males be raised to recognize their abilities to transcend this particular period of societal upheaval, which requires spiritual, mental, and intellectual energy. This chapter speaks to how black males can attain greater determination by both emulating the tenacity of the great men who left behind a legacy of fearlessness and recognizing their talents as world citizens and cultural ambassadors in the 21st century. In this chapter, I hope to foster greater discussion around the need for black males to embrace their multiple identities to position themselves on the world stage.

Reimagining the Traditional View of Black Male Identity

President Obama's capacity to negotiate and transcend his multi-racial and cultural identities while remaining true to his deep connection to the black American community is a deep reservoir of wisdom for black males to draw from. The intersectionality of Obama's multi-ethnic heritage and religious experiences as a child and young adult wasn't easy to negotiate. In his autobiography, we learn that Obama struggled with his identity as he acknowledges:

> [...] I learned to slip back and forth between my black and white worlds, understanding that each possessed its own language and customs and structures of meaning, convinced that with a bit of translation on my part the two worlds would eventually cohere. (Obama, 2004, p. 82)

His ability to reconcile those tensions proved critical to his success, for they enabled him to connect with diverse groups of people. As teacher educators, especially those of us of color, how can we begin to reimagine traditional monolithic views of black male identity? How might this message be transmitted to black males, particularly in the school environment and the larger culture?

One way to reimagine the traditional view of black male identity is to share counter-narratives of the multidimensionality of being African American. I will share my own story as a starting place, capitalizing on the memories of growing up looking up to Muhammad Ali and El Hajj Malik Shabazz, known as Malcolm X, as two of my heroes—two Muslim men who redefined their black masculinity on their own terms and whose ascension to the world stage broadened my horizons. Crowned heavyweight champion of the world, Ali was literally the most renowned and loved human on the planet, whereas Shabazz is known for renouncing the white racist ideology and embracing the spirit of humanity during his Holy pilgrimage to Mecca. Forerunners to President Obama, both men were trailblazers who did not accept restrictive, society-imposed, black male identity. While I drew inspiration from both men as a child, my formative development and educational experiences were complex and contradictory, requiring me to juggle multiple identities as an African American Muslim woman.

As the Civil Rights Movement and struggles for African independence formed the backdrop of my youth, my stepfather provided me with a regular heavy dose of my *true* identity. Because his beliefs were strongly rooted in Garveyism, he taught me to view myself as an African despite the fact that I had no language or specific African ethnic group to identify with. In fact, this deficit became a positive since I did not have to practice ethnocentrism, which is a common problem in many African nations. My African identity developed decades before the adoption of the *African American* identity label, for we had barely evolved from being referred to as *Negros* to being labeled *blacks*.

The historical legacy of Islam in the United States dates back as early as 1920, with the arrival of the first missionary from India. By the time I came to the world, decades later, belief in one God—Allah—learning prayers in Arabic, and attending instruction in the religion became a central part of my life. Essentially, my cultural biography as a Muslim girl represents a "story of the unchurched," which stands in direct contrast to dominant narratives about the black experience. For me, as an "outsider within the Black Church community," my story helps me connect with the diversity that is often overlooked within the black male experience (as African, Caribbean, South American, Central American, etc.).

When I spent a decade living abroad, in Nigeria, I came into contact not only with Nigerians from diverse ethnic and socioeconomic backgrounds, but also with a variety of foreign nationals. My narratives required me to embrace the complexities of my own identity. As a result, I developed a greater value and respect for global understanding and diversity. I also learned valuable lessons about persistence and resilience that continue to inspire and support my professional and personal experiences. Today my family embraces Nigerian, Ghanaian, and African American identities.

Although female, I believe that the notion of a singular identity of the black experience has been particularly harmful to black males. Daily, unflattering media messages reinforce the viewpoint that the young black male can only aspire to be a rapper, athlete, or drug dealer. I have chosen to discuss this issue in my attempt to counter the untruthful depiction of black males and bring to the forefront the complexity of black identity in general. This discussion centers on the use of the counter-narrative genre as a tool to support the achievement of black men and challenge negative portrayals.

As a teacher educator, I acknowledge the critical need to educate young black males as citizens of the world through the lens of critical race theory, culturally responsive pedagogy, and the disability studies in education framework. I am keenly aware of how structural racism and special education classification converge to exclude minority students in general and black males in particular from access to equitable public education. During the tumultuous Civil Rights Era, a new form of segregation, which emerged in Dunn's classic work (1968), identified the overrepresentation of minorities in special education. Today, half a century later, it continues to persist in various forms.

Each year a significant number of minority students with disabilities are suspended and/or expelled. African American students are twice as likely to be identified as having an Emotional Disturbance (ED) while black male students are particularly prone to the ED classification with services provided in segregated school settings. In addition, they are more susceptible to repeated juvenile and prison incarceration. Deeply sobering is the fact that black students are 40 percent more likely to be identified as having disabilities than the general population (U.S. Department of Education, 2016). Under these circumstances, the tendency of schools of education to prepare largely white middle-class females to become special educators presents its own challenges, particularly when they hold ideas and beliefs that reify the privileges they enjoy. Central to their beliefs is a critical understanding of Carter G. Woodson's (1933) cautionary message, which states, "To point out merely the defects as they appear today will be of little benefit to the present and future generations. These things must be viewed in their historical setting" (p. 9). It is imperative that black scholars center stories of black male excellence, which are quasi absent in the ideologies and practices of schools and misrepresented in the mainstream media. Counter-narratives allow students of color to challenge assumptions about them, their world, and ultimately their aspirations.

Black Males Are Meant to Be World Citizens and Cultural Ambassadors

Black males ought to assert their position as world citizens and cultural ambassadors, drawing inspiration from prominent role models, such as Ali, Shabazz, and Obama, as well as pan-Africanists W. E. B. Du Bois and Paul Robeson. Muhammad Ali's transcendental career as a boxer and later a global goodwill ambassador for cultural understanding—or Shabazz's civil rights advocacy particularly during the last year of his life spent in various countries in Africa, Europe, and the Middle East—speak to this possibility. Shabazz's cultural background and identity, born of a Caribbean black woman who spent years in Montreal, Canada, deserves recognition.

It is also important not to forget earlier forerunners, such as Paul Robeson and W. E. B. Du Bois. Active during the 1920s, Paul Robeson[1] was a visible key contributor to the Harlem Renaissance. Furthermore, his legacy as an international social justice activist, actor, singer, and intellectual left an indelible footprint on America's cultural landscape. One of the first three black men to graduate from Rutgers College, Robeson went on to obtain a law degree from Columbia University, almost five decades before the birth of Obama. While living in England, he deliberated with African intellectuals who would eventually become leaders of their countries. By the 1940s, Robeson was considered the most famous black man in the world. Because of his travels to Russia, he became perceived as a communist, which led to his passport revocation.

Like Robeson, W. E. B. Du Bois[2] was the first African American to obtain a Ph.D. from Harvard University. He too championed the cause for blacks in the diaspora as well as those on the continent. He was also a well-traveled man (Germany, China, and the Soviet Union). Du Bois, too, was stripped of his passport due to adherence to communism. Respected by Ghana's first president, Kwame Nkrumah, he became a citizen of Ghana and began work on the *Encyclopedia Africana*. W. E. B. Du Bois died in Ghana and was buried there.

Without a doubt, Obama's legacy connects to these forerunners and trailblazers who weren't afraid to forge their own paths. While President Obama embodies multiple ethnicities and world nationalities like Robeson, Ali, Shabazz, and Du Bois, his life experiences resonate to a great extent with

---

[1] Paul Leroy Robeson. https://www.paulrobesonhouse.org/paul-robeson/
[2] Du Bois, William Burghardt. 1868-1963. http://www.blackpast.org/aah/dubois-william-edward-burghardt-1868-1963

21st-century young black males. The two-term president's resilient character is an important trait that should be inculcated in young African American males as part of the many important lessons to be learned from his life.

Black (Male) Children Deserve to Be Given Chances at Success

No doubt, Barack Obama experienced significant life challenges during his journey into world citizenship. This process must not have come easy for him, as a son of an absentee father, mainly raised by white grandparents in a racist world. Yet, his resilient life offers a counter-narrative to typical stories of fatherlessness in the black community which, in part, foster a sense of despair and hopelessness for African American males. Obama's realization that he must persist and develop his potential despite his inner turmoil, as a fatherless child, provides a salient connection with brown and black boys who face similar trials. During his White House launch of My Brother's Keeper, an initiative to address the troubling issues that black males face in society, he identifies with the majority of black males in America as he says:

> I was a lot like them. I didn't have a dad in the house. And I was angry about it, even though I didn't necessarily realize it at the time. I made bad choices. I got high without always thinking about the harm that it could do. I didn't always take school as seriously as I should have. I made excuses. Sometimes I sold myself short. [. . .] I could see myself in these young men. And the only difference is that I grew up in an environment that was a little bit more forgiving. So when I made a mistake, the consequences were not as severe. I had people who encouraged me, not just my mom and grandparents, but wonderful teachers and community leaders. And they pushed me to work hard and study hard and make the most of myself. And If I didn't listen, they said it again. And if I didn't listen, they said it a third time and they would give me second chances and third chances. They never gave up on me, and so I didn't give up on myself. [. . .] I firmly believe that every child deserves the same chances that I had. (Capehart, 2014, n. pag.)

Today's teaching force, school leadership, and political climate, unfortunately, are intrinsically linked with educational structural inequalities which further exacerbate the difficulties that black males face. Without teachers and community leaders who encourage them to persist despite the odds, positive adult outcomes for males of color are severely threatened.

The story of Miko Chardin, founding principal of the Putnam Avenue Upper School in Cambridge, MA, further reinforces Obama's message. In his keynote address at the 2017 Universal Design for Learning (UDL) Social Justice Conference in Boston, Chardin passionately shared with the audience the challenges he faced, as a child of Haitian descent, growing up and attending school in U.S. society. He explained that his difficulties were mainly complicated by the absence of a father figure similarly to Obama. Where he differed from Obama, however, was that his identity felt threatened because of the influx of Haitians who drew mockery and ridicule from African American peers. Chardin's stories about the anger and frustration he experienced growing up as a black male were particularly compelling when he shared his encounters with police brutality. Perhaps, of notable importance, were the positive school experiences, which resonate with Obama's message of giving children chances. He highlighted that educators who did not give up on him were instrumental in enabling him to reconstruct his own identity as a thoughtful individual who could succeed academically and overcome his anger issues. It is thanks to the nurturing schooling experience that, in his professional role, he has opted to act as an advocate and a nurturer for the students. Narratives of optimistic outcomes by compassionate local leaders of color who show empathy to black male children, who are mischaracterized as trouble kids by the dominant narrative, are significant for their inspirational value. Black and brown young males need to hear and learn from resilient black males accessible within the communities, who beat similar or more odds than they have and went on to achieve greatness.

Reflections on the Importance of Black Male Counter-Narratives

The great black men of the 20th century, who had to endure atrocities eerily similar to the Trump era, gave meaning and pride to their black maleness. We see examples of strong spiritual values in Shabazz, Ali, and Dr. Martin King. Each of the three leaders epitomized the intersection of faith, persistence, and racial uplift. Moreover, they all ascended to the world stage and did not allow themselves to feel limited by societal expectations. Their life narratives contain valuable lessons that should be unpacked and repackaged to inform present-day conversations about black male multiplicity of identity and capability of achievement in the post-Obama era. I am strongly advocating that educators and advocates in urban school settings and communities should ensure that black male counter-narratives are embraced and ritualized, as they call into question deeply entrenched stereotypical stories of what it means to be a black male.

The post-modern black male has already achieved ubiquity on the world stage as cultural ambassador; it just needs to earn global recognition. Across continents, from Palestine to South Africa, Korea, and France, the hip-hop culture is a phenomenon that imbibes black male masculinity and agency. However, there is an urgent need for black men to resist being put in a box—the wrong box. This will happen if the young black male grows up exposed to empowering messages, such as those in Dr. Jawanza Kunjufu's (1982) famous poem "Pledge on Black Manhood," which center the possibility of the black male to achieve greatness educationally, morally, and spiritually—the possibility to believe in success as:

> ... the Black man who
> From this day forward
> Pledge my life to the liberation of my people,
> Put God first in my life,
> Will be a supportive, responsible,
> and loving husband;
> will hug, talk and listen to, and educate my children.
> [...] The Black man—the original man,
> The one and only,
> The one that other men are afraid of,
> because they know whenever
> I've seized the opportunity—
> I succeed.
> (Adapted from "Pledge on Black Manhood," 1982, p. 77)

References

Capehart, J. (2014). *Obama urges nation to be "My Brother's Keeper."* Retrieved 08/06/2018. From: https://www.washingtonpost.com/blogs/post-partisan/wp/2014/02/28/obama-urges-nation-to-be-my-brothers-keeper/?noredirect=on&utm_term=.38759486bb64

Du Bois, William Burghardt. 1868-1963. http://www.blackpast.org/aah/dubois-william-edward-burghardt-1868-1963

Dunn, L.M. (1968). Special education for the mildly retarded, is much of it justifiable? *Exceptional Children*, 55, 5-22.

Kunjufu, K. (1982). *Countering the conspiracy to destroy black boys.* Chicago: African American Images.

McCann, E. (2017). *Coretta Scott King's 1986 Statement to the Senate about Jeff Sessions.* Available: https://www.nytimes.com/2017/02/08/us/politics/elizabeth-warren-coretta-scott-king-jeff-sessions.html

Obama, B. (2004). *Dreams from my father.* New York: Three Rivers Press.

U.S. Department of Education. (2014). *36th Annual Report to Congress on the Implementation of the Individuals with Disabilities Education Act.* Washington, D.C.: Office of Special Education and Rehabilitative Services. Retrieved from https://www2.ed.gov/about/reports/annual/osep/2017/parts-b-c/39th-arc-for-idea.pdf

U.S. Department of Education. (2016). *38th Annual Report to Congress on the Implementation of the Individuals with Disabilities Education Act.* Washington, DC: Office of Special Education and Rehabilitative Services. Available: https://www2.ed.gov/about/reports/annual/osep/2016/parts-b-c/38th-arc-for-idea.pdf

Woodson, C. (1933). *The miseducation of the Negro.* Trenton, NJ: First African World Press, Inc.

SECTION VI
PARADISE TO REGAIN: CHANGE MUST COME AGAIN

Chapter 25

"Oh, Mercy, Mercy Me"— "A Change is Gonna Come"...Again

Gillian U. Bayne

IN THE WAKE of the 2016 presidential election, and my being struck by its outcome, the writing of this piece emerged spontaneously, as did the whirling of songs and their resonating lyrics in my mind. While the harmony of the songs remained the same, some of the words became modified, ever so slightly. In the midst of my bewilderment, I experienced, almost simultaneously, my head spinning and my stomach turning. I was trying to shake off the truth of what was coming into view. Then, recollections of the outcome of the 2008 presidential election, and reminiscing about the elated feelings I often experienced throughout President Barack Obama's terms became juxtaposed with my concerns about how collectively we would now have to face the reality of the unknown state of affairs locally, nationally, and globally, at least for the next four years.

> Oh, mercy, mercy me
> Things ain't what they used to be
> Where did all the blue skies go?
> Poison is the wind that blows from north and south and east
> —*Marvin Gaye, "Mercy, Mercy Me"*

Throughout Mr. Obama's presidency, I had a strong desire to visit the White House—especially since it was not so white anymore—at least figuratively—but now it was the home of a powerful black man and his family. As the 2016 presidential election approached, the need for that visit progressively intensified. I was fortunate enough to finally do so with my 12-year-old son on October 29, 2016, exactly 10 days prior to the 2016 election. We had such a warm and memorable experience—taking pictures at the entrance, inside and outside, as well as viewing photos displayed on the walls as we moved more deeply inside of the White House. The photos shed light on the nature and normalcy of everyday life—the president playing catch with one of his dogs, a beautiful family portrait, the president with young children looking through a telescope, and one of the president and the First Lady together with my all-time favorite artist and musical genius, Stevie Wonder. We imagined what it might have been like for the First Family of the United States to live at 1600 Pennsylvania Avenue, N.W., and being the first black family to do so. We were overcome with emotion throughout our visit. The feeling of being welcome to this, *their* home, our collective home, was something we thoroughly enjoyed during the beautiful two hours of our visit. It was an experience we will never forget. Somehow, because of the Obamas' dispositions, the sense of them being not so distant from us, as human beings, and of them working *for* all human beings, was and continues to be very real for us.

> It's *our* house and *we* live here—It's *our* house and *we* live here
> There's a welcome mat at the door
> And if you come on in—You're gonna get much more
> There's *our* chair—We put it there
> Everything you see—Is with love and care
> It's *our* house and we live here—It's *our* house and you're all welcome here
> —adapted from *Diana Ross, "It's My House"*

And so, when thinking about the Obamas, and what it means to *be* human in the world, I am drawn to the Jamaican novelist, critic, and essayist Sylvia Wynter (2003), and her call for a *re*envisionment of being human—one that beckons us to think more deeply about the intricacies of human thought and action.

Our experience that day at the White House, though, our good feelings about it, and the thought of the country progressing toward strengthening our beliefs and practices toward becoming more human, came to a screeching halt as we left the White House and waited to cross Pennsylvania Avenue onto New York Avenue. First, we heard a type of chanting in the distance, which became increasingly louder as we began to see the bopping heads of all white people—except for one black man—wearing red t-shirts and holding signs that supported Trump. They were all gruff looking. We could not believe our eyes, as we had never experienced such a forceful and loud endorsement face-to-face of the one who only a few months later would try to undo the progress made during the past eight years. Simultaneously, my son and I turned to each other, seemingly able to read each other's mind, and blurted out together, "What?" in disbelief. We quickly realized the reality of what was in front of us.

> There's a natural mystic
> Blowing through the air
> If you listen carefully now you will hear
> This could be the first trumpet
> Might as well be the last
> Many more will have to suffer
> Many more will have to die
> Don't ask me why
> Things are not the way they used to be
> I won't tell no lie
> One and all got to face reality now
> —Bob Marley, "Natural Mystic"

I asked my son as we stood in shock, "What do you notice about those approaching people?" The teacher in me came to the fore. My son looked at me sternly, and with a disappointed tone to his voice replied, "Come on, Mom! Can't you see? They all have the same expression. They look very angry, and their eyes are glazed over and cold." Well, what could I say to that? His observation was spot on. I observed the same. The crowd displayed characteristics and dispositions all counter to Mr. Obama—highly educated, soft spoken, a caring warm spirit, and an interested citizen.

> They've been spending most their lives
> Living in a pastime paradise
> They've been spending most their lives
> Living in a pastime paradise
> They've been wasting most their time
> Glorifying days long gone behind

> They've been wasting most their days
> In remembrance of ignorance oldest praise
> Tell me who of them will come to be
> How many of them are you and me?
> Dissipation
> Race relations
> Consolation
> Segregation
> Dispensation
> Isolation
> Exploitation
> Mutilation
> Mutations
> Miscreation
> Confirmation, to the evils of the world
>   —Stevie Wonder, "Pastime Paradise"

All in all, though, we did not let the end of the visit mar our delight in having visited the home of the president, our president. To the contrary, the entire experience took me back to the night when Mr. Barack Obama became elected the first black president of the United States.

***

I recall leaving from my home, which is in a diverse section of Brooklyn, New York, for work the morning after the 2008 presidential outcome. As I walked toward my local subway station, I noticed that there was a special energy that seemed to radiate from every person whose gaze crossed mine. The sky above was clear, the temperature was a comfortable 75 degrees, and the neighborhood streets had much less traffic than they normally had at that time during morning rush hour. Positive emotions were highly palpable and bubbling forth during the friendly exchanges of many approaching the subway. One could feel the excitement, an emotional lift, and hope permeating every molecule of air. Eyes were bright, and smiles were on the faces of those passing by the newsstand to pick up their daily paper. I also recalled a bittersweet memory, as told by a relative of a dear colleague who passed away shortly after President Obama's victory.

My colleague, a black male history teacher of predominantly white high school students, came rushing into my classroom waving a *Newsweek* magazine that featured the young black senator from Illinois. He asked me in disbelief, "Can you imagine that when I asked the students if they had heard about Mr. Obama, no one had? All I got were blank stares." I did not know how to respond to him; I was embarrassed to admit that I did not know at that time, either, who the man was. At my colleague's memorial service, I learned that after hearing about the outcome of the 2008 presidential election, he balled himself up in the corner of his bed and wept heavily. I was also told that he could only think of his parents at that moment—how he wished they would have experienced the victory, and had they lived long enough to have done so, they too would have been taken over by tears of joy.

Juxtaposing this flashback moment to that of the next, and most recent, presidential election was very emotional for me as well. Just like my colleague, I cried. But this time the tears were not happy ones—they were those of disbelief and worry.

> Joy and pain
> Are like sunshine and rain
> > —*Maze* featuring Frankie Beverly, "Joy and Pain"

The morning of November 9, 2016, had a totally different feel to it. Whereas people of all sizes, shapes, and colors walked quickly with a "pep in their step" just the day before, this day, the air was heavy. Eyes were cast downward, heads hung low, and steps on the pavement seemed to resemble the sound of chalk grating sharply on a blackboard.

Entering the subway car, as I normally do, I was greeted with soft, almost inaudible talk. Faces looked worn out; eyes were red—many frozen and seemingly in shock. Three women and a man entered the subway car. Two of the women stood erect and spoke in loud voices to each other, in between the emotional wailing of the third woman. They could not get over the fact that their candidate, *Hillary*, had lost the election. Finally, there was a pause. Silence filled the car. It was soon broken by the visceral reaction of a seated black woman whose lungs appeared to almost pop out of her chest. Her crying could be likened to that which is experienced upon learning by surprise of a close loved one's death. Her breaths were deep, and streams of tears ran down her face faster than any part of her six-foot scarf could absorb. People turned toward the direction of her wail, immediately after which she tried to contain herself. Her attempt was to no avail, though, and was quickly followed by her exiting the subway car—the disturbing sound reverberating even as the doors closed.

> Mother, mother / There's too many of you crying
> Brother, brother, brother / There's far too many of you dying
> You know we've got to find a way/ To bring some lovin' here today
>
> Father, father / We don't need to escalate
> You see, war is not the answer / For only love can conquer hate
> You know we've got to find a way / To bring some lovin' here today
>
> Picket lines and picket signs / Don't punish me with brutality
> Talk to me, so you can see / Oh, what's going on
> What's going on / Yeah, what's going on
> —Marvin Gaye, "What's Going On"

The next stop on the subway was a five-minute walk from the previous one; yet it felt as though the train took twenty minutes to finally reach it. After what seemed to be a long while, a black man rose from his seat and took a strong stance in front of the doors of the car. He looked at his reflection through the glass which covered the upper half of the doors, cleared the lump in his throat, stiffened his coat collar, and tightened the strap on his messenger bag. He took a deep breath. Then he gave his reflection a forceful affirmative nod upon leaving the train. His gestures made me think of those taken by African American soldiers I remember seeing in the movie *Glory*. I likened the man's gestures to those that the soldiers would take when preparing for battle.

We arrived at my stop on the train. I was very anxious—my heart was beating fast. I was sweating even though it was quite cold in the car. My breathing pattern had quickened tenfold—at least it seemed that way. My eyes were wet and my mind was consumed with worries about how my two colleagues and I would face the group of high school students we were scheduled to teach. "How," I wondered, "could we give these black and brown youth hope about the prospects of pursuing science careers during the political climate in which we would all soon be entrenched?" My mind raced back to the image of that man preparing for "war."

> Get up, stand up / stand up for your rights
> Get up, stand up /don't give up the fight
> —Bob Marley and Peter Tosh, "Get Up, Stand Up"

The thought that then came to me was that I have to brace myself for a fight, together with my students and colleagues, to defend Mr. Obama's legacy as an advocate for the advancement of science:

> Whether it's improving our health or harnessing clean energy, protecting our security or succeeding in the global economy, our future depends on reaffirming America's role as the world's engine of scientific discovery and technological innovation.
> —Barack Obama, "Educate to Innovate"
> (U.S. White House, 2009, n. pag.)

When there is a detectable spark in an individual's mind or heart with inherent potential that is not activated because of forces outside of the individual's control, it can be argued that the act or inaction of those forces is criminal. With increasing movements toward disrespecting the need to understand the natural world and beyond, we all are currently suffering locally, nationally, and globally from the loss of being able to move that engine of scientific discovery and technological innovation forward. In thinking about the need to change the developing mindsets of disregard for science and progress in general under our current regime, I recall a young child at seven years of age who, thankfully during Mr. Obama's presidency, had in him an exemplar of anything being possible irrespective of racial and/or ethnic background.

> I believe that children are our future
> Teach them well and let them lead the way
> Show them all the beauty they possess inside
> Give them a sense of pride to make it easier
> Let the children's laughter remind us how we used to be
> —George Benson, "The Greatest Love of All"

I was at the American Museum of Natural History for a special educators' meeting with a host of other educators—one of whom had brought her young child with her. After a long day of being the only child at the event, the little boy found some relief from sitting by engaging in a bit of solo "free play," as he ran around the large conference room, with his arms out, imitating a flying bird. In the words of Bob Marley, and in his soft, barely audible voice, he sang,

> . . . sweet songs of melodies pure and true . . . singing, this is my message to you . . . Don't worry about a thing, 'cause every little thing is gonna be alright.
> —Bob Marley, "Three Little Birds"

Soon he found a blank whiteboard and instinctively was drawn toward it. Without hesitation, the child quickly and gracefully picked up a black marker and carefully translated what was circling in his brain onto the whiteboard with his little brown hands. What materialized from him was an outpouring of a series of chemical reactions, structural formulas, along with bonding probabilities of chemical elements. Video cameras emerged quickly from backpacks, as those who were witnessing what was happening could not believe their eyes. One educator mentioned that she wished her high school chemistry students could see what was happening, as she knew that those who were convinced that they could not, would not, or should not understand the content would have a radically different perspective once they saw differently from the seven-year-old's actions. At the end of the child's depictions, a spontaneous caption emerged that had scientists and science educators in the room aghast. The caption read, "Chemistry is the best! Go on to be a chemist!" With the feeling of satisfaction came a smile that quickened upon the little boy's face at the adults' surprise of what they had witnessed. His eyes lit up as photos were taken to mark the event, and positive emotions were shared among all.

> To be young, gifted and Black,
> Oh what a lovely precious dream
> To be young, gifted and Black,
> Open your heart to what I mean

> In the whole world you know
> There are a billion boys and girls
> Who are young, gifted and Black,
> And that's a fact!
> —Nina Simone, "To Be Young, Gifted and Black"

From this unprompted event, what can be noted is that when all share capable and positive outlooks, as they had been by many during Mr. Obama's presidency, much progress is indeed possible. Hope can be kept alive.

As a result of the 2016 election, however, progress toward creating a better physical environment and healthier world for all is being challenged and quickly dismantled. The critical need to depend on each other for support so that proper care can be taken to protect all aspects of life is at its pinnacle now.

> Sometimes in our lives we all have pain
> We all have sorrow
> But if we are wise
> We know that there's always tomorrow
>
> Lean on me, when you're not strong
> And I'll be your friend
> I'll help you carry on
> For it won't be long
> 'Til I'm gonna need
> Somebody to lean on
> —Bill Withers, "Lean on Me"

As a black female science educator, and as a result of the 2016 election, I cannot stay silent, and I will not be discouraged from keeping hope alive. I will not be dissuaded from promoting hope for a better planet. Today's generation of black and brown children need educators who will uphold the tenets of humanity and not lose faith in the possibility that another black or brown person will become the next agent of change. I vow to be the type of educator who will educate "the young and fearless at heart, the most diverse and educated generation in our history, who the nation is waiting to follow," as was so passionately emphasized by President Barack Obama during the 50th Anniversary of the Selma Marches on March 7, 2015. And, in anticipation of the future, I sing the words to the melody of Sam Cooke's notable song:

> It's been a long time, a long time coming
> But I know a change is gonna come, oh yes it will.
> —Sam Cooke, "A Change is Going to Come"

References

Ashford, N., and Simpson, V. (1979). *It's my house*. [Recorded by D. Ross]. On *The Boss* [Vinyl record]. Detroit, Michigan: Motown.

Beverly, F. (1980). *Joy and pain*. [Recorded by Maze featuring Frankie Beverly]. On *Joy and Pain* [Vinyl record]. Los Angeles, California.

Cooke, S. (1964). *A change is gonna come*. On *Ain't That Good News* [Vinyl record]. Los Angeles, California: RCA Records.

Gaye, M. (1971). *Mercy mercy me* (The ecology). On *What's Going On* [Vinyl record]. Detroit, Michigan: Tamla Records.

Gaye, M. (1971). *What's going on*. On *What's Going On* [Vinyl record]. Detroit, Michigan: Tamla Records.

Irvine, W. (1969). *To be young, gifted and Black*. [Recorded by Nina Simone]. On *Black Gold* [Vinyl record]. New York, New York: RCA Records.

Marley, B. (1977). *Natural mystic*. [Recorded by Bob Marley and the Wailers]. On *Exodus* [Vinyl record]. Kingston, Jamaica: Island Records.

Marley, B., and Tosh, P. (1973). *Get up, stand up*. [Recorded by The Wailers]. On *Burnin'* [Vinyl record]. Kingston, Jamaica: Island Records.

Marley, B. (1977). Three little birds. [Recorded by Bob Marley and the Wailers]. On *Exodus* [Vinyl record]. Kingston, Jamaica: Island Records.

Masser, M., and Creed, L. (1976). *The greatest love of all*. [Recorded by George Benson]. On *The Greatest* [LP]. New York, New York: Arista Records.

U.S. White House. (2009, November 23). *Remarks by the President on the "Education to Innovate" Campaign*. Available at: https://obamawhitehouse.archives.gov/realitycheck/the-press-office/remarks-president-education-innovate-campaign. Accessed: 8/8/18.

Withers. B. (1972). *Lean on me*. On *Still Bill* [Vinyl record]. Los Angeles, California: Sussex Records

Wonder, S. (1976). *Pastime paradise*. On *Songs in the key of life* [Vinyl record]. Detroit, Michigan: Motown.

Wynter, S. (2003). Unsettling the coloniality of being/power/truth/freedom: Towards the human, after man, its overrepresentation—An Argument. *CR: The New Centennial Review, 3*(3), 257-337. Retrieved from http://www.jstor.org/stable/41949874

Chapter 26

Yes, She Did: Following Queen Mother Sanford Wherever She May Go

Lindamichelle Baron

I HAVE TO admit that during the 50 years that I have voted in elections for the president of the United States, I only thought of the possibility of a president as a change agent twice. And both times it was because of the same person, Barack Hussein Obama. It was not his blackness that made me believe he could change historic hatred, and economic inequities into a new world order. It was his persona, his passion, his mantra of "Yes, we can!!!" that led me to believe.

"Yes, we can" was a mightier statement of power than the refrain of an earlier black presidential aspirant, Reverend Jesse Jackson, who proclaimed, "Keep hope alive!" Hope is good but it has no grip. To me, hope is what we have when we don't have power. Until the 44th president, I saw the position of president as merely a leadership role. Certainly, it was the most powerful leadership position on the planet. But it did not entice me.

I never wrote, thought, or even joked that "I wanted to be president when I grew up." Perhaps my perspective toward my desire for the position of power was in some ways skewed by a belief system infected by American society's gender-based devaluation of women's occupational and leadership capacity. In any event, I always wanted to do something and be someone who could change the world. Until the ascent of the 44th president, I could only envision "teacher" as having that capacity.

Of course, there were politically astute women leaders vying for president prior to the 2008 election cycle in which Hillary Rodham Clinton ran for president the first time; and again in 2016 when she actually won the nomination. In fact, in 1972, the same year I became a teacher, Shirley Chisholm became the first black woman to run for a major party's nomination for president. She had already led the way as the first black woman to be elected to the United States Congress. She proclaimed throughout her political career that she was "unbought and unbossed" (as cited in Vaidyanathan, 2016). Some of her words of wisdom, were "If they don't give you a seat at the table, bring a folding chair" (as cited in Vaidyanathan, 2016). When announcing her candidacy for president she told supporters,

> I stand before you today, to repudiate the ridiculous notion that the American people will not vote for qualified candidates, simply because he is not white or because she is not a male. (as cited in Vaidyanathan, 2016)

And yet, even with the powerful political female figure before me, I saw teacher, not politician, as a potential revolutionary force—Harriet Tubman-like, guiding enslaved people to the Promised Land.

As a teacher, I could guide children, whose minds were enslaved, to the land of knowledge, insight, and critical thinking. I could be a change agent. That's what I wanted to be. A teacher could mold, support, and manifest a child's transformation right before his/her eyes. I wanted to change the world, one child at a time, one class at a time, one school at a time, one community at a time, one person at a time. I even crafted poems to extol the virtue and prowess of the educator, as this excerpt from one of my poems—about the teacher—attests.

> *This rhymes about a teacher*
> *Who is tough enough.*
> *When some say, "These kids can't learn."*
> *She says, "You're talking stuff."*
>
> *She really piles it on,*
> *She knows that we can do it.*
> *We know we'll make the grade,*
> *Because she helps us through it.*
>
> *We don't come from homes*
> *where life is peachy keen*
> *We walk down cracked up sidewalks*
> *Where the streets are mean.*

She guides us to the mountaintop
So we can see a wider view
She helps us fill our backpacks
With the strength to make it through

Success, she says, is something
Even money cannot buy.
Don't forget mind, body and soul
When you're soaring toward the sky.
...

Our teacher has it going on,
And we're doing what we need to do.
We're power charged and cannot stop.
Look out world we're coming through.

(Excerpted from Baron, 2007, pp. 36-37)

In 1972, as a newly minted childhood education teacher, a graduate from NYU, and Martin Luther King Jr. Scholar, I was interviewed by the principal, Mrs. Adelaide Sanford, for a position in the Crispus Attucks Community School 21 in Bedford-Stuyvesant, Brooklyn. I realized during the interview that Sanford was a leader who encompassed all of the capacities and vision of a revolutionary. I hadn't thought about the power of a principal until I met her. But then I rationalized a principal must be a teacher who empowers other teachers. I don't know where I initially developed that idea, other than from the questions she asked me. I felt embraced and empowered because her questions guided me toward expressing all that I believed. I believed all children could learn. I believed all children had a right to learn. I believed in children's unlimited capacity to excel under the guidance of a skilled and caring educator.

Although Ms. Sanford was asking the questions in the interview, within those questions were embedded expectations for those she would entrust with her children. My belief systems were unquestionably consistent with hers. Before the interview was over I knew I had a job and a mentor.

Although I had not been familiar with the school, I was very familiar with the community. I was about four blocks away from Nazarene Congregational Church where my father had been the pastor. I went to that church every Sunday from the age of 12 until I was about 17 years old. As far as I was concerned, the Brevoort Projects, across the street from CS 21, was not part of the ghetto, but it was where my father's and mother's friends, Uncle Artie and Aunt Shirley, and one of my best girlfriend's, Paulene, and her family lived. Sanford was known to insist that new teachers, black or white, visit the school's families in the projects if they planned on teaching at Crispus Attucks. There was no need for me to do so. Although I lived in Springfield Gardens, Queens, this Brooklyn neighborhood was also my home.

Actually, rather than having fear of the community, based on my experiences, I considered the community as an aspiring middle-class one. Most of the members of the church were long-standing residents of Bedford-Stuyvesant. They were teachers, administrators, judges, and politicians as well as city, state, and federal employees. As far as I could tell, their quality of dress, immaculate homes, and conservative affect identified most of the congregation as such. Many of the parishioners owned their own brownstone homes. In fact, several also had summer homes in Sag Harbor, a resort community, primarily inhabited by people of African descent, located near the tip of Long Island.

I was not aware of the Bedford-Stuyvesant I later discovered in the headlines in newspapers. I had no knowledge of the "black community," used as a pejorative to describe a crime-ridden, impoverished community. If I had, it wouldn't have mattered. I was going to be a teacher in a school with a leader who was going to support me as an educator. I was being chosen to teach where I could change the world... one child at a time.

During the five years I taught at CS 21, Principal Adelaide Sanford encouraged, supported, and guided educators who then did the same for their students... guiding them to the mountaintop "to see a wider view." She was a leader from the tradition of mentorship. I did not perceive her leadership, as she practiced it, as burdensome to her. She had not planned to be an administrator. It became her purpose in response to the parents who begged her to take administrative responsibility as assistant principal, and then as principal. One parent actually went so far as to say, in an attempt to convince Mrs. Sanford to lead the school, "You know, if I had another child that had to come to this school, I'd kill it. I'd commit infanticide. That's how bad it is. Can you please stay and help us? Could you please become principal of this school?" (HistoryMakers, 2003).

Then again, if burden is defined as a responsibility or even as a heavy load, it was a self-imposed burden. It was a burden that Mrs. Sanford relished, embraced, and owned. Not only did she accept this challenge—this burden, but she also supported other educators of African ancestry and encouraged them to get their administrator's license, in order to pick up their burden as leaders.

Her decision-making was informed by cultural considerations and community concerns. Her educational philosophy and later her legacy, as she espoused it during a video interview in 2015, was what was apparent to me, as a young teacher, in the 1970s when I taught under her as my mentor. Sanford spoke of "The importance of our responsibility for children as a paradigm that must be shifted" (HistoryMakers, 2003):

> Our children are neglected, our boys in particular. The prisons are full of our very, very bright youngsters. I think that during integration, we abdicated our responsibility to tell our story, and we let the oppressor define our children. And those definitions were majority negative. And because they were heard in a vacuum, they didn't hear any other voices; they began to think that's what being African, that's what being Black, is. (n.p.)

The words of the renowned author and activist James Baldwin are consistent with Mrs. Sanford's perspective,

> Every street boy—and I was a street boy, so I know—looking at the society which has produced him, looking at the standards of that society which are not honored by anybody, looking at your churches and the government and the politicians, understands that this structure is operated for someone else's benefit—not for his.
> (Baldwin, 1996, n. pag.)

Folk singer Odetta sang a Negro Spiritual about laying her burden down. The burden seems to reference slavery, Jim Crow, and the historic racism that Baldwin and Sanford decry.

Glory, glory, hallelujah
Since I laid my burden down
Glory, glory, hallelujah
Since I laid my burden down
I'm gonna ask my dearest brother
Help me lay this burden down
Gonna ask my dearest sister
Help me lay this burden down
   (Garrison Institute, n.d., n.p.)

Yet, I can't imagine that song being sung by Adelaide Sanford. Her song would be informed by the same backdrop of racial inequality and pain, but her rendition would also seek to unite others to help transform the system that bludgeons and burdens her people. Perhaps:

Glory, glory, hallelujah,
Time to pick our burden up! . . .
. . . I'm gonna tell my sisters and brothers
Help me pick our burden up . . .
   Adapted by Lindamichellebaron

Adelaide Sanford was conferred the title of Queen Mother on one of her many visits to Africa. A Queen Mother in some African societies does not have to be a blood relative of the reigning monarch; she is one who is ceremonially vested with the ritual essence of departed queens. She led the Crispus Attucks School as Queen Mother even before the title was conferred upon her. Her mission was to enrich and advance the brilliance within our children and their families. There are times when being "pro" your people is seen as "anti" others. Throughout Sanford's career, she was called anti-Semitic, and a racist, primarily because of her unequivocal support of people of African ancestry. In response to teachers of European descent who said our children are not "deprived, they are depraved," she worked as an activist administrator who proved her own positive perceptions through documented successes. To quote her:

> And my position was that the children are brilliant. Their parents, regardless of the condition in which they come to school—and at that point some were alcoholics and some were addicts, they wanted the best for their children. (HistoryMakers, 2003, n. pag.)

Although she refers to some parents with shortcomings, Sanford actually encouraged, engaged, and developed the best in the parents in support of their children. I witnessed her capacity to manage the school while leading it with a philosophy of student excellence, teacher efficacy, and community empowerment. Her career took her beyond traditional school management to the broader community. She was an activist in every sense of the word. After she retired, she was voted onto the New York State Department of Education as a state regent. In fact, after several terms as regent, she became deputy chancellor for the department. The next step, for which she was eminently qualified, was as New York State Department of Education chancellor. A virtual war ensued, in which copies of newspaper articles, from the 1960s and 1970s accusing Adelaide Sanford of anti-Semitism, and pro-Ebonics, were used to defame her. Although she didn't reach that pinnacle of state leadership as chancellor, her reach has become international.

At over 90 years old, Queen Mother Adelaide Sanford still defies sexism, ageism, racism, and even character assassination to emerge in majesty and grace to encourage us to research and critically analyze all that we are exposed to and corrupted by. She is a role model of one who "speaks truth to power." She risked her livelihood to create an enduring model of excellence in one school and continued in retirement to work toward New York State educational reform, which had the potential, as a model of excellence, to change teaching pedagogy and perhaps create or inform a new paradigm of leadership.

Queen Mother Adelaide Sanford never made lifting her heavy load seem like a burden. She lifted us and inspired us to do our part to lift each other and ourselves. I think of the definition of a black woman as described in an excerpt from Mari Evans' poem "I Am a Black Woman" when I think of our Queen Mother.

> *I am a black woman*
> *tall as a cypress*
> *strong*
> *beyond all definition still*

> *defying place*
> *and time*
> *and circumstance*
> *assailed*
> *impervious*
> *indestructible*
> *Look*
> *on me and be*
> *renewed.*
>
> (Evans, 1993, n. pag.)

Queen Mother Sanford had and continues to have the qualities of a leader who could not only lead a school and state but lead this country. Yes, she could. But her power is far beyond her own self-empowerment. Her gift is in utilizing her persona, her passion, her scholarship, and her very being to empower each of us to believe in our collective and individual greatness and change the world.... Yes, lead the world, with that power, in whichever field we choose or in any form we create. Yes, we can!!!

References

Baldwin, J. (1996). A talk to teachers. In William Ayers and Patricia Ford. (Eds.), *City kids, city teachers*. Pp. 219-227. New York. The New Press.

Baron, L. (2007). Poem about a teacher. In *For the love of life*. New York: Harlin Jacque Publication.

Evans, M. (1993). I am a black woman. In Howe, F. (Ed.). *No more masks!: an anthology of twentieth-century American women poets*. HarperPerennial

Garrison Institute. (n.d.). *Odetta Sings "Glory Halleluja."* Available: https://www.garrisoninstitute.org/blog/odetta-sings-glory-halleluja/

HistoryMakers. (2003). Education Makers. *Adelaide Sanford*. Available: http://www.thehistorymakers.org/biography/adelaide-sanford-39

Vaidyanathan, R. (2016). Before Hillary Clinton, there was Shirley Chisholm. BBC News. Retrieved from https://www.bbc.com/news/magazine-35057641

Chapter 27

As Long as There Is Life
Elections That Shaped My Transnationality

Immaculée Harushimana

IN 1935, LANGSTON Hughes, an anti-slavery poet and activist, titled his poem "Let America Be America Again." Fourscore years later, in 2016, a pro-nationalist presidential candidate chose "Make America Great Again" as the slogan for his campaign. From a nostalgic point of view, one can only wonder what greatness a friend of white supremacists is referring to, especially given his unapologetic, defensive stance toward violent demonstrations by his die-hard supporters. My African immigrant/refugee experience resonates with Langston Hughes' interpretation. To me, America had become America again when the Clinton administration opened America's doors to African refugees for resettlement and extended the Diversity Visa Lottery program to African immigrants.

It will soon be a quarter century since I moved to the United States of America. My arrival in 1993 coincided with the first year of Bill Clinton's presidency. Students at New York University, where I had been placed as a Fulbright exchange student, were very active in politics. They followed Clinton's agenda very closely. The instructor of cultural politics, Ms. S. L., who proudly identified herself as a Democrat, was extremely critical of the previous administrations, especially the Reagan administration, which she (and she is not alone) accused of being anti-black. BET commentator Joe Davidson did not mince his words in accusing the late president of implementing anti-civil rights policies (Davidson, 2004). Thanks to him, Davidson observes, black America embraced Clinton as their redeemer, a hope that was short lived. It did not take long before interest in Clinton's implementation of his political agenda shifted to the scrutiny of his private life. All of a sudden media coverage became dominated by this intern whom he was allegedly having an affair with—Monica Lewinsky. I remember asking myself whether democracy meant shaming a leader in public, and what one's private life had to do with his professional life anyway. Despite the public shaming and impeachment, Clinton rose above waters and completed his second term. There goes the French saying again, *"Le chien aboie, la caravane passe,"* translated as "the dog barks and the caravan goes on."

Four years later, we entered a new election era. I breathed a sigh of relief when the Clinton saga subsided. President G. W. Bush succeeded him and went on to also serve two terms. The 9-11-2001 tragedy shook me to the core. Somehow, President Bush associated the bombing of the World Trade Center with Saddam Hussein and, therefore, authorized the war in Iraq. The anti-immigrant sentiment which ensued nullified all my efforts to become reunified with my children, whom I had left behind at the ages of two and four. My heart sank when my hopes to bring my children fell over into the water.

The G. W. Bush era coincided with my official immigration status change to permanent resident of the United States and later to naturalized citizen, which gained me entry in the professional world. I found a faculty position in my area of expertise—which happened to be English. I never anticipated, nor was I ready for, the encounters of racism and xenophobia I endured from American-born students, whites and non-whites, who questioned my qualifications solely based on my African origin and accent. I became more aware of my being and non-being in a world that was not mine, as an immigrant woman from Sub-Saharan Africa. I was accused by the students of "taking their jobs," despite their confusion of *than* with *then; could have* with *could of; went* with *gone,* etc. I, too, felt the *Kanye West fury* (Robertson, 2005), and I wished for the Bush presidency to come to an end; eventually it did. Little did I know that the 2008 election would make an indelible imprint in my life.

I remember the buzz that went on, in 2004, about a certain Obama, senator of Illinois, who had made a landmark speech at the 2004 Democratic National Convention. A student in my class highlighted Obama's support for the teaching and learning of Spanish to American children (Carpenter, 2008). It turned out this Obama was the blend of an African father and a white American mother, and he denounced America's insensitivity toward slavery, poverty, and immigration. Regardless of how he identified himself, I identified with him, as a direct descendant of an African man—a Luo man. As an immigrant mother of two young black men, I nodded vigorously when he talked about "the hope of immigrants who set for different shores," when he talked about "the hope of the skinny kid with a funny name who believed that America had a place for him, too," when he denounced the "slander that says that a black youth with a book is acting white." His words became prophetic to me when, one month after he said these words, on August 8, 2004, I was sworn in as a naturalized citizen of the United States of America. It was a glorious moment for me to be sworn in, in the company of my two children who had finally joined me—two skinny kids with funny names whose mother believed that America had a place for them, too! Four years later, in 2008, I witnessed history—a history like the one I had witnessed in 1993, before I left my home country, when the first Hutu president ascended to power in Burundi through a democratic process.

I felt special that I should witness the victory and "crowning" of the first democratically elected African American as president of the United States of America. Perhaps that is the tale of the two elections I should tell. The election of Barack Obama, an African American man, to the presidency of the United States reminded me of the victory of President Melchior Ndadaye, in 1993, as the first Hutu president of Burundi—a country whose population comprises 85% Hutu and 15% Tutsi. Never had Burundian Hutus anticipated that a day would come when they would go to the urns and elect a president who looked like them. Never had a campaign generated so much euphoria in the country. Even village girls, with no schooling, were lifting their fists in support of their Hutu candidate. To the rumor-turned-true that he might be assassinated, the girls said in confidence, "If they kill him, we will elect another [Hutu]." The day of the election came, and Ndadaye won in a landslide. It was too good to be true, and the next day was a day of calm. In celebration, Hutu people shared drinks and food indiscriminately, just as they had shared the victory. Those with money treated those with none. For two months, before my date to travel to the United States arrived, I felt like I truly belonged to my country. For the first time, as Michelle Obama confessed and took heat for it, "I was proud of my country." I was hoping that, finally, the days of fearing senseless assassinations were behind me. It was unfortunate that I was utterly wrong. How could I be so naïve to think that an ethnic group that had maintained itself in power for scores of years was going to accept defeat without a fight?

During the three decades of my life in Burundi, my motherland, I barely spent a decade living in peace. The hostilities between two fictitious ethnic groups—Hutus and Tutsis—turned Burundi into a living hell. I grew up hearing about the tragic assassination of the Burundian hero of independence, Prince Louis Rwagasore, in 1961. I was barely one year old when it happened. There was a lot of unrest following this assassination; the so-called conspirators in the prince's death were subjected to death by hanging while the public watched. In 1962 Burundi became an independent nation, and four years later through a military coup the country was declared a republic. The monarchy was dissolved, and the last prince—Charles Ndizeye—sought exile in Belgium. For the next 25 years, Burundi was led by military regimes which succeeded each other through military coups and arbitrary arrests, led by army generals from the Southern region of the country. The first massacre of Hutus took place in 1972, under the reign of Lieutenant Colonel Michel Micombero.

I was 11 years old when the event that shook me to the core took place. I was at the stream fetching drinking water when I saw an airplane hovering over me in the sky. I had a phobia of planes, so I hurriedly filled my jar and went home. In those days, nobody in my neighborhood owned a radio, so we did not know what was going on. I came home and spent the night normally, as I was used to. In the middle of the night, however, I was wakened by huge sounds of heavy artillery, which thundered in my ears as if they were being launched from our backyard. My stomach started grumbling; I called my mother to take me to the toilet, and she told me to go where the cows slept. Yes, our cows slept in the house to shelter them from thieves. I could not sleep anymore.

Morning came, and my mother woke me up to get ready to go to school. I was young and naïve, so I went to school as if nothing had happened. To my surprise some teachers were absent, and children who lived in the military barracks and were used to being dropped off by the military bus did not come to school. Rumors went around that both the absent teachers and the children's parents had been arrested and taken somewhere for questioning. During the day, rumors also circulated that the last prince, who had been living in exile in Belgium, had forcefully entered the country to seize power with the support of mercenaries that he had recruited in the neighboring Tanzania. Talk about "fake news"! There was panic in my village.

The following days, the arrests intensified and a lot of Hutu men from the civil society, as well as Hutu males attending secondary schools and the university, were arrested and taken away. A few escaped and many never came back. On the news, the president referred to those people as *abamenja* (traitors). A curfew was imposed on the whole country from eight at night until six in the morning. Gatherings of more than three people were prohibited. The crisis spread in the villages, and several Hutus died of tragic deaths in the hands of their Tutsi neighbors. The worst death, I heard, was through sodomy with a sharp bamboo.

There was panic throughout the country. Every Hutu male feared that he would not live to see the next day. Burundi was never going to be the same again. Cycles of tensions between Hutus and Tutsi, which resulted in Hutu killings, were to happen at regular intervals. As I grew up and qualified to attend secondary school and, later, the university, I lived in constant fear that I would be next. Whenever tensions mounted on campus, and I felt threatened, my mother's proverbial warning that "the caterpillar died from wanting more" kept coming in my head. I still refused to quit.

Eventually, I graduated while the young Hutu men who had sought refuge in Rwanda and Tanzania began to organize and plan their possible return. The first of these men to return was a psychologist by the name of Ndadaye Melchior, who was pursuing his fiancée who lived in Burundi. He was a leader of a liberation movement founded by exiled Hutu students in Rwanda. On his return, he founded a branch of the same movement in Burundi, and he suffered for it. He was jailed and tortured until the international community intervened and put pressure on the military government to release him and implement a multi-party political system. Ndadaye was finally released, and his party—FRODEBU (Burundian-Democratic-Front)—was the first opposition party to be approved. The man went on to become the first democratically elected Hutu president in 1993. Unfortunately, his regime did not last; he was assassinated three months after his inauguration. It is with this trauma that I watched the electoral campaign of Barack Obama with a similar fear, i.e., that he might not live to savor his victory.

Given my intersectionalities as an African-born, black woman in U.S. academia, I could not help feeling excited about the possibility of Obama being elected to the presidency of the United States of America. I followed the Obama campaign with lots of hope. Having a voice in U.S. academia, as a black African-born woman with an African accent, had been a real challenge for me. In class, I found myself having to apologize for the way I spoke and list my degrees to be trusted, for being respected seemed totally out of the question. Among my colleagues, I felt the same tension even if the discrimination did not occur as overtly (program coordinators' reluctance to assign me courses spoke volumes). I was definitely a victim of the "savage African" mischaracterization. I still wonder if some of the hostility Obama endured throughout his presidency was not due to his Kenyan heritage. It is one thing to be black American; it is another thing to be a direct offspring of a black African parent! In the eyes of some white people, an African was destined to be a white man's servant.

As more and more electoral campaign analysts predicted Obama's victory, and endorsements accrued, my sense of optimism increased. On the night of the elections, I could not sleep, nor did the people in my neighborhood, the majority of whom consisted of Hispanic Americans. When he was declared the winner, I leapt for joy like the days of my childhood when my father would present me with a new dress on Christmas Eve. For the first time, I felt like I too had a shot at being who I wanted to be in the country that had adopted me as its citizen. For the eight years that he served as president, I looked up to him as my invisible mentor. I learned from how he kept his cool and composure when some hostile people questioned his legitimacy, disrespected him, and called him names. I learned from watching people inside his own race, at times, turn their backs on him. Most importantly, I learned from his fulfillment of his third-grade dream—to become president of the United States of America. His story made me believe that if I worked hard and abided by the law, I too could one day achieve my dream.

Having witnessed history being made, I never imagined that a day would come when I would sink back to the insecurities of the past. Unfortunately, it happened sooner than I anticipated. I painfully watched a thick cloud cover my sky on the night of the 2016 elections. The shocking victory of a ferocious opponent of Obama, and an anti-everything he stood for, has dug a deep hole in my hopeful heart. How am I to relate to a president who has never mentioned the word "Africa" throughout his campaign? Watching President 45 deny refuge to helpless refugees broke my heart. Hearing him vow to terminate the DACA (Deferred Action for Child Arrivals) program for innocent, law-abiding youth sounded surreal. I can't help thinking back to the decade of emotional turmoil I lived when my loved ones were trapped in the war with no hope of getting out. I empathize with some of the students we teach, who live in constant fear of brutal deportation or of witnessing their hard-working parents being stripped of their humanity because they are undocumented immigrants. I miss the inspirational speeches from Obama and his reassuring voice that no one should any longer doubt that "America is a place where all things are possible." It is painful to watch a paradise gained slipping out of one's hands without any assurance that it might be regained. Another ten-score years' wait for change would be unbearable. When I see nostalgic people forwarding each other video clips of Obama's speeches on Whatsapp, I feel comforted by the fact that I am not alone in missing him. I will miss his message of hope. I will miss his tears of humanity.

As a black educator, though, I cannot afford to be a crybaby when the young generation needs a strong guide. As an instructor of language and literacy, I have the crucial responsibility to ensure that Obama's message lives on and his audacity of hope is cultivated among young generations of black and brown children, starting with assurance that they are "articulate." The pen is mightier than the sword.

References

Carpenter, A. (2008). Obama: Kids Should Learn Spanish. Available https://townhall.com/columnists/amandacarpenter/2008/07/09/obama-kids-should-learn-spanish-n758559

Davidson, J. (2004). Reagan: A Contrary View—The 40th President Led a Sustained Attack on Programs of Importance to African Americans. Available: http://www.nbcnews.com/id/5158315/ns/us_news-life/t/reagan-contrary-view/#.WZdHGSiGPIU

Robertson, J. (2005). Kanye West Blasts President Bush—Grammy Winning Rapper Says President Does Not Care about Black People. Available: http://www.rollingstone.com/music/news/kanye-west-blasts-bush-20050906

Chapter 28

From Barack Obama to Donald Trump:
Two Extremes of Making History

Aminata Diop

Back in the presidential election of 2008, half of the nation would have sworn that racism died the night the first African American president was elected. That same night, there was no such thing as discrimination. However, looking back, it almost feels like the 2008, 2012, and 2016 elections brought back front stage the issue of race and racism in America. For the longest time, these topics were not addressed openly as they are today. Many people felt the election of President Barack Obama made them feel different because they were able to identify with him. Some successful people of color were seen as a token of success for the entire minorities group, but their success was used as a hush card to anyone who dared to voice any civil rights issues. The election of President Donald Trump did the same for other groups. They felt he would address their true and biased feelings on their behalf. Depending on which race one is, the elections of Presidents Obama and Trump could be seen as good or bad history. Those who supported President Obama felt good during his presidency while feeling angry with the election of President Trump and vice versa.

The Election That Made World History

Tuesday, November 4, 2008, was a day I will never forget. I can still see myself on my couch with the TV volume so high, running back and forth screaming at the top of my lungs, as the decisive results were coming in favoring Barack Obama both on the popular vote and the Electoral College. In the moment, I regretted not hosting an election party where all my friends could share a space to celebrate with me. As Barack Obama was being declared the

44th U.S. president by multiple media outlets, I heard screams from various apartments in my building. On a normal day, I would have thought about calling 911, but this day was anything but normal. I paused and thought about my kids and how, one day, I could tell them the way it felt to have lived through such a historic event. I was happy and proud because that year was also my very first time voting in a presidential election after becoming a U.S. citizen. I felt powerful and proud as if I alone had elected Barack Obama. There is something to be said about the power of our imagination when combined with so much excitement. There I was, in my living room, not only being part of a big moment in our historical time, but I was also involved in making that history because after all I did vote for Barack Obama. Mixed emotions ran through my body.

Obama's Identity from an African Lens

To me, then, Barack Obama's win was not merely a way of sweeping away the silent racial barriers that existed (and still exist) in American politics, and among different racial groups; it felt more like a deep sense of connection that went beyond the fact that he was black. This extended sense of connection was more about the fact that he was an African American with strong ties to Africa. To me, Barack Obama was not only black, but a black figure from the motherland. I was not just proud of his accomplishments and the fact that he was forever the 44th president of the U.S.; that sense of pride was even sweeter to me and, I assume, those who were born and raised in Africa. To me Barack Obama being elected president validated not only the African American race, but also the black race from Africa.

For the longest, we, African-born living in America, spent a lot of time feeling marginalized and occasionally treated as if we were from a different planet—the jungle. Our successes sometimes come as a shock to the Westerners. At times, it felt as if being an African was good for only living and staying in the motherland. I have felt a lot of times as if I was displaced and misunderstood being on U.S. soils. I questioned many times the meaning of the African identity—from Africa—once it crossed the Mediterranean Sea, the Indian and Atlantic Oceans. That is why there is a sense of liberation and inexplicable connection that overcomes us when we visit our families in Africa.

The True Face of America Revealed through Trump's Victory

Fast-forward eight years later; November 8, 2016, was anything but what I remembered from 2008 when Barack Obama was elected. Definitely, I did not watch it from the couch; I was in bed as the results started coming in. I was switching back and forth from one TV channel to another in disbelief and afraid to accept what was about to come. As the results were leaning toward a Donald Trump win, I turned off the TV and pretended to be asleep. Though the TV was off, I was still conscious about the likelihood that my reality would soon be changed forever. At some point during the night, I looked at my cell phone and, there it was; Donald Trump had been named the 45th president of the U.S. My body went through various emotions. At first, I felt that life would never be the same. Then, my thoughts went to the women, the African Americans, the immigrants, people affected by the Deferred Action for Childhood Arrivals act (DACA), undocumented students, and people from various religious backgrounds.

After Donald Trump was officially named president of the U.S., an unusual number of people went to the various social media and, within a short time, #NotMyPresident went viral. This hashtag had a deeper meaning for people as they worried about the challenges and threats we would face for years to come. As Elizabeth Currin and Stephanie Schroeder said, "Each of the threats surfaced within the Trump administration—including racism, nativism, sexism, anti-Semitism, homophobia, Islamophobia, Afro-phobia, white supremacism, and unbridled neoliberalism—has its own history" (Blumenreich, Baecher, Epstein, & Horwitz, 2018, p.2). In fairness, each of these has existed within the American schools and society in general for the longest time. However, as stated in "Preparing and Supporting New Teachers during the Trump Era," "The election brought these issues forcefully out into the open in a new way that many of our country's students and educators find frightening" (Blumenreich, Baecher, Epstein, & Horwitz, 2018, p. 2).

I could clearly remember hearing so many times Barack Obama state that the job of the president is to unite people for the common good. As people took their disbelief to social media, some felt even more frustrated that Donald Trump, unlike Barack Obama, had won the Electoral College, but not the popular vote. People took to the streets across the country because they felt that their voices were silenced during this election. Most New Yorkers felt deeply sad. There was a sense of sorrow in people's eyes. The disbelief was real, and it felt almost as if everyone looked to one another for comfort. There was a palpable silence. It felt as if people lost their morning smiles and needed their own space to process the reality of what was happening. The professors walked into their classrooms not knowing how to talk about the election results with their students. The teachers struggled to explain to their young students the end result of the election. Moreover, teachers were left to answer questions filled with fear from their students. The administrators turned to each other to get through the day. At City College, the then interim president, Vincent Boudreau, wrote this message to the college community:

> To many of you, the world today must feel a colder and more lonely place. Over the past months, we have watched the parameters of what is acceptable in our political and social life, and in the speech acts associated with that life, shift radically away from established norms of racial justice, gender fairness and basic equality before the law. I write these lines to you [not] as a partisan in our political process, but as someone who has been asked to steward, for the time being, an institution that is not neutral on these questions, and that cannot remain neutral. (Boudreau, 2016, n. pag.)

Paulo Freire wrote long ago, "When the teacher is seen as a political person, then the political nature of education requires that the teacher either serve whoever is in power or present options to those in power" (Freire, 1987, p. 212). Similarly, the great Nelson Mandela used to always say, "Education is the most powerful weapon which you can use to change the world." Teachers, educators, and leaders knew there was a conscious choice that needed to be made in order to pinpoint strategies on how to proceed after the last election because Freire made it clear that simply deciding to do nothing is supporting the status quo. Therefore, teachers went as far as asking if there was a way for them to get workshops that would help them address the meaning of the election to the young students and address their fears. However, it was not only the students who were fearful; a lot of people shared similar fears.

The mood of the country showed us how a new history, unlike the one Barack Obama made, was unraveling in front of us. The people who voted for Hillary Clinton, and felt she should have been president, were in disbelief and uncertain about what the future would hold with a longtime businessman such as Donald Trump in power and how he would act as president. Today, as I walk the streets of New York City and ride its subways and buses, I let my mind go back in time and put Barack Obama's legacy into perspective. I wonder, "How legitimate was Barack Obama's time as a president?" Is there a difference already felt after his spending eight years in office versus Donald Trump's two-plus years?

As the days have gone and I've made my way to various places in New York City, my mind goes to the time Donald Trump nurtured the so-called *birther* movement, which had one goal and one goal only: force Barack Obama to produce his birth certificate—evidence that he actually met (or did not meet) —one of the main requirements to be president of the United States. In other words, Barack Obama needed to prove that he was in fact born on American soil. Politics is often a mind game where the major players would dig anywhere possible to expose their opponents' flaws and weaknesses rather than tell people why they should vote for them.

The Power of Identity Politics

During the 2008 presidential campaign, many Republicans tried to label Barack Obama as non-American, or simply an immigrant, who doesn't understand what it means to be an American. They tried to label him as an African who doesn't share the same American democratic values and rules of law. However, if we think about this at a much deeper level, we may realize that portraying Barack Obama as a foreign-born president corroborates the idea that Trump acts like a tyrant who, rather than accepting the notion of balance of powers, chooses to impose his radical views by bypassing Congress on issues of critical importance. After playing the non-U.S.-citizen card during the campaign, many Republicans complained that Barack Obama overused his constitutional power and signed too many executive orders. However, the reality, according to Chris Cillizza of *The Point*, is that Donald Trump, less than a year into his presidency, was on pace to sign more executive orders than not only Barack Obama, but any other president for the last 50 years.

There was a point when Barack Obama even was labeled as a Muslim because he spent part of his childhood in Indonesia, which is the world's largest Muslim country. This reminds me of an interesting moment, during a John McCain town hall meeting, when a woman from the audience called Barack Obama an Arab. Parallels were being drawn from the fact that his middle name is Hussein. Very quickly, McCain clearly expressed his disagreement with the woman's comment that Barack Obama was Arab. Many people thought and still believe that John McCain rose to the occasion and took the high road by praising and presenting Barack Obama as a decent family man. However, to me as a foreign-born American, I argue that John McCain's response insinuated that Arab Americans are not decent citizens. He should have stated that Arab Americans are also decent citizens. "Indeed, what is justice if not equality of opportunity given from the beginning to all men regardless of race or condition?" asked Leopold Sedar Senghor, former President of Senegal (Senghor, 1964, n. pag.).

For those on the far right of the Republican Party, Obama was not supposed to be the president of this great nation, given the fact that he didn't fit the description of what an American president should look like. He was an African American whose father was not from America, but from some "s*hole" country in Africa, of all places. Race discrimination gets to the soul of a person. That is why the legendary peace and freedom hero Nelson Mandela, always said that he hated race discrimination most intensely and in all its manifestations. He fought it all during his life; he fought it until the end of his days.

By all indicators, however, Barack Obama's presidency was a successful one based on social and economic data between 2008 (when he took office) and 2016 (when his presidency era ended). On January 20, 2009, Obama's inauguration date, the Dow Jones Industrial closed at 7,949 (Jagerson, 2018). That same month the unemployment rate was 7.6 (US Department of Labor, 2019). Eight years later the Dow finished the day on January 20, 2017, at 19,732 with an unemployment rate of 4.8. Numbers are usually powerful, and people believe in them, as they should. But was President Obama held to a different standard than other U.S. presidents? How much did race play in these standards?

For some people, Barack Obama was all but an authentic American. The fact of the matter is that many people voted or did not vote for him because of his racial/immigrant background, which was highlighted enough to cast doubt in some people's minds during the campaigns. What is real, however, is that Barack Obama will be remembered as one of the most polarizing presidents in American history. On one hand, his detractors (among them Senate Minority Leader Mitch McConnell) were determined to make him look like he failed as a president. On the other hand, his presidency was viewed by the minority group as a confirmation that America is a land of opportunities where no matter where you come from, what you look like, and what your socio-cultural background is, you can be everything you dreamed, which includes being the commander-in-chief or chief of state. No matter what, one thing was clear to Barack Obama. He was aware that beyond his person, his successes and/or failures as the first African American president would forever be attributed to the entire African American community.

As I think back on how proud I felt to be part of his legacy by voting for him during his 2008 presidency, I can imagine how much pressure it must have felt to wake up every day being in the White House and being Barack Obama. There is no doubt that he was carrying his history, legend, and legacy on his shoulders from the moment he was named the 44th president of the U.S. to the time Donald Trump was named the 45th president of the U.S. Perhaps, might we even think, the weight of being the first African American president will never go away from the moment Barack Obama entered one of the biggest chapters of U.S. history. Was his audacity pushing him hard to try to achieve something as big as his historical presidency? Or, deep down, did he believe that he could succeed as the first African American president? Only he can give the answer.

The Danger of a Double Identity

Unlike in the case of President Obama, who easily identified as African American, African-born immigrants do not necessarily find it easy to self-identify. When I am filling out a form, whether it is for a job application, an immigration document, and the like, I do not fit in any of the listed racial categories, i.e., White, Black or African American, American Indian or Alaska Native, Asian, Native Hawaiian or Other Pacific Islander, and Other (US Census Bureau, 2018). I consider myself African-born, which to me is not the same as black or African American. If for most U.S.-born citizens this is a straightforward question, many foreign-born people, like me, are tempted to check the option that says "other" and elaborate on this selection. For one thing, I am not Hispanic or African American. Moreover, where we come from, we are not called black or African. We are identified by our countries of origin (Senegalese, Nigerian, etc.); therefore, being asked to identify as anything else is troubling to me. But then circling back to the so-called first African American president of the United States, where does Barack Obama fit in all of this? Is he an African American? Why can't he be Kenyan American? The question may sound provocative to some, whereas others may find it inappropriate and racially sensitive, because of the emotional capital that was invested in his election as president. Factually, however, not only is Barack Obama a person of mixed race; he is also of mixed nationalities. And for that reason, some black people saw him as not black enough, just like some African immigrants did not connect with him. Yet again, what does it say about me as an American citizen who was born and raised in Africa? Furthermore, what would this mean to my children?

Many immigrant families send mixed signals to their children trying to raise them in two different cultures. While the children can certainly benefit from both cultures, as they grow up and go through different phases of personality changes and identity formation, they find themselves in conflict with society, their family and peers. I always find it very interesting to hear children of immigrant backgrounds responding in English when their parents speak to them in their mother tongue. A lot of times, there is a clear attempt to silence that voice simply because it does not speak or sound authentically American. However, speaking with that voice reaffirms the true sense of belonging to the U.S., which is those children's country of birth. In a country such as the U.S. that is known for its racial diversity, why is race creating such a division among people? Why can't there be diverse ways of thinking, speaking, worshiping, believing, etc.? Why can't one express oneself, be valued, accepted, and promoted without contrast or comparison? Again, to borrow from Senghor, "The civilization of the 20th century cannot be universal except by being a dynamic synthesis of all the cultural values of all civilizations. It will be monstrous unless it is seasoned with the salt of négritude, for it will be without the savor of humanity" (Senghor, 1965, n. pag.).

References

Blumenreich, M., Baecher, L., Epstein, S. & Horwitz, J. (2018) Preparing and Supporting New Teachers during the Trump Era, *The New Educator*, 14:1, 1-4, DOI: 10.1080/1547688X.2017.1406228

Boudreau, V. (2016). *A post-election message from president Boudreau*. Email to the CCNY Community. Retrieved November 9, 2016.

Freire. P. (1987). Letter to North American teachers. In I. Shore (Ed.), *Freire for the classroom*. Portsmouth, NH: Boyton/Cook. pp. 211-214.

Jagerson, J. (2018). *Where was the Dow Jones when Obama took office?* Retrieved from https://www.investopedia.com/ask/answers/101314/where-was-dow-jones-when-obama-took-office.asp

Senghor, L.S. (1964). *Leopold Sedar Senghor on Religion and Justice*. Retrieved from https://berkleycenter.georgetown.edu/quotes/leopold-sedar-senghor-on-religion-and-justice

Senghor, L.S. (1965). *Prose and Poetry*. Selected and Translated by John Reed and Clive Wake. London.

US Census Bureau. (2018). *What is Race?* Retrieved from https://www.census.gov/topics/population/race/about.html

US Department of Labor. (2019). *Labor Force Statistics from the Current Population Survey*. Retrieved from https://data.bls.gov/timeseries/LNS14000000

Chapter 29

Supporting the Village That Raises the Children
From the Perspective of a Community Advocate

Patricia Mason

UPON THE INAUGURATION of President Obama, some people—both privileged and marginalized—saw the potential for a change in America. Hope was associated with President Obama's election to the highest office in the country. Obama's intelligence, empathy, and politics continuously conveyed his belief in the possibilities for America to become a just and fair country. His voice was the hope that change could be achieved. For a very short time, it appeared that the madness of racism would be challenged.

People of color are frequently judged and condemned by the errors of a few; thus, having a brilliant, articulate black man elected to the White House gave the country pause to challenge the negative stereotypes of black people. Was there a possibility that talents and strengths of black people were overlooked due to the country's ignorance about race and skin color? Well, as America's willingness to address racial discrimination and disparity waned, there seemed to be an increase in the daily harshness black people experienced.

Unfortunately, this harshness entered the classroom and the needs of students were compromised. The effect of this continues be detrimental to black students' learning and self-esteem. Concerned adults have a responsibility to advocate for these students' futures. A proactive approach is needed to ensure that students' academic, cultural, and social developmental needs are addressed using creative energies from a "village" of concerned adults—the village I am proud to belong to.

> *"If You Don't Stand Up for Children, Then We Don't Stand for Much"*
> —M. W. EDELMAN

I identify as a black female, mother, wife, educator, mentor, and campaigner for justice and fairness. My profession is education, so my disposition and skills enable me to teach, demonstrate, and model the value of learning and education. I have taught in private and public schools from elementary through graduate school. My experiences are shaped by my tenure in upper-middle-class schools as well as those in extremely poor communities—but I have always imagined the endless possibilities for all students, no matter their diversity. Volunteering in community programs for parents and youth has enabled me to observe children's talents. As I currently teach graduate education students, I purposefully emphasize the importance of recognizing all children's talents and abilities and provide culturally relevant recommendations on how to efficiently support children. I believe that my colleagues and community partners would agree that I constantly ask, "why not," for justice and fairness always require a struggle to untangle unknown and hidden miscues. In many circumstances, the best solutions have been ignored or hidden by biases and assumptions about students, parents, or/and the community. I remain determined to create the village I experienced growing up—one that recognized my value and both encouraged and made space for me to accomplish my goals.

> *"Education Is a Precondition to Survival in America Today"*
> —M. W. EDELMAN

I am a first-generation American. My parents came from Panama, where they both spoke fluent Spanish and English due to their Caribbean background. My grandparents left the islands for Panama in the early 1900s to build the Panama Canal. Then in 1952, my parents left Panama for America to make a better life for themselves. Although they valued education, this new country did not value the education they had received in Panama. Their school credentials were not accepted in New York, so they were forced to accept clerical employment below their education levels. However, they both worked hard to create a pleasant home life for my brother and me. My parents owned their own home within seven years of arriving in New York and provided well for my family. I was raised in a comfortable home that valued education and emphasized that it would enable me to have a good life. I heard the word "college" before I even knew what it meant. Having been educated in religious schools, my parents enrolled me in Catholic schools through high school to ensure I would be prepared for higher education.

As I attended school in a predominantly white community with a small grouping of black and Latino students, my parents did their best to shield me from the discrimination they faced and what was going on during the Civil Rights Movement. This was significant for my family, who was the second black family to move onto our block, with all of my classmates living in private and public apartments. I have memories that my neighbors were friendly and their kids and I played together. It was only when I began to watch the evening news with my father that I quickly saw that black people were mistreated. My parents would shake their heads and speak in hushed tones doing their best to protect me. Now as I reflect, I think that my parents, due to their immigrant status, were unsure if they could or should join the Civil Rights Movement. However, they made me feel safe.

> "Our Destiny Is Not Written for Us but by Us"
> —BARACK OBAMA

The privileges of my childhood education keep me acutely aware of the disparity and lack of access that many youth experience in underfunded communities. I was fortunate to have both my parents and Catholic nuns demanding effort and achievement from me. The value of education and its benefits were clearly outlined by the adults in my life; my parents' goal for me was that I would have a better job than they were able to obtain, and my teachers' expectation for me was to remain on the honor roll. As I reflect on my educational journey from elementary school through the completion of my doctorate, and now presently while teaching in higher education, I am continually angered and frustrated by the lack of support and resources that I seemingly took for granted in my youth. Believe it or not, I was privileged as a young black girl attending school in New York City on the heels of the Civil Rights Movement, which definitely influenced my future possibilities.

My early experiences teaching in private and public schools was a rude awakening for the disparities I observed in both educational settings. The value placed on a child's future seemed to correlate with the expectations of the classroom teacher. It was easy to connect how the teachers' comments about children and their families influenced what transpired in many classrooms. Students were judged and condemned by the zip code that their parents or guardians could afford. The ramifications of a teaching profession that, both intuitively and cognitively, instructs "other people's children" without an appreciation of the cultural and political climate of the country, or even the school district, are very unsettling. Maya Angelou signified the damage done to children's learning and self-esteem when she stated: "Prejudice is a burden that confuses the past, threatens the future and renders the present inaccessible" (Angelou.1986 [rpt 1991], n. pag.)

I may never confirm that watching the brutal treatment of black people demonstrating for justice in the '60s did not shape my teachers' interactions with their black students. I have recently overheard "majority" teachers and teacher candidates express less than sympathetic comments about black and other marginalized people demonstrating against police brutality. Their comments appear to reflect a culture that has shaped the teaching and learning dynamics in the 21st century. The tolerance of excuses for the damage done to families of children in low-income communities and the absence of advocacy by school personnel is disheartening because children are the first to suffer the ramification of these actions. Schools continue to refuse to provide many kids a safe harbor from the hate and ignorance of our society. Many teachers can be seen as the gatekeepers who refute the presence of implied racism in every aspect of education in our country and in their schools.

Furthermore, children cannot be perceived by school personnel as the enemy of the state. Teachers who cannot see the damage done to the black community by negative stereotypes shown in the media remain blind to the strengths of the child and his or her cultural diversity. The school experience of children whose teachers claim to be afraid, unaware, or non-empathic is short-changed. Such teachers must find it difficult to imagine the possibilities of their students' achievement and success, whether it is to get promoted to the next grade, attend college, or even become the president of the United States. It saddens me that, in 2018, students will learn in an environment that is completely opposite of my recollection of elementary school. My memories built both my skills and self-esteem, for I felt valued by my teachers. Somehow the color of my skin didn't stifle their ability to remain positive with me so that I never felt less than others.

Unfortunately, my experiences lead me to believe that in today's climate teachers might have used my socioeconomic status or my parents' immigration status to define my academic trajectory. What if the nuns saw my dark skin or heard my parents' accent and didn't encourage me to aim for the honor roll or attain my goals? I think some children are left to feel marginalized because of how they are categorized: poor, black, immigrant, English as a Second Language, or special education students. This thinking hampers students' growth, for their strengths and abilities are compromised by the assumptions and low expectations of their teachers. In addition, when immigrant parents are unfamiliar with school expectations, they are criticized instead of provided with the resources necessary to support their child. In an era with so many possibilities and choices, students' melanin remains one of the most significant roadblocks which can be overcome with efforts of concerned adults.

> "It Takes a Whole Village to Raise a Child"
> —AFRICAN PROVERB

The combined strengths of individuals are needed to energize a paradigm which allows students to dream and see their future possibilities of success and safety. Parents, as well as concerned adults, can use their resources to both push back the negative treatment of children of color as well as provide supplemental enrichment activities. Black adults generally have experienced discrimination, and their approach to overcoming such experiences is what leads them to encourage and assist younger people. The combined efforts are what drive the "village" to help the next generation.

My experiences of creating avenues where individuals of various professions can intersect with children and families remain rewarding for all participants. Consider this reflection an invitation I offer educators and concerned adults to think of ways to support students outside the school system. I will share a few examples of how I choose to engage students while enriching their learning experiences in my role as an educator. My goal is to help them see beyond the boundaries of what their schools and society perceive for them and, in small ways, challenge the disparities that inhibit achievement. My programs also involve parents in order to strengthen their understanding of how schools should support their children's needs. I include my college colleagues and resources to expose students to higher education. As youngsters sit in college classrooms and are given tours, they can be overheard saying, "So this is what college is like?" I carefully choose colleagues on campus who are sensitive to the developmental needs of youngsters and have humor as they creatively present information about their topic. Classroom teachers and/or school districts should consider reaching out to local colleges or former professors to create partnerships so that college experiences are possible for these students.

I also invite former graduate students who are teaching to bring their classes to campus. A class of fifth graders came to perform at the college and was given the opportunity to be accompanied by the college music majors. Youngsters benefit from listening to older students who are working toward their goals. When one of the college students mentioned that she was a first-generation student, a fifth-grader asked for the definition. Once the definition of the term was stated, the fifth-grader turned to her classmates and, said, "I guess we will be the first generation when we attend college later." The seed was planted. I share this example with professionals in any field so they can make arrangements for local students to visit their organization. I would suggest soliciting younger personnel to discuss their journey to accomplish their professional goals. Youngsters benefit from hearing the school experiences of others along with the determination and persistence maintained.

Over the years, I have also purposely created enticing, relevant, and academically enriching afterschool and summer programs for local students. Since I was not always satisfied with the academic rigor or culturally relevant learning opportunities for my own children, I consistently worked on bridging the gap between the standard curriculum and the curriculum I believe black children are entitled to. Teachers should be on the lookout for adults who will donate time and resources to help students make the connection between their current education responsibilities and later career opportunities. I would suggest that sororities and fraternities as well as local church and community organizations are places where schoolteachers will find professionals who want to give back and be part of the village.

Another example of adults using their talents and resources are parents planning activities for their children and friends. Parents would be very surprised that these occasional functions can help students gain knowledge about their culture and heritage. When my children were in upper elementary and middle school, a parent and I began a program where families met at each other's home and invited professionals to discuss their careers and the importance of prioritizing academic success in spite of roadblocks and distractions. Parents were always impressed with their child's respectful attention to the presentation as well as the relevant questions they would ask. They also came to appreciate the skills of their children so that they could confidently challenge the negativity experienced in school. In addition, parents would be pleasantly surprised that college students and professionals in the community would gladly volunteer their time to speak to the children in these workshops.

> "We Have a Powerful Potential in Our Youth, and We Must Have the Courage to Change Old Ideas and Practices So That We May Direct Their Power toward Good Ends"
>
> —MICHELLE OBAMA

Expose students to the richness of their culture and heritage. See this as a template to invite the readers to use their talents and resources to reach out to children and their families and supplement what local schools might not be providing. Michelle Obama's idea is the harness that can drive the development of a program. Black and other students of color need adults in the village to continually create opportunities for the students to see themselves as strong and purposeful. In order to dream BIG, children need exposure to new ideas and visions of themselves as future leaders. The adult villagers who share their maps of success demonstrate models which can encourage the next generation. Teachers in their classrooms need to provide varied and challenging experiences that reflect the culture and interests of their students. Classroom activities should encourage children to use their learning preferences to both explore and inquire to gain knowledge. Students should be able to clearly understand that classroom demands can be related to later career and life choices. This way of knowing about school and learning is extremely important, especially for first-generation college students. Children and families who struggle pushing society's roadblocks aside benefit from the communal support from the village stressing determination and resilience.

Finally, if it takes a village to raise a child, it is most helpful if the parent is part of that village. The struggles that challenge families can be overwhelming and, in cases that I have experienced, the families with the least resources often face the most demands from schools and society. The pushback on parents who either want to discuss their child's progress or who disagree with the teacher's comments about their child can be intimidating for some. Since some parents' experiences with their own schooling were not pleasant, the art of negotiating with school personnel can be frustrating. Students with big dreams benefit from parents who understand the intricacies of schools' and teachers' demands and expectations. The village can also support parents in this area.

I have presented parent workshops in libraries and community centers where information was shared about parenting skills, special education prevention and referral processes, and preparing for teacher conferences. These workshops encouraged parent engagement, which is another component that supports teaching and learning in local communities; administrators and teachers could see that black parents are partners in educational success. Discussions at my workshops remind parents to attend parent-teacher conferences throughout high school mainly to learn how their child is progressing, but also to subliminally leave a message that "I want my child to succeed." My last suggestion is to encourage parents to move forward with any complaint they may have to individuals who have the authority to address it; complaining to each other does not bring about change. In my experiences parents are always appreciative of a forum to discuss their thoughts about their child's learning or school issues.

In conclusion, schools and the educators who teach students of color, especially black children, still struggle to be effective. The education of children cannot be left to chance, especially in a country where racial views hamper the services that children might receive. Children are sent to school in good faith that they will receive services and resources to enhance their abilities to develop skills to successfully address adulthood. Minority students deserve a more receptive education system than their parents experienced so that they can become the leaders that our communities and the country need. Mobilized, adults can be a force to address the biases and assumptions that interfere with teaching and learning in black and brown communities. It will take an informed and united village to make it happen.

Reference

Angelou, M. (1986) (rpt 1991). *All God's children need traveling shoes.* NY: Vintage books

Chapter 30

"We Danced in the Streets"
Obama Era, Civil Rights Generation, and Voting Rights

Mary E. Dillard

WHEN BARACK OBAMA was elected as the first black president of the United States in 2008, I was overjoyed! On election night, friends and I rushed to 125th Street in Harlem and literally danced in the streets as we celebrated Obama's historic victory. I had campaigned for Obama in Pennsylvania, debated with friends about the merits of a "first" black or woman president, and dreamt of a change to the conservative political climate in the United States, my country of birth, citizenship, and disappointment. I had also entered into the adoption process. My daughter, Halima, was born in March 2010. I adopted her in July of the same year, and, for the first six years of her life, a black president was all that she ever knew. I marveled over how fortunate she was and wondered if she would eventually take Obama's achievements for granted. My parents and I giggled along with her when my father would ask her, "Who's the president?" and she would happily, loudly reply, "ObAAmaaaaaa!"

In contrast, when Donald Trump was elected, I woke Halima up the next morning and said, "Honey, Donald Trump is president." Her first response was, "Oh *no*! He's going to kill more black people." Even though she was only six, it had proven impossible (and possibly unwise) to keep the images of Ferguson, MO, Trayvon Martin, or the existence of the #BlackLivesMatter movement from her. The other people in my family who were deeply disappointed about the rise of Donald Trump were my parents. They were both born in the 1940s and had grown up in environments that restricted opportunities for black people. My father was raised in Philadelphia, and although he describes a family life that sheltered him from much of the reality of racism, Philadelphia's history speaks volumes about the struggles of black people to gain an even playing field in that city. My mother grew up under a system of legalized segregation in North Carolina and Virginia.

In contrast to my parents' experiences, I am a full beneficiary of the Civil Rights Movement and the women's movement, having been born less than two months after Dr. Martin Luther King was assassinated. As a result, I have had the ironic experience of debating with my parents about whether or not African Americans were "better off" under segregation. My mother, in particular, argues that black children at least had positive role models, teachers who cared about them, and people who taught them to strive for excellence. For this essay, I interviewed my parents, who are now in their early 70s, to get an understanding from them of whether or not they still think it is important for black people to vote.

Family History

I teach my students that orality and storytelling are prized among African Americans for a very important reason: storytelling is how we survive. In my own family, I have been fortunate to listen to multiple generations of excellent storytellers. I am happy to see that my daughter, siblings, and I are intent upon continuing these traditions. As a child, teenager, and adult, I loved listening to my father's mother's voice. It was something of a baritone, and because she was a smoker, she often had a raspy laugh. Her laugh came from deep within her gut and she had a wonderful sense of humor. Even though she had suffered numerous losses and disappointments in her life, her resilience rubbed off on some (unfortunately not all) of her children and grandchildren. I learned from my grandmother the history of black people in Philadelphia and the history of our family. But I was shocked to learn the history of segregation in Woodstown/Mullica Hill, New Jersey, which she just started reminiscing about one day while I was in the backseat next to her. We were with my parents, driving to visit relatives. She mentioned stores that blacks could not enter and invisible lines that black people could not cross. Because I had grown up with an "Abraham Lincoln freed the slaves, the North was good to black people" kind of post-Civil War history, this was one of the first times that I had heard about *and paid attention to* details of segregation in the North from a family member.

In contrast with my grandmother, I never asked my mother's father about the history of segregation. He had grown up in Hollister, North Carolina, and raised his family in both North Carolina and Virginia. Those stories of segregation were ones that I took for granted, partly because they reflected a national narrative of the North being "better" to black people than the South. My mother, aunts, and uncles often discussed their experiences. These stories were also the ones that were covered during Black History Month celebrations and television programs that my parents forced us to watch on PBS when they kept us home from school to celebrate the life of Dr. Martin Luther King Jr. When I was a child, Martin Luther King Jr.'s birthday was not a federal holiday. As a result, my parents staged their own form of protest by keeping us home from school on his birthday and forcing us to watch educational television (!). I honestly believe that this yearly protest and honoring of King's life is part of what made me want to become a historian.[1]

Like my father's mother, my grandfather was a very intelligent and interesting man. He was full of ideas. Watching television news with him and listening to his observations was like looking at the equivalent of a calm, simply stated, deeply insightful, verbal Twitter feed. He often uttered one-liners on politics and the state of the world that were simply brilliant. Because it is so easy to take present circumstances for granted, I didn't start to wonder until I was an adult what his life could have been had he not grown up in a segregated environment.

These two examples of grandparents on both sides whom I loved very much remind me in my teaching and as a parent that our history is alive. It is carried on through us, passed on to our children. If we will listen, this history can teach us some incredible things and remind us of that elusive, magical word that was the cornerstone of Barack Obama's presidential campaign: HOPE.

In order to continue to value the stories that my family members tell, I interviewed my parents, Stanley and Bernice Dillard, for this essay. Both were born when the U.S. was emerging from WWII and beginning the nascent stages of becoming a global superpower. Many U.S. historians identify the 1940s and '50s as a time of rising consumer power, the expansion of the middle class in the United States, and the introduction of time-saving devices into American homes. While this formulation is true for vast swathes of the U.S. population during that era, it was not true for African Americans, who struggled to develop a toehold on voting rights and economic security. For people of my parents' generation, the Civil Rights Movement of the 1960s offered a hint that the political freedom and economic prosperity promised by the Statue of Liberty would also be extended to African Americans. In this regard, voting rights was a cornerstone of forcing

---

[1] Martin Luther King Jr. Day became a federal holiday in January of 1986, the second semester of my senior year of high school.

America to live up to its promises. With this history in mind, I asked my parents four questions:

1. What did it mean for you in your own life when you couldn't vote?
2. What do you think about young people who say that voting doesn't matter?
3. How would you respond to young people who feel that politicians don't care about them?
4. If there is any inspirational message that you could give to young people about voting or politics, what would it be?

Parents' Memories

The following is a condensed version of their responses:

Bernice

> Well, we actually as a race got the right to vote in 1964. I don't know that I even thought about it back then because in 1964 I was what? 19? [unsure voice-Researcher's Comment]. And so, I was just at an age when I would be able to vote. I just know from the things that my parents and grandparents talked about was how many of them tried to vote but couldn't because of the restrictions that were placed. Things like you had to own land. They would ask you to recite the Constitution. All kinds of things just really designed to keep you from voting.
>
> So, having the opportunity to vote, it really felt more like an opportunity and at the same time a duty. You just couldn't not go and vote because you knew and had seen all the news footage and all the demonstrations where people were asking for the right to vote and reading about all of the people who had died trying to get the right to vote.

I don't know that [a lot of young people today] would understand it but I do remember that there was a saying, "If you don't vote, you don't count." I don't think that most of the young people really appreciate the struggle that occurred for them to get the right to vote and so they don't see any real value in it because it's not something that they have had to work to get. You know, it's just something that's there. They don't really realize that when you vote and those votes are counted there are decisions that are made by politicians based on those numbers. For example, if you are talking about school funding and people didn't go and vote about it, then the decisions may be different than if you had gone and at least expressed an opinion whether you are Republican, Democrat, or Independent, you know? To me, to not go and vote is a vote for whatever it is you would be against.

I think that I would remind [young people] that it happened once and it can happen again. The reason Obama got elected once is because—actually he got elected twice!—because of the people who went out and actually voted, participated in the election. Who were part of the process. I think that what they lost though was the importance of local elections because that is what has changed many things since then, the local picture.

Stanley

Well, it's interesting I was raised in the North so we always had the right to vote. Matter of fact, when we got married, shortly after we got married because the voting age was 21 then it was the Republicans who approached us to register us to vote. And there was a reason for that. We were young. We were Republicans [in Philadelphia] because the mayor who was a Democrat was so corrupt and the police commissioner was so corrupt. He was a bigot. Plus, the Democrats had a history of excluding black people from jobs such as street car driver, bus drivers, and they kept us out of unions.

We saw what was going on in the South because of the television network news and I think that's what motivated the civil rights marches of the '60s, having this come into our living rooms. Because people had no idea how bad things were, until we could see the dogs attacking people only because they just wanted to vote, exercise their right to vote. So that's how it affected me.

Back then the Democrats in the South were no picnic either. Because George Wallace [of Alabama] and Strom Thurmond [of South Carolina], the "Southern Dixiecrats," they were all Democrats. The Voting Rights Act was passed when President Johnson came into office. Well, President Johnson basically got us most of our civil rights. When the Voting Rights Act came into being, that's when the South turned Republican. [White voters] left the Democratic Party in droves because I remember President Johnson saying, "We've essentially lost the South." I mean, my sentiments were with the Democrats because my parents were Democrats. I had no feelings one way or the other except I *could not stand* the racist police commissioner in Philadelphia. He used to brag about how he would take his billy club in his tuxedo to formal banquets so that he could run out and direct the beating of black people.

Voting matters because here's what happens. When you vote the choice is yours. When you don't vote that's the same as a vote. But what you've done is you've ceded your vote to the other side. You've essentially voted by not voting. You've essentially voted for the other side [because] you haven't stood up for your ideals.

I also feel that the future of the Democratic Party is not with older people because the surveys that I've seen say that it's the older white voter who wants to look back. They are calling themselves "conservative." They want to return things to the way it used to be. But if I think about what used to be. Well, if we go back to the '50s or even further, my father and my uncle served this country. And my grandmother, they all worked *hard* but when Social Security became available it was *not-for-black-people*. When my uncles and cousins and father fought in World War II, the VA benefits were not available to them. They also could not get loans. The FHA—Federal Housing Administration—had "whites-only" policies. But what we have with this current president is people who want to go back to that, and I never thought that I would be saying this in this day and age.

We saw in the election that Donald Trump won Florida by a very small fraction. As a matter of fact Hillary Clinton won the popular vote by 2.2 million votes, so every vote counts.

I'd say don't take your vote for granted. I look at the color of my skin; when I look in the mirror, and I say that people died just for the right to pull a lever. I know it's true. That's what people forget—those people who don't go out there. People had dogs turned on them. They were beaten with billy clubs, had fire hoses and this is not like watering the lawn; these things can knock you down the street and carry you for several hundred feet. That's how much force was directed on them. So those are the things that I remember from the '60s, as my brother and I watched that in our living room. How they treated us. If you left your pet in a car and it was overcome by heat or something like that they would arrest the owner. But if you killed a black person in the South, nobody paid the consequences and unfortunately we are starting to see that again with police. So yes. It's so important. And I'd say don't take anything for granted. Plain and simple. If you don't exercise your right to vote you're being very foolish, because there are other countries that don't have these rights and I look at what happened in South Africa.

Conclusion

I have read Millennials' arguments against voting. Many of them echo the sentiments of Socialist and Communist activists of earlier generations that, for the average worker, voting is just an endorsement of the demands of elites. While

I recognize that politicians of every stripe have disappointed their constituents, I do not completely agree with the Millennials' assessment. As a historian, there is something deeply troubling to me about the North American propensity to gloss over, ignore, or superficially understand our bloody history, with our eyes turned firmly toward either the present or the future. It is even more distressing when I hear black people do this. I am dismayed when I hear progressive activists use bits and pieces of U.S. history to patch together the arguments they want to make against voting. I cannot help thinking about previous generations of activists who were tortured, harassed, maimed, permanently disabled, and lynched so that we could have the right to dismiss their efforts, sacrifices, and dreams. Or, so that we could allow cynicism to erode, not our sense of democracy and but, even, of civic good? I am acutely aware of the fact that the vast majority of black people won the right to vote a few years before I was born. Because I now see that right actively being taken away, especially from black and brown people, I still believe that voting matters *especially* in local elections. I pay attention to who is running for mayor in my city, who my state senator is, who the president might be, and even who is on the local school board. I pay attention because whether I know the full magnitude or not, that person has the potential to help or harm my life in ways that I often cannot even imagine. The individuals whom we elect to political office also have the opportunity to help or harm people who are most important to me: my family, my students, friends and loved ones in Africa. Perhaps most important, I vote because not doing so would dishonor the memory of all of the people who sacrificed so much so that I could have the opportunities that I have. U.S. history is truly heinous in this regard. It is not possible to be a historian and disregard the legacy of people who dreamed of a better future for me, for women, for so many black people, both citizen and non-citizen alike. We ignore this history at our own peril because both popular culture and government structures in the United States are very good at perpetuating historical amnesia for political purposes.

CONCLUSION

Looking Back to Move Forward
A Black Women's Collective (Re-)Imagining and (Re-)Membering of Hope and Change

Sherry L. Deckman

> *Sankofa: "It is not wrong to go back for that which you have forgotten."*
>
> *"I have come to believe over and over again that what is most important to me must be spoken, made verbal and shared, even at the risk of having it bruised or misunderstood."*
>
> —AUDRE LORDE (1984/2007, P. 40)

"TELL ME WHERE *I've* been." It was more of an imploring statement than a demand. I was sitting at my brother's kitchen table decorating gingerbread people with my then seven-year-old nephew, Isaiah, and my fifteen-year-old niece, Andrea, or Shuggie, as she is referred to by our entire family. Isaiah was very interested in the Cold War and video games at the time and, consequently, fashioned his gingerbread people after soldiers and vampires replete with icing fangs and menacing eyes. I had never seen anything like it.

We had been playing a game Isaiah invented, in which he tried to guess a state or country I hadn't travelled to. "Hawaii?" "Yes." "Idaho?" "No." It was a good way for him to learn geography more than anything else. After a few rounds, Isaiah paused and looked at me, and that is when he said, "Tell me where *I've* been." As a seven-year-old, it was an earnest request. He was too young to know all the places he might have visited. To me, the questions and meanings implied were far deeper: Did I know where he had been? Did I know his story, his history? Was the story of where he had been intertwined with the story of where I had been?

I begin this concluding chapter of *Paradise to Regain* with Isaiah's story, by telling where he has been, as intertwined with my own story, in order to connect to the histories recounted by the 30 contributors to this volume. Indeed, given the important focus of this volume on youth and change, it is essential that this chapter include the story of my nephew, joining the four other chapters in which mothers, including Faith Muturia's and Shirley Mthethwa-Sommers', have touching conversations with their children in the form of letters. The collective story of *Paradise to Regain*, then, is very much one about *Sankofa*—looking back to move forward—and, to borrow from the words of Audre Lorde, speaking what is important, despite the risks, because the risks of remaining silent are equally or even graver yet.

So, what happened on that December day when Isaiah seemed to ask an innocuous question, how does it connect to my story, and why does it matter on these pages? Together he, Shuggie, and I re-created memories of the places he had travelled and the family members who had joined him on those journeys. In a way, that day we looked back together at Isaiah's past as part of our family in order to look forward and dream together of the future that might await him to pursue, the journey he might discover for himself, and the path he might forge. That conversation would ultimately plant the seed of inspiration that would take us to Washington, DC, in March of 2010. But we didn't know that then, that December evening, we weren't yet able to imagine a black family in the White House.

As a little girl growing up in central Pennsylvania, like Isaiah, I was told regularly by my parents and teachers that I could be anything I wanted when I grew up. In my mind, nothing could stop me from pursuing my dreams. A teacher or two even offered, president of the United States of America. I believe that they believed their own words and that I did as well. But, maybe I accepted this particular fiction, not because I believed I could be president, but because I never allowed myself to desire something so grand, so out of reach for a scrawny brown-skinned girl whose father graduated from high school in East Texas years before the Supreme Court ruled legally mandated segregation unconstitutional in the *Brown v. Board* decision. Of course, one can be whatever one wants if one's dreams are bounded by what is "realistic."

That all changed on Tuesday, November 4, 2008.

I had heard of this "Barack Obama" when he won a Senate seat from Illinois in 2005. Given that to this date there have only been 10 black United States senators, that election was also a big deal. I was proud when the upstart organizer from Chicago seemed to come out of nowhere to be elected to Senate. Though I had no real connections to Illinois, the election of Senator Obama felt very much like a win for black people across the States. One of our own had made it and could influence policies that mattered to black communities all over the country. To hear, though, that this man had secured the Democratic nomination for the presidency after a very brief tenure in the Senate was beyond my wildest imagination.

Throughout the campaign season for the 2008 election, I lived in a perpetual state of worry. I worried that even if Barack Obama did win the presidency, he wouldn't live to assume the position. From my history classes, it appeared the United States knew only one way of dealing with black men who seemed to become "too big for their britches," black men who would defy the power of the white hold on our country's institutions. As a result, images of assassinated black leaders of the past such as Martin Luther King Jr., Malcolm X, Medgar Evers, and on and on, haunted me. These were the only referents I had that came close to approximating with what Barack Obama dared to do.

As I reflect further, I wonder, was it possible that throughout my elementary and secondary schooling we had *only* learned about black men leaders at the U.S. national level who had died fighting for their rights and ours as a community? What message does that send to our young people? Fear? Was the message that if you're foolish enough to take on white supremacy, there was one assured outcome? Where was the possibility of hope offered by the likes of U.S. Representative John Lewis or James Meredith, black men who indelibly changed U.S. institutions for the betterment of black Americans and all who lived to tell the tale? Where were the stories of women like Angela Davis, whom in my younger days I foolishly believed to be long dead—because stories of her revolutionary activism were always presented as bygone—but who continues to be active in civil rights work as a professor emerita from the University of California, Santa Cruz? To what extent had we really written our own history?

This is not dissimilar to Diane Price Banks' indictment of the erasure of black contributions to science history (this volume) and isn't even to mention the neighborhood heroes like Adelaide Sanford, the principal in Bedford-Stuyvesant, Brooklyn, of whom Lindamichelle Baron in this volume writes, "Sanford was a leader who encompassed all of capacities and vision of a revolutionary. I hadn't thought about the power of a principal until I met her." This recalls Wendell Hassan

Marsh's (2015) powerful words for the diasporic black community: "History is the science of the state. While memory is the art of the stateless" (pp. 18-19). It seemed, even our (collective) memory was failing us, having been subjected to a history written by others about us. This is part of the promise of *Paradise to Regain* in memorializing a living black hero for young black and brown children.

My unrealized fears aside, it looked like everyone in liberal-leaning Massachusetts was excited by the prospect of breaking the color barrier of the United States presidency. One friend, a graduate school classmate, a social-justice-minded white woman, invited me and others over to watch the election results come in. She too had put her hopes in the possibility of a "President Obama." At the same time, the only other black woman and an Arab American woman in my graduate school cohort suggested that we three watch the election results together. These classmates, perhaps uncertain what their—or others'—reactions would be—given either potential outcome—wanted to hold a space just for us women of color to be together for this moment. Indeed, we sat stunned as the polling numbers rolled in. Then, like so many others who share their voices in this volume, like Faith Muturia, we wept quietly and hugged when it was clear Senator John McCain would be conceding the election.

A day we thought we would not see in our lifetimes had come. That day would go on to last for eight years, during which time white Americans would exclaim that our country was "post-racial"! Even some well-meaning white allies in the struggle for racial justice would go on about how race no longer mattered because a black man held the highest office and was, as the aggrandizing, U.S.-exceptionalist phrase goes, "leader of the free world." Perhaps because of the intoxicating sweetness of this dream, the bitterness of Tuesday, November 8, 2016, was that much worse.

This time, there was no collective of women of color holding space together watching the election results. Hoping that I would wake up on November 9 and the nightmare of the Trump campaign would be a distant memory, I went to bed early, checking beforehand that Secretary Clinton was still ahead as the polls closed. As people of color seemed to know, but white liberals couldn't accept, perhaps still clinging to the tattered shreds of the hope of a post-racial society, I knew the threat of a Trump presidency was real. In the line to vote that morning, a middle-aged white woman told me that tomorrow we'd be celebrating, surely suggesting Secretary Clinton would win. I responded, "I hope you're right." Incredulous that I could fathom a different outcome, she reprimanded me, "We *will* be celebrating tomorrow." I still wonder what thoughts were going through her mind as she saw the numbers coming in from the polls closing across the country. In any event, I got out of bed on November 9th expecting to have received messages of relief and excitement. I naively wondered why I hadn't been woken in the middle of the night by horns blaring and cheering as I had heard on the streets of Cambridge, Massachusetts, after Barack Obama had been elected. Instead, I awoke to a seeming funeral in New York City. My fears about President Obama being assassinated were replaced with fears about increased, widespread, targeted acts of violence against blacks across the country, fears that did bear out. But on that day, I found myself attending solidarity gatherings where people of color could collectively mourn and consider what would come next, how we would resist the backlash to our communities.

Isaiah's experiences with these two elections largely mirrored mine. He even felt a minor celebrity during President Obama's first term as people in his small town often commented that he looked so much like the president—same caramel complexion and close-cut dark hair, same pensive, yet playful eyes. This prompted another kitchen-table conversation. "I would like to visit the White House," declared Isaiah, looking at me with his characteristically serious expression. I felt privileged to be in a position to make a visit to the West Wing possible as my dear friend Sarah was working as a White House Fellow and offered to give Isaiah and Shuggie, and their siblings, a tour.

Unlike Gillian Bayne's experience visiting the White House with her son (this volume), my family was not met with an angry white mob. Instead, on a chilly March morning, five of my nieces and nephews were ushered into the building through a secluded entrance for a private tour. Sarah showed Isaiah and the others the Oval Office, from which the president—*our* president—led the country. They also stopped in the press room where they took photos in front of the White House insignia, perhaps imagining that they could one day return here to work. This dream was now possible. During the tour, Isaiah and his siblings said the president waved to them from a window in his private residence. Be that true or wishful thinking, Isaiah added the Obama White House to the places where he had been. That someone who looked like him had assumed this office was of the utmost importance to this now 10-year-old.

This hopeful moment was a distant memory on Wednesday, November 9, 2018. On that morning, Isaiah got off the school bus and headed to class as he would on any Wednesday. Only, on this morning, he was greeted by classmates roaming the halls shouting, "White Power!" The story was reported on NPR along with a spate of similar incidents that had been inspired by the election results. The students at Isaiah's school had equated Donald Trump's win with a nod of support for white supremacy. A result that, while sad, was unsurprising, given the actions of candidate Trump and his subsequent excusing of white supremacists' actions resulting in one fatality in Charlottesville, VA, after the election. At Isaiah's school, the teachers and administrators immediately sprang into action, voicing love and support for all their students and rebuking the racist actions of the few. While this mattered very much to the school community, hearing Isaiah recount this story, I wondered how we could make our white brothers and sisters understand that the motivation for these actions ran far deeper than just being the racist proclivities of the few.

This incident, too, became part of Isaiah's story; it was now part of where he had been and will be part of where he journeys forward from. It is my hope that Isaiah—and those of his generation—will take the memory of the pride of the Obama presidency along with the anger and frustration of the aftermath of Donald Trump's election, to incite action toward change that will become part of our collective story. It has always been the younger generations who have led the movement for racial justice in the United States and elsewhere, as Mthethwa-Sommers' story relates in this volume. It was, for instance, college students who rode buses through Mississippi during Freedom Summer, risking life and limb to register black voters. It was nine determined high school students who faced a jeering white mob, being spat at, who integrated Little Rock High School in Arkansas. Similarly, it was high school students in Soweto, South Africa, who on June 1976 paid with their lives the price to be educated in their language (Michigan State University, n.d.). This is why I share where I have been and where Isaiah has been as part of *Paradise to Regain*, and why the women who have penned these pages share their voices: we must remember where we have collectively been in order to move forward. This is the meaning of *Sankofa*.

Across history, *Sankofa* has been drawn upon by African Americans in the call to "remember our past to protect our future." It is an idea that has connected the diasporic black community from Africa throughout, following the slave trade, as a call to remember our collective strength and past, as the authors do in *Paradise to Regain*. In a way, that is the intended legacy of this volume—to provide a collective (re-)imagining and (re-)membering of hope and change surrounding the election and presidency of Barack Hussein Obama. I deliberately use the phrasing (re-)imagining and (re-)membering to suggest how the collective voices intertwine on these pages to not only recount a past, but to put forward a vision for and a path toward a different future than the present.

The black women scholars and educators whose voices commingle to create this volume offer a vision, a dream—a substantive dream forged of real blood and bones—as Tracy Cook-Person reminds us (this volume)—of possibility and hope to present and future black youth. Indeed, collectively the authors of *Paradise to Regain* tell black youth where they and we have been as a diasporic people and community—particularly around the moment of the first president of African heritage of the United States—so that black youth might know the limitlessness of where they can go in our collective journey and anticipate the struggle it might take to get there. We want black youth to know that they are not alone in their struggles, and they can gain strength from the rich legacy of those who have come before. We have taken risks—some personal and others professional—in telling our stories because of the power of providing this legacy.

We also want black youth to hear the call to act in this volume. As the poet Audre Lorde, who was a masterful storyteller, knew, we cannot wait for change to come to us. Lorde urged us to make our own change—and—in ways that had previously been thought un-imaginable. While history might have laid a foundation, through working together change would be inevitable. Here, Meahabo Dinah Magano's (this volume) words resound in speaking of how she was able to bring about change as a black woman professor at a university slow at making change following apartheid. As the South African saying suggests, "Motho ke motho ka batho," meaning, "*I am because you are*—if you want to go fast, go alone; if you want to go far, go together with others"; we have collectively dreamt of not only where we have been, but also where we as a people may go. "Tell me where *I've* been," the future child might ask, and *Paradise to Regain* will respond.

References

Lorde, A. (1984/2007). *Sister outsider.* Berkeley: Crossing Press.
Marsh, W. H. (2015). Re-membering the name of God. *Chimurenga Chronic.* Available: http://chimurengachronic.co.za/re-membering-the-name-of-god/
Michigan State University. (n.d.). South Africa: Overcoming Apartheid. Retrieved from http://overcomingapartheid.msu.edu/sidebar.php?id=65-258

Contributors

Rasheeda Ahmad received her master's degree in special education and doctoral degree in curriculum and instruction from West Virginia University where she received the highly competitive W.E.B. Du Bois Fellowship for Academic Excellence. She also received a pre-doctoral dissertation fellowship at Le Moyne College. Dr. Ahmad has presented at various workshops and conferences on multicultural education and the preparation of teachers of learners with diverse abilities. Her publications have focused on how power and privilege shape educational experiences for marginalized students. She has served on a variety of advisory boards and task force committees related to strengthening educational practices for students with disabilities and urban students. She has also been a reviewer for the *International Journal for Multicultural Education*. Her service has taken her to faraway Ghana, where she provided teacher training and helped create a library with 2,000 donated books in collaboration with the Humanity First non-profit organization.

Mary V. Alfred is Professor of Adult Education in the College of Education and Human Development (CEHD) at Texas A&M University. She is also the Executive Director of the Texas Center for the Advancement of Literacy and Learning (TCALL), the statewide professional development and resource center for adult and literacy education providers in the state of Texas. Her research interests include women of color in STEM, international adult education, sociocultural contexts of immigration and adult learning, social welfare and economic disparities among low-income and low-literate adults, and issues of diversity and equity in higher education and in the workplace. She received her Ph.D. in Education Administration with a focus in Adult Education and Human Resource Development Leadership from the University of Texas at Austin.

Diane Price Banks is Assistant Professor of Biological Sciences at Bronx Community College (BCC), where she also serves as Program Director for the Medical Laboratory Technician Program. In 2019, she anticipates completing her Ph.D. in Urban Education for Math, Science and Technology, City University of New York (CUNY). Her research specializes in microbiology with a focus in soil and water microbiome; epidemiology with a focus in sexually transmitted infections; STEM education with a focus on faculty preparation and learned helplessness; and science history education with a focus on rediscovering the contributions of African Americans in science education. Her book, *The Business of Education: Networks of Powers and Wealth in America*, was published by Taylor and Francis in 2017. Furthermore, her work has been published in *Theory, Research, and Action in Urban Education*. Mrs. Banks' awards and honors include a 2017-2018 Science Teaching Fellowship with the American Society for Microbiology and National Certification as a Medical Laboratory Scientist from the American Society for Clinical Pathology in 2015. Her research has been funded by grants from the CUNY Research Scholars Program and BCC's Student Government.

Dr. Lindamichelle Baron, a former New York City public school teacher, is Associate Professor in the Teacher Education Department at York College, CUNY. She holds a Doctorate in Cross Categorical Studies from Columbia University's Teachers College, and a Master's Degree in Reading. She teaches undergraduate courses in educational psychology, classroom evaluation and assessment, content area literacy, and human development. Her academic journal articles and book chapters focus on literacy and social and emotional intelligences, and culturally responsive, critical pedagogy. Dr. Baron has been publisher and president of Harlin Jacque Publications for over 30 years. Lindamichellebaron (Dr. Baron's pen name) is an accomplished author, poet, and storyteller. One of her poetry collections, *The Sun Is On,* is included on a list of recommended books for New York State middle schools. She also authored several narratives for children, and her work is featured in several children's books and anthologies. She has co-authored a language arts textbook series for Pearson. Her creative work has been produced dramatically in community theater, college productions, and off-Broadway. Dr. Baron has received numerous awards as an educator, author, entrepreneur, inspirational speaker, and performing artist. For more about Dr. Baron, visit www.lindamichellebaron.com.

Gillian Bayne is Associate Professor of Science Education at Lehman College of CUNY. She also holds an appointment in the Urban Education Department at CUNY's Graduate Center. Dr. Bayne's research interests involve utilizing cogenerative dialogues and coteaching to improve the teaching and learning of science, examining the personal and professional trajectories of underrepresented scientists of color, and addressing equity issues that are embedded within STEM. An additional and recent research focus involves helping to strengthen the leadership qualities and experiences of Ethiopian professional women in STEM.

Ronisha Browdy is an assistant professor in the English Department at North Carolina State University where she teaches rhetoric and writing courses. Her research focuses on black women's rhetorical and literacy practices, particularly how black women use language to name, define, and give meaning to their identities. This includes engaging black women's practices of self-definition within everyday contexts and private settings, as well as more public acts of self-determination employed by black women in popular culture. Her work has been published in *Reflections: A Journal of Public Rhetoric, Civic Writing, and Service Learning* and *Women & Language*.

Marcia Burrell, Ph.D., is an innovative leader with more than 30 years of experience in secondary and higher education settings. She has served as chair of the Department of Curriculum and Instruction at SUNY Oswego and as co-director for Project SMART, a teachers' professional development program in New York State. Her publications include topics such as comparative education, mathematics teaching techniques, and global education. She has presented internationally on topics such as investigating teaching math through technology and educational assessment. Her most recent work includes creating and posting to a blog about her journey as a mathematician and educator. Born in Great Britain to West Indian (Jamaican) parents, Dr. Burrell came to the United States in the 1970s. Her immigrant identity motivates her to ensure that the next generation of students has the opportunity to learn mathematics to their full capacity.

Eleanor T. Campbell is Associate Professor of Nursing, Lehman College, and the Graduate Center, CUNY. She holds a B.S. in Nursing from Alfred University, NY, and an M.A., M.Ed., and Ed. D. from Teachers College-Columbia University, NY. Professor Campbell's educational expertise is in curriculum and teaching, but she is also a registered professional nurse with a pediatric nursing specialty. She is a Fellow in the NY Academy of Medicine, a member of Sigma Theta Tau

International Nursing Honor Society, and leader in the Transcultural Nursing Society. Her areas of research and publication include child and adolescent health and clinical decision making in nursing. Currently, Dr. Campbell is Director of the Graduate Nursing Program at Lehman College.

R. Deborah Davis is Professor Emeritus, State University of New York (SUNY) at Oswego, in Curriculum & Instruction, where she taught culturally relevant teaching and foundations of education courses for 17 years. She also served as Diversity Coordinator for Recruitment in the School of Education. Her primary areas of research are: school climate; persistence to graduation; and socialization in a racist society for African American/ethnic students. Dr. Davis served as education subdivision editor for the series Black Studies Critical Thinking from 2012 to 2017 at Peter Lang Publishing, Inc. She is author of *Black Students' Perceptions: The Complexity of Persistence to Graduation at an American University*, as well as monographs, book chapters, and articles. Including this publication, she is also co-editor of three books: *Activist Art in Social Justice Pedagogy: Engaging Students in Glocal Issues through the Arts*, and *"How Do We Know That They Know?": A Conversation on Teaching for Social Justice*. Dr. Davis was awarded a Teacher Opportunity Corps grant from the New York State Department of Education and served as the Director (2008-2017). William V. S. Tubman University in Maryland County, Liberia, invited Dr. Davis to be Dean of the College of Management & Administration (2013-2014).

Josephine J. Dawuni is Assistant Professor of Political Science at Howard University, Washington, D.C. She holds an LL.B. from the University of Ghana, and is a qualified Barrister-at-Law before the Ghana Superior Courts of Judicature. Her doctorate in political science is from Georgia State University. Her primary areas of research include judicial politics, women in the legal professions, gender and the law, international human rights, women's civil society organizing, and democratization. She is the editor (with Judge Akua Kuenyehia) of *International Courts and the African Woman Judge: Unveiled Narratives* (Routledge, 2018). Her first edited book (with Gretchen Bauer), *Gender and the Judiciary in Africa: From Obscurity to Parity?*, was published in 2016 by Routledge. She is respectively a 2016 Carnegie African Diaspora Fellowship recipient and a 2018 Fulbright Specialist

(Ghana) awardee. She is currently a Global Scholar at the Wilson Center for Women in Public Service Project.

Sherry L. Deckman is assistant professor of education at Lehman College, CUNY. Her current research explores how undergraduate students from diverse backgrounds negotiate race, class, and gender while participating in culturally focused performing arts groups. She is also interested in how educators are formally prepared to work with students from diverse race and class backgrounds as well as how they address issues of race, class, and gender inequity in schools. Dr. Deckman's selected publications include "Leaving the Space Better Than You Found It through Song: Music, Diversity, and Mission in One Black Student Organization," published in the *Harvard Educational Review* in 2013, and "Managing Race and Race-ing Management: Teachers' Stories of Race and Classroom Conflict," published in *Teachers College Record* in 2018). She is also a 2018 recipient of the Transformative Teacher-Educator Fellowship from Arcadia University.

Mary Dillard is the director of the Graduate M.A. Program in Women's History at Sarah Lawrence College. Prior to joining Sarah Lawrence, Dr. Dillard was a postdoctoral fellow at the Columbia University Society of Fellows in the Humanities. She earned a B.A. with Honors from Stanford University and her M.A. and Ph.D. from the University of California Los Angeles. Her research interests center around four major themes: gender, education, migration, and representations of Africa. Her grants, awards, and honors record includes the Major Cultures Fellowship from Columbia University's Society of Fellows in the Humanities, a Fulbright Fellowship, a Spencer Fellowship, two U.S. Department of Education Foreign Language and Area Studies (FLAS) fellowships, and a grant from the National Endowment for the Humanities. For several years, she served on the editorial board of *JENdA: A Journal of Culture and African Women's Studies*. In 2012, she guest-edited a special issue of *JENdA* on gender and education in Africa. She currently serves on the editorial board of *Ìrìnkèrindò: A Journal of African Migration*. Her current research project, *A Permanent Inheritance: Determinants of Nigerian Immigrants' Educational Success in the United States*, is a book of oral history interviews with Nigerian families. Most important, Mary is the proud single mother of eight-year-old Halima Dillard.

Aminata Diop is a Ph.D. candidate in Urban Education at the CUNY Graduate Center and the Executive Assistant to the Dean at the School of Education at City College, CUNY. She holds a B.S. in Information Systems, an M.A. in Culture and Communications, and an M.P.A. from New York University. Her dissertation research focuses on the intersectionality between culture, language, and social identity of returning American-Senegalese youth. She is also the author of "Policy Networks and Political Decisions Influencing the Dream Act: The Power of Dreamers," a book chapter published in *The Business of Education: Networks of Power and Wealth in America*. Ms. Diop is also recipient of the 2018-19 CUNY Advanced Research Collaborative (ARC) Fellowship at the CUNY Graduate Center.

Janice B. Fournillier is a highly productive and dedicated associate professor and researcher in Georgia State University's (GSU) College of Education and Human Development (CEHD). Dr. Fournillier's research spans international borders and has impacted her academic peers, practitioners, graduate students, policymakers, and community members in Trinidad and Tobago, Barbados, Jamaica, Canada, the United Kingdom, and Finland. During her decade-long tenure at GSU, Dr. Fournillier has made important innovative, scholarly contributions to her discipline that employ qualitative and quantitative research methods in the study of teacher education and educational policy. As a seasoned evaluator and consultant on a range of school and community-based programs and initiatives, she has played an instrumental role as the qualitative methodologist and co-principal investigator on several externally funded mixed-methods, multi-year evaluation studies for the Georgia Department of Education and the Georgia Department of Human Resources, helping fulfill mandated reporting and performance requirements.

Mary N. Ghongkedze is Assistant Professor in the College of Education, at Grambling State University. Her bachelor's degree is from Yaoundé University in Cameroon. Her master's and doctorate degrees are from Texas A&M University. She has more than 30 years of experience teaching elementary and secondary students both in Cameroon and in the United States. She is an ardent educator with passion and commitment in the following interest areas: preservice teachers' knowledge, reading intervention for struggling readers, emergent literacy, early childhood education, and culturally responsive teaching. She worked with Katy Independent School District in the reading improvement program for four years. Her research and teaching reflect her desire for creating awareness on issues of diversity and equality. She has made several presentations at national and international conferences and written articles on education and women issues. She loves to travel, cook indigenous food, and listen to Makossa music.

Immaculée Harushimana is a 2018-2019 Fulbright Scholar (Malawi) and Associate Professor of TESOL and English Education at Lehman College, City University of New York (CUNY). Her major area of inquiry is in critical linguistics and its implications for literacy instruction to adolescents in a globalized world. The underlying theme of Harushimana's research is linguicism as reflected through African-born immigrants' academic and professional integration, multilingual identities, and alternative discourses. Harushimana's research and writings have been published in refereed professional journals and edited volumes. She is lead editor of two books: *Reprocessing Race, Language and Ability: African-Born Educators and Students in Transnational America* (2013), and *A Paradise to Regain: Post-Obama Insights from Women Educators of the Black Diaspora*. She is also co-author of *African Immigrants' Experiences in American Schools: Complicating the Race Discourse (2016)*, with Dr. Shirley Mthethwa-Sommers.

Rosaire Ifedi is Associate Professor in the College of Education, Ashland University. An educator, scholar, wife, parent, and community activist, her teaching and school leadership career span over 30 years at all levels in both Nigeria and the U.S. Dr. Ifedi teaches graduate courses in curriculum, qualitative inquiry, English language education, and a global perspectives in education capstone experience that included a study abroad tour to London, England, from 2010 to 2014. Her scholarship examines the intersections of race, identity, gender, and achievement in the lives of immigrant, transnational, and second language learners as well as in the professional lives of those who educate them. She has presented nationally and internationally, and written and co-authored many articles and book chapters, including *African-Born Women Faculty in the United States: Lives in Contradiction* (2008, Mellen Press). Her leadership service includes work in academic, non-profit, government, and faith-based organizations, including the New African Immigrants Commission of Ohio, Central Ohio Parent Leadership Training Institute, Ohio TESOL, African Christian Fellowship, Christ International Community Church, FWD. US, and Central Ohio End Ebola Task Force. She holds B. A. Ed. English and M.A. ESL degrees from the University of Nigeria Nsukka (U.N.N.) and an Ed.D. from Ashland University.

Patricia Isaac is an associate professor and teacher educator at SUNY Empire State College in the Master of Arts and Master of Education in Adolescent Special Education programs. She earned her doctorate in Educational Psychology-School Psychology and M.Ed. in Counseling-Human Relations from Northern Arizona University. Formerly, she was a high school teacher and practiced as a school psychologist for a northern Arizona Native American community. She currently holds an Arizona secondary teaching certification, 6-12, Guidance Counselor Pre-K-12 certification, and an Arizona and New York State School Psychology certifications—Pre-K-12. Her research agenda focuses on childhood and adolescent mental health, trauma-sensitive schools, and teacher preparation.

Jaye Jones is Executive Director of the Institute for Literacy Studies (ILS) and an adjunct assistant professor in the social work department at Lehman College-CUNY. She received her Ph.D. in Social Work from the University of Chicago, an M.S. degree from Columbia University's School of Social Work, an M.A. in Women's Studies from George Washington University, and a B.A. in Psychology from the University of Iowa. As ILS Director, Dr. Jones oversees professional development, program evaluation, direct services, and research activities conducted under four affiliated programs: the NYC Math Project, the NYC Writing Project, the Adult Learning Center, and Writing Across the Curriculum (WAC). Jaye's interdisciplinary research agenda focuses on adult literacy learners with histories of trauma, and the creation of emotionally responsive learning contexts that both honor learners' diverse knowledges and foster collective empowerment.

Meahabo Dinah Magano is a full professor in the Department of Psychology of Education at the University of South Africa (UNISA), specializing in psychology of education, with a passion for teacher education. Professor Magano is currently a manager for teaching, learning, community engagement, and student support in the College of Education at UNISA. She is leading a research project in Correctional Centre schools about the wellness of juveniles in correctional schools and teachers' professional development. Her research niche is wellness dimensions, and she has authored book chapters and published articles in accredited journals. She is also involved in a number of projects intended to empower communities. Currently she is an ex-officio member of UNISA Women's Forum, where she mentors women. She is passionate about community engagement and was the recipient of the Woman of the Year award in Community Service at UNISA in 2014.

Faith Maina has been Professor of Curriculum & Instruction at Texas Tech University since 2015 and possesses a wealth of knowledge and experience as a teacher educator and clinical supervisor of field experiences for pre-service teachers. She has taught multicultural, culturally responsive pedagogy and action research courses. Her expertise is in the area of qualitative research, action research, and teacher inquiry particularly in the area of supporting the development of culturally responsive curriculum designs and instructional strategies. She previously taught at SUNY at Oswego in the same capacity and held the position of McNair Post-Baccalaureate Program Director, a federally funded program to support students from underrepresented populations to pursue STEM and academic careers at the graduate level. She is also a 2011-2012 Fulbright Scholar and a Carnegie Fellow in summer 2018.

Patricia Mason is an associate professor in the Division of Education at Molloy College, Rockville Centre, New York, where she teaches graduate classes in special and inclusive education curriculum and methods. She has more than 30 years' experience in teaching and administration in private and public schools and higher education. She offers workshops focusing on adolescent engagement and mentoring strategies. Dr. Mason builds community partnerships for the enrichment of local youth.

Sizakele M. Matlabe obtained a doctoral degree in Adult Education from the UNISA in 2016. Her academic career began in 2009 at UNISA, as a temporal lecturer. In 2010 she served as a permanent lecturer in the Department of Adult

Basic Education and Training (ABET). In 2016, she joined the faculty of the Department of Educational Foundations at UNISA. She has received funding from the South Africa-Netherlands Research Program on Alternatives in Development (SANPAD), which was a wonderful opportunity that opened spaces for her to interact with other SANPAD scholarship recipients through scheduled research workshops. She credits the training for introducing her to productive and advanced ways of doing research. Currently she is a leader of a community project titled "Empowerment of Teachers in Peter Haboniwe Lepai Moraka High School" and "Conversations from the South: Experiences of Bereaved Women."

Esther Milu is Assistant Professor of Rhetoric and Composition at University of Central Florida. She earned her B.A. and M.A. degrees in literature from the University of Nairobi and a Ph.D. in Rhetoric and Writing from Michigan State University. Her research interests revolve around multilingual literacies, identities, and pedagogies. She is interested in understanding how people construct and perform their linguistic identities in multilingual contexts. Some of her work has been published in *International Multilingual Research Journal*, *Research in the Teaching of English*, and several edited collections. She is currently working on a project that examines how African immigrant students construct and perform their linguistic identities in American writing classrooms.

Gladys Kedibone Mokwena is an academic of the College of Education in the Department of Adult Education and Youth Development at the University of South Africa (UNISA). She is author of *An Auto-Ethnographic Life Story of a Black Academic Woman: A Story of Triumph in the Face of Adversity* (2016). A recent Ph.D. completer in the same institution, she continues to make a difference for marginalized communities, particularly women, through adult literacy and vocational training. Her chapter authorship includes "Teaching of Arts and Craft to Adult Students" in M. D. Magano and U. Ramnarain *Including the Excluded: Educating the Vulnerable in the 21st Century* (2015).

Shirley Mthethwa-Sommers is Associate Professor of Social and Psychological Foundations of Education and Director of Service Learning at Nazareth College in Rochester, New York. She was the founding director of the Frontier

Center for Urban Education and Institute for Pluralism at Nazareth College. She is the author of numerous chapters and articles. Her books are *Narratives of Social Justice Educators: Standing Firm* (Springer); *Reprocessing Race, Language and Ability: African-Born Educators and Students in Transnational America* (co-edited volume, Peter Lang), and *African Immigrants' Experiences in American Schools: Complicating the Race Discourse* (co-authored book, Lexington Books). Her teaching and research focus on social justice education as well as anti-oppressive and anti-bullying pedagogy. She is the mother of a 20-year-old woman and a 15-year-old son, to whom the chapter in this volume is dedicated.

Faith Muturia is a lecturer (Doctoral Schedule) of special education at Lehman College, CUNY. She received her bachelor's degree in education (Ed.B.) at the University of Nairobi, Kenya; and she holds an M.Sc. and Ph.D. in Education, Curriculum and Instruction from Iowa State University. Faith teaches various special education courses and supervises student teachers in the Student Teaching of Diverse Learners with Disabilities course. Her areas of research interest include the recruitment and retention of special education teachers in urban settings, research-based practices in meeting the needs of culturally and linguistically diverse students in inclusive classrooms, mentoring novice special education teachers, as well as the portrayal of disability in children's books.

Tracy Cook-Person is an educator, lecturer, professional storyteller, and a published poet. Currently a doctoral candidate at CUNY in the Urban Education program, Tracy is full-time lecturer at Long Island University in the School of Education, Information and Technology. Recently she was the sole instructor of pedagogy and clinical practice for the Teaching Residents at Teachers College (TR@TC2) program in the Office of Teacher Education at Teachers College, Columbia University. Tracy is also the World Council for Curriculum and Instruction's delegate to the United Nations under UNESCO. She has collaborated with such NYC cultural institutions as the Brooklyn Museum, the Schomburg Center for Research in Black Culture, the New York Botanical Gardens, and the Brooklyn Historical Society. An 11-year veteran of the NYC public school system, she is in Who's Who of American Teachers (2004-2007) and received the Claes Nobel Prize for Outstanding Educator (2008-2014).

Yolanda Sealey-Ruiz (Ph.D., New York University) is as Associate Professor of English Education at Teachers College, Columbia University. Her research interests include racial literacy development in urban teacher education (with a specific focus on the education of black and Latino males), literacy practices of black girls, and black female college reentry students. At Teachers College, she is founder and faculty sponsor of the Racial Literacy Project, where for the last 10 years, national scholars, doctoral, and pre-service and in-service master's students, and young people have facilitated informal conversations around race and other issues involving diversity and teacher education for the Teachers College/Columbia University community. She is also the co-founder of the Teachers College Civic Participation Project which concerns itself with the educational well-being of young people involved with the juvenile justice and foster care systems in New York. Yolanda and two of her students appeared in Spike Lee's 2 *Fists Up: We Gon' Be Alright* (2016), a documentary about the Black Lives Matter movement and the campus protests at Mizzou. She is recipient of the AERA 2018 Revolutionary Mentor Award.

Eleanor Williamson has been an educator for the past 19 years. She has taught various science and math courses at the secondary and graduate levels. Her teaching career began in Jamaica where she also completed her undergraduate studies at the University of the West Indies, Mona Campus. She also has a Master's Degree in Science Education from CUNY, Lehman College. Eleanor is very passionate about developing strong, rigorous, fun, and creative curriculum, which she has shared with teachers across the nation at various science teacher conferences. Other highlights of her career include being one of the recipients of the Shell Urban Science Educators Development Award in 2018, a two-time recipient of the Math for America Master Teacher Fellowship, 2013 and 2017, and a Master Teacher in the New York State Master Teacher program.

Index

#MeToo, 61, 75
90210 (TV show), 181

A

Abamenja (traitors), 257
absent fatherhood, 218, 221
academic freedom, 25
activist administrator, 252
acts of racism, 74
Adult Basic Education (ABE) 85, 87
Affordable Care Act (ACA), 201
African American Vernacular (AAVE), 113
African American experience, 54
African American-Hispanic, 179, 180
African American identity, 226
African American Muslim women, 226
African Americans, 1, 3, 22, 64, 89, 154, 177, 200, 224, 294
African-born female, 11
African cultural beliefs, 95
African Diaspora 168, 174
African feminism, 77
African patriarchy, 93
African proverbs, 213
African traditions, 68
Africanizing the curriculum, 32
Afro-Caribbean, 22
Afrocentric, 13
Afro-phobia, 265
Agar, Muller-Hinton, 154
agent of change, 243
Ali, Muhammad, 226
alien immigrant, 22
alienation, 158
alternative epistemology, 31
Aluta Continua, 145
Amandla Awethu, 145
American dream, 106, 170
American immigration policy, 24
American non-Hispanic, 180
American Press survey (2011), xiii
Americanness, 113

Angelou, Maya, 31, 64, 76, 276
Anti-apartheid activist, 142
anti-black, xv
anti-civil rights, 255
anti-immigrant, xv, 256
anti-immigrant America, 12
anti-Semitism, 265
anti-slavery, 255
Apartheid, 78, 79, 94, 122, 139, 141
Apartheid-free president, 139
applied linguistics, 121
"articulate," 2
Articulatedness, 123
A-team, 143
Audacity of Hope, The, 207, 210
authentic American, 268

B

Baldwin, James, 251
Barack Hussein Obama Sr. Sports and Vocational Training Facility, 220
basic interpersonal communication skills (BICS), 125
Benson, George, 243
Beverley, Frankie, 239
bi-racial, 71, 139, 177
birther conspiracy, 107, 267
birtherism, 12, 208
black academics (young), 31
black aesthetic, 189
Black arts movement, 190
black comic superhero, 201
Black English Vernacular (BEV), 190
black excellence, 12
black faculty, 16
black female educators, 66, 89, 95
black female immigrants, 158
black female lecturers, 97, 98
black feminist scholars, 53
Black History Month, 68, 283
black identity, 190
black immigrant woman, 105, 164
black introspection, 190
black leadership, 11, 17
black lecturer, 96

Black Lives Matter (BLM), 144, 145, 194, 283
"black luck," 95
black male experience, 226
black male identity, 225
black man as America (a), 70
black man in America (a), 70
black Muslim, 189
black nationalism, 189
Black Nationalist Movement, 191
Black Panther Party, 189, 201
black perspective, 155
black pride, 200
black professors, 29
black respectability, 69
blackness, 11, 184
black professors, 29
black women, foreign-born, 157
black women leaders, 30
"born free," (a)139
botho-humane, 30
Bre'er Rabbit, 167
"Brit," 22
Brown, Michael, 144, 209
Brown v. Board of Education, 290
Burundi, 121, 257, 259
Bush, George W., 3

C

call and response, 68, 112
Caribbean exams, 132
Caribbean mentality, 23
Carmichael, Stokely, 189
Carroll, Diahann, 200
Chardin, Miko, 230
Chisholm, Shirley, 247
Civil Rights Act, 188
Civil Rights advocacy, 228, 263
Civil Rights Movement, 64, 152, 187, 212, 226, 275, 282, 283
Clayton, Adam, 194
Cliff, Jimmy, 131, 133, 135, 138
Clinton, Hillary Rodham, 6, 60, 77, 194, 213, 247, 286
cognitive academic language proficiency (CALP), 125

collective consciousness, 223
collective memory, xvi, 294, 295
collective physical action, 73
collective story, xvi
collective voices, 295
colonial mindset, 114
colonization, 122, 212
Comer, James, 195
concentration camps, 160
Congress of South African students (COSAS), 142
consciousness raising, 51
Cooke, Sam, 244
"cool kids," 85
counternarrative genre, 227
Creole/Patois dialect, 160
critical and constructive feedback, 138
critical discourse analysis, 179
critical feminism, 78
critical literacy, 85
critical pedagogy, 88
critical race theory, 185, 227
critical social justice, 223
cultural ambassador, 225
cultural heritage, 185
cultural and linguistic enslavement, 114
cultural and linguistic heritage, 117
cultural communities, 68
culturally relevant pedagogy, 153, 154
culturally relevant recommendations, 274
culturally responsive instructor, 88
culturally responsive pedagogy, 227
cyberbullying, 185

D

Dangerous Minds, 136
deconstruction theory, 78, 79
Deferred Action for Childhood Arrivals (DACA), 13, 24, 25, 27, 87, 163, 201, 260, 265
deictic expressions, 124
Democratic party, 23
demonization, 17
Diallo, Amadou, 209
discrimination, 158

Index

disparity of access, 275
dominance of English and American cultures, 117
Dominant American English variety, 114
dominant-and-popular culture, 68
dominant narrative, 230
double identity, 269
Douglas, Frederick, 144, 211
Dream Act, 24
Dreams from My Father, 207, 218
Drew, Charles, 153
Du Bois, W.E.B., 228

E
early socialization, 159
Ebonics, 114
Edelman, Mary W., 274
educational inequities, 43
Electoral College, 14, 60, 265
emancipatory classroom environments, 49
emotional capital, 270
Emotional Disturbance (ED), 227
Encyclopedia Africana, 228
engaged pedagogy, 88
English as a Second Language (ESL), 122, 277
epistemologies of the oppressed, 32
ethic of care, 95
ethnic identity, 182
ethnicity, misportrayal of, 180
ethnocentrism, 109
Eurocentric (science) curriculum, 152, 153
Eurocentric perspective, 150
Evans, Mari, 253
Evers, Medgar, 291

F
false consciousness, 142
family structure,
fatherlessness, 229
Federal Housing Authority (FHA), 287
female objectification, 79
female-of-color parents, 87
feminist idol, 78
feminist principle, xvi
feminist theory, 31

Freedom Charter of 1955, 78
Freire, Paulo, 106, 265
FRODEBU (Burundian Democratic Front), 259

G
Garveyism, 226
Gaye, Marvin, 235
gender-based devaluation, 247
gender bias, 75
gender equality, 75, 154
gender inequality, 79
gender justice, 154
generational oppression, 171
Ghandi, Mahatma, 212
Gingrich, Newt, 211
Glory, 240
Grant, Oscar, 144
Great Depression, 223
Great Migration, 89
Great White Hope, 188
grounded theory, 185
guided collaboration, 42

H
H-1B visa, 136
hard right, 12
Harlem Renaissance, 190, 228
Head Start program, 151
Hebert, Christ Tambu, 28
hegemony, white, 38
hidden curriculum, 43
hidden figures, 13
High School Equivalency (HSE), 87
higher education, 157, 159, 164
higher-order thinking, 42
Hinton, Jane, 153
Hinton, William Augustus, 153
hip-hop culture, 231
historical amnesia, 286
Historically Black College and University (HBCU), 50, 171
history of hope, 199
HIV epidemic, 152
Holocaust, 122

homophobia, 265
Hughes, Langston, xiii, 188, 189, 192
humanness, 69
Hurricane Katrina, 192
Hutu, 257, 258, 259

I
"I have a Dream," 70, 200
identity affirmation, 185
identity confusion, 185
identity politics, 267
immigrant (African) woman, 50
immigrant women's invisibility, 157
immigrants, 11
immigraphobia, xvi
immigration policies, 73
implied racism, 276
In Living Color, 181
inclusive social order, 109
Indigenous Americans, 64, 180
indigenous knowledge, 32
indigenous languages 114
inherited Africanness, 209
institutional ethnography, 33
institutional power, 90
institutional racism, 200
instructional coach, 136
Integrated Performance Management System (IPMS), 97
Integrative Transformative Learning, 98
internalized borderland conflict, 113
International Adult and Continuing Education Hall of Fame, 164
intersecting and overlapping identities, 50
intersectionality, 225, 259
intra-peer respect, 50
invisible mentor, 260
Islamophobia, 256

J
Jackson, Jesse, 208, 247
Jacob Lawrence, 89
Jim Crow Laws, 69, 89, 153, 200, 251

K
Kalenjin, 118
Kaunda, Kenneth, 211, 212
Kennedy, Jackie, 187
Kennedy, John F., 187
Kennedy, Robert, 188
Kenyan cultural identity, 112
Kenyanness, 113
Kenyata, Mzee Jomo, 212
Khan, Khizr, 109
Kikamba 113, 115, 118
King, Coretta, 76, 224
King, Reverend Martin Luther, 2, 8, 13, 64, 70, 109, 187, 189, 223, 249, 282, 283, 291
Kirundi, 121
Kisii, 118
Kogelo, 222
Kunjufu, Jawanza, 231
Kuu, Sauti, 222

L
Lajos posas, 42
landscape of the dream, 174
language of communication, 121
language of literacy, 121
linguicism, 122
latent racism, 12
Latinx, 90
learned helplessness, 171
learning conversation, 82
legacy of hope, 159
legacy of self and others' affirmation, 160
legalized segregation 281
Lewis, John, 291
LGBTQ, 87
Lincoln, Abraham, 202, 282
literacy practices, 68
literacy-rich families, 127
literate culture, 124
lobolo, 80, 81
Lorde, Audrey, 295
Lumumba, Patrice, 212
Luo man, 207, 256
Lynch, Loretta, 211

Index

M
Machel, Graca, 76
madness of racism, 273
Maher, Bill, 12
Make America Great Again, 4, 73, 163
Malcolm X, 175, 212, 226, 291
Mandela, Madiba, 106
Mandela, Nelson, 2, 14, 29, 32, 34, 37, 80, 93, 139, 143, 144, 265, 268
Mandela, Winnie, 29, 30, 76, 77, 79, 143, 144
marginalization, 158
Marley, Bob, 243
Martin, Trayvon, 72, 144, 209, 281
mass incarceration, 73
Math for America, 137
Mathai, Wangari, 114
mathematical ways of knowing, 44
McConnell, Mitch, 16, 268
Melchior, Ndadaye, 259
Meredith, James, 291
micro-aggression, 108, 125
minorities, 11
minority status, 22
misogynistic rhetoric, 64, 182
Morehouse College, 171
mother of the nation, 78
Motlanthe, Kgalema, 2
Mueller, J. Howard, 154
Mugabe, Robert, 212
Muhammad, Elijah, 189
multiculturalism and inclusivity, 54
multiethnic heritage, 225
multilingual literacies, 116
multiple boundaries, 50
multiple identities, 31, 49
multiplicity of identity, 231
Museum of Natural History, 242
My Brother's Keeper Initiative, 55, 229
myth of white supremacy, 141
Mxenge, Griffin, 142
Mxenge, Victoria, 142

N
narcissistic personality disorder, 108
narratives of hope, 4

nation of immigrants, 158
National Alliance of Black School Superintendents (NABSS), 59
nativism, 265
naturalized citizen, 22
Ndizeye, Charles, 258
Negritude, 270
Negro National Anthem, 191
Nelson Mandela Foundation, 42
neoliberal growth agenda, 93
neoliberalism, 265
New York City Department of Education, 136
New York City Housing Authority (NYCHA), 200
New York City Public Schools, 136, 170
New York Public School culture, 136
New York State Educational Reform, 253
Newton, Huey, 189
Ngoyi, Lillian, 144
n'krumah, Kwame, 212
Nlum-nnam, 106
No Child Left Behind, 151
"no drama Obama," 13
No Justice—No Peace, 73
non-compulsory language, 121
non-violent activism, 189
non-whites, 12
novel paradigm, 106
Nyerere, Mwalimu Julius, 212

O
Obama, Auma, 222
Obama, Barack Hussein Obama, xii, 1, 2, 3, 8, 23, 42, 49, 68, 77, 85, 93, 122, 131, 138, 139, 149, 150, 158, 185, 200, 207, 211, 229, 235, 244, 265, 267, 269, 270, 275, 295
  administration of, 67, 172
  as first black president, xv, 269
  generation of, 171
  identities of, 71
  Senator, 177, 185
Obama Hope, 70, 71
Obama, Michelle, 49, 65, 72, 76, 86, 108, 136, 137, 159, 185, 279

Odetta, 252
one-drop rule, 177
oppression, 90
oppressive environment, 89
oppressive men, 78
oppressive patriarchy, 79

P
pan-Africanists, 228
Paris Agreement, 140
Parks, Rosa, 31, 144, 212
partisan politics, 223
patriarchal academia, 93
patriarchal and misogynist society, 79
patriarchal mindset, 79
patriarchy, 75, 76, 78, 80
patriarchy (oppressive), xvi
Pedagogy of the Oppressed, 78
permanent resident, 22
"personal diaspora," 179
perspective transformation, 162
planned shrinkage, 152
"Pledge on Black Manhood," 231
police brutality, 73, 230
political activism, 173
political left, 11
popular vote, 14
post-apartheid South Africa, 29, 99, 139
post-Obama, xv, 21, 49, 231
post-racial America, 11
post racial/racist era, 192, 193, 292
Powell, Colin, 200
Predominantly White Institution (PWI), 22, 50, 159
probationary assistant teacher, 160
problem solving, 40, 42
professional immigrants, 158, 164
project-based learning, 183
psychological odyssey, 218

Q

R
race and gender consciousness, 50
Race to the Top, 151
racial fairness, 154
racial hatred, 187
racial identity, 106, 190
racial marginalization, 145, 252
racially-profiled, 73, 224
racism (white), 2
racism and sexism, 97, 265
Raggedy Ann doll, 180
repression, 88
resistance and survival strategies, 88
rhetoric and linguistics, 122
rhetorical discourses, 68
Rice, Condoleezza, 3, 200
Rice, Susan, 211
Rice, Tamir, 144
rituals of silencing, 90
Robeson, Paul, 228
Robinson, Michelle La Vaughn, xiv
Ross, Diana, 236
Rosewood Massacre, 69
Rwagasore, Louis, 258

S
Sankofa, 289, 290, 294
Sanford, Adelaide, 250-254
Savage African mischaracterization, 260
school-to-prison pipeline, 224
Seal, Bobby, 189
segregation, 187, 200
self-affirm, 15
self-awareness, 160
self-efficacy, 42
self-empowerment, 254
self-identity, 179
self-knowledge, 160
self-perception, 179
selfless leadership, 35
Selma Marches, 244
sense of identity, 220
servant leadership, 34
Sessions, Jeff, 224
sexism and racism, xv, 265
Shabazz, El Hajj Malik, 226
shades of black, 21
Sharpton, Al, 208

Sheng, 113
Simone, Nina, 243
single black mother, 54
singular identity, 226
Sirleaf, Ellen, 2
Sisulu, Albertina, 76, 77
slavery and colonization, 1
slavery, legacy of, 169
social change, 68, 88
social justice, 90, 106
Social Justice Activist, 228
social mobility, 170
social responsibility, 93
Socratic seminars, 137
Southern Dixiecrats, 286
Standard American English (SAE), 113
standpoint theory, 31
status quo (oppressive), xvi
STEM education, 6, 202
storytelling, xiv
structural inequalities, 86, 230
structural racism, 227
Student Nonviolent Coordinating Committee (SNCC), 189
"students as empty vessels," 134
supplemental Security Income, 86
Swahili, 113, 115, 118

T
Temporary Protected Status (TPS), 163
terrorism, 200
textbooks, contemporary science, 154
Tosh, Peter, 241
toxic social change, 175
transfer of learning, 162
transformative initiative, 31
transformative leaders, 32
transformative paradigm, 33
transnational feminism, 56
transnational students, 17
triple invisibility, 158
Trump, Donald, 4, 75, 87, 90, 105, 108, 157, 267, 269, 281, 287, 294
Tubman, Harriet, 144, 212, 248
Tutsi, 259

Tutu, Bishop Desmond, 2, 118, 210

U
Ubuntu, 82, 95
Ubuntu principle, 26, 31, 32
universal healthcare, 223
Universal Design Learning (UDL), 230
University of West Indies, 132
upper echelons of power, 85

V
vision of hope, 169
Vision Keeper grant, 96

W
Waiting for a Miracle, 195
Wasserman Laboratory, 154
Weldon, James, 191
wellness theory, 32
Western viewpoints, 76
What Gender is Motherhood?, 53
"white America," 108
white devil, 189
white plantation, 22
white racism, 190
white supremacy, 90, 255, 265, 294
white working-class America, 108
"whites only' policies, 286
wholeness, 71
Winfrey, Oprah, 14
Withers, Bill, 241, 243
women academics, 49, 97
women, changing role of, 75
women educators, 49
women, objectification of, 75
women, oppression of, 75
Women Reading for Education, Affinity and Development (WREAD), 88, 89
Wonder, Stevie, 236
world citizenship, 229
World War II, 154

X
xenophobia, 256

Y
Yes We Can, 4, 29, 40, 67, 73

Z
Zimmerman, George, 73
Zuma, Nkosana Dlamini, 76, 80